Economic Restructuring
and
African Public Administration

Economic Restructuring and African Public Administration

Issues, Actions, and Future Choices

Editors

M. Jide Balogun

Gelase Mutahaba

African Association for
Public Administration
and Management

KUMARIAN PRESS

Copyright ©1989 African Association for Public Administration and Management
Published by Kumarian Press, Inc.
630 Oakwood Avenue, Suite 119, West Hartford, Connecticut, 06110-1505
All rights reserved under International and Pan-American Copyright Conventions. No part of this book may be reproduced or transmitted in any form or by any means, electronic or mechanical, including photocopy, recording or information storage and retrieval system, without prior written permission of the publishers.

Printed in the United States of America
93 92 91 90 89   5 4 3 2 1

Cover design by Marilyn Penrod

Typeset by The Type Galley, Boulder, Colorado

Library of Congress Cataloging-in-Publication Data

HC
800
.E278
1989

Contents

Contributors	ix
Preface	xi
Keynote Address by His Honour, P. S. Mmusi, Vice President and Minister of Finance and Development Planning, Government of Botswana	xvii
An Address by the President of AAPAM, W. N. Wamalwa	xxiii

PART I ORIGIN, SCOPE, AND RESPONSES TO CRISIS

Chapter 1 The African Economic Crisis: Origins and Impact on Society   3
Eshetu Chole

Chapter 2 The Adaptation of Government to Economic Crisis: Philosophical and Practical Considerations on the Role and Scope of the State in Society   29
Ibbo Mandaza

PART II POLICY AND MANAGERIAL RESPONSES TO CRISIS

Chapter 3 Economic Crisis, Organization, and Structure of Government for Recovery and Development: A Comparative Review of Experiences and New Perspectives   51
P. M. Efange and M. Jide Balogun

Chapter 4 Public Sector Management Improvement in Sub-Saharan Africa: The World Bank Experience   67
Ladipo Adamolekun

Chapter 5 Economic Management in Africa: The Reform of Organization and Process   91
David Fasholé-Luke

PART III IMPACT OF RESTRUCTURING MEASURES ON THE PUBLIC SERVICE

Chapter 6 The Impact of Structural Adjustment Programs on the Performance of Africa's Public Services 109
William N. Wamalwa

Chapter 7 The Impact of the Economic Crisis on the Effectiveness of Public Service Personnel 121
James Nti

Chapter 8 Economic Crisis, Budgetary Constraints, and Effectiveness of Government: A Critical Review 131
Michael A. Bentil

PART IV COUNTRY AND SUBREGIONAL CASE STUDIES

Chapter 9 Government Response to Economic Crisis: The Experience of Ethiopia 149
Asmelash Beyene

Chapter 10 The Adaptation of Government to Economic Change: The Case of Senegal 177
Amadou Sadio

Chapter 11 The Adaptation of Government to Economic Change: A Case Study of Tanzania 187
B. Mulokozi, W. H. Shellukindo, and R. Baguma

Chapter 12 The Adaptation of Government to Economic Change in Zimbabwe 203
S. Mahlahla

Chapter 13 ECOWAS Contribution to West African Efforts at Economic Recovery and Development 211
Momodu Munu

PART V MANPOWER DEVELOPMENT AND CAPACITY-BUILDING IMPLICATIONS

Chapter 14 The Role of Management Training Institutions in Developing the Capacity for Economic Recovery and Long-term Growth in Africa 225
M. Jide Balogun

Index 239

Tables

3–1   IDA-Eligible Sub-Saharan African Countries Implementing Structural Adjustment Programs, March 1987, p. 57
3–2   Annual Percent Change in Kenya's GDP at Constant 1982 Prices, p. 57
3–3   External Public Debt Service Charge and External Debt Service Ratios: Kenya, 1974–85, p. 57
3–4   Summary of Policies/Decisions Reported To Have Been Taken by Selected African States on the Launching of APPER, p. 61
4–1   Technical Assistance Loans and Credits for Administrative Reform, 1981–83, p. 68
4–2   PSM Components in Bank Operations Implemented as of April 1987, p. 69
4–3   PSM Components in Bank Operations Under Preparation as of April 1987, p. 70
4–4   Checklist of Bank-Supported Measures for the Improvement of Public Sector Management, p. 70
4–5   Countries in which Bank-Supported Civil Service Management Improvement Measures Were Being Implemented or Planned by April 1987, p. 72
4–6   Countries in which Bank-Supported Economic and Financial Management Improvement Measures Were Being Implemented or Planned by April 1987, p. 74
4–7   Selected Technical Assistance Projects Including Credits for Public Sector Management Improvement, 1980–87, p. 85
5–1   Trends in Policy and Institutional Reform among African Countries, p. 92
5–2   African Countries with Major Structural Reform Programs Planned or Underway as of March 1987, p. 92
6–1   GDP Growth Rates in Asia, the Middle East, and North Africa, 1960–83, p. 111
6–2   Number of Countries Implementing Structural Adjustment Programs by March 1987, p. 114

7–1   Growth Rates of Manufacturing, Agriculture, Food, and Mining Sectors in Africa, p. 122

8–1   Changes in GDP, Population, and GDP Per Capita in Sub-Saharan Africa, 1960–86, p. 132

11–1   GDP and Per Capita Income (PCI), 1976–86, p. 189

11–2   Economic Growth in Different Sectors, 1978–86, p. 191

11–3   Tanzania's External Trade, 1975–85, p. 191

11–4   Tanzanian National Consumer Index, 1977–85, p. 192

11–5   Producer Prices for Peasant Export Crops, 1973–79, p. 193

11–6   Minimum Import Requirements, p. 200

12–1   External Debt and Debt Service Ratio, p. 206

12–2   Exchange Rates, 1979–86, p. 206

12–3   Agricultural Output, 1980–86, p. 208

Contributors

Ladipo Adamolekun, Senior Training Officer, Economic Development Institute of the World Bank, Washington, D.C., U.S.A. Former Professor of Public Administration, Obafemi Awolowo University, Ile-Ife, Nigeria.

Rweikiza Baguma, Professor, Institute of Development Management, Mzumbe, Morogoro, Tanzania.

M. Jide Balogun, Senior Regional Adviser, Division of Public Administration, Management and Manpower Development, United Nations Economic Commission for Africa, Addis Ababa, Ethiopia. Former Director-General of the Administrative Staff College of Nigeria.

Michael A. Bentil, UNDP Chief Technical Adviser, Ministry of Public Service and Cabinet Affairs, Government of the Republic of Uganda, Kampala, Uganda.

Asmelash Beyene, Ethiopian Institute for Nationalities, University of Addis Ababa, Addis Ababa, Ethiopia.

Peter M. Efange, Regional Adviser, Public Administration, Management, and Manpower Division, UNECA, Addis Ababa, Ethiopia.

Eshetu Chole, Ethiopian Institute for Nationalities, University of Addis Ababa, Addis Ababa, Ethiopia.

David Fasholé-Luke, Assistant Professor, Department of Political Science, Dalhousie University, Halifax, Canada.

S. Mahlahla, Deputy Secretary, Ministry of Finance, Harare, Zimbabwe.

Ibbo Mandaza, Commissioner, Public Service Commission, Harare, Zimbabwe.

Bernard Mulokozi, Principal Secretary, Ministry of Labour and Manpower Development, Dar es Salaam, Tanzania.

Momudu Munu, Executive Secretary, ECOWAS, Lagos, Nigeria.

Gelase Mutahaba, Secretary-General, AAPAM, Addis Ababa, Ethiopia. Former Professor of Public Administration, University of Dar es Salaam, Tanzania.

James Nti, Chief Technical Adviser, UNDTCD Project, Management Development Institute, The Gambia.

Amadou Sadio, Administrateur Civil Conseiller Technique, Secretariat General de la Republique, Dakar, Senegal.

W. H. Shellukindo, Deputy Principal Secretary to the President, Dar es Salaam, Tanzania.

William N. Wamalwa, President, AAPAM and Director, Administration, Finance, and Conference Services Division, UNECA, Addis Ababa, Ethiopia.

Preface

As the contributions to this book readily acknowledge, Africa's socioeconomic crisis has received so much attention that sustaining a claim to originality in the realm of ideas or with regard to empirical data may, in the present circumstances, prove difficult. Yet by broadening the empirical base and by providing new interpretations of the existing body of data, the current volume offers possibilities of looking at the crisis in a new light.

The book comprises fourteen chapters, and is divided into five parts. In part 1, Eshetu Chole and Ibbo Mandaza focus attention on the broad theoretical and philosophical issues in Africa's development. According to the two contributors, it would be difficult to assess the character and magnitude of Africa's socioeconomic crisis unless we fully grasp the fundamental structural barriers to growth. In chapter 1 Chole discusses the crisis of production, which he relates to another crisis—that of dependence. He advances reasons in support of his thesis that the costs of dependence have been very high. In chapter 2, Ibbo Mandaza proceeds from the premise that a neocolonial state is incapable of undertaking the needed radical structural changes in the economy. Yet, as he sees it, unless the neocolonial state is transformed into a genuinely independent one, the existing structure of dependence would be maintained to the detriment of the growth and development of the various African countries. While endorsing Samir Amin's advocacy of "de-linking," Mandaza recognizes that there are practical and serious obstacles in the way of such a policy option.

Part 2 is devoted to the analysis of the policy, institutional, and managerial measures adopted by African countries to stem the economic crisis and generate growth. Thus in chapter 3, Peter Efange and Jide Balogun carry out a comparative review of experiences in policy and administrative reform. In chapter 4, Ladipo Adamolekun discusses the World Bank experience in public sector management improvement in sub-Saharan Africa. In chapter 5, David Fasholé-Luke concentrates on the reform of organization and process.

On the basis of available evidence, the public service in Africa can no longer be accused of failing to undertake reforms. Apart from those imposed upon it from outside, the public service has adopted a series of measures designed to accelerate the process of economic recovery and development. In examining some of these measures, Efange and Balogun, in chapter 3, underscore the importance of policy flexibility and managerial innovativeness. Moreover, as a means of promoting inter-African economic cooperation, and the cause of self-reliance, they (Efange and Balogun) emphasized the need to give priority to monetary reform.

With respect to the reforms sponsored or supported by the World Bank, Adamolekun, in chapter 4, focuses on the interactions between, on the one hand, governments in sub-Saharan Africa, and on the other, the World Bank and the IMF. He debunks the popular notion that all reform measures are externally imposed. As a matter of fact, a number of countries in sub-Saharan Africa have initiated policy and managerial reforms. However, the World Bank's stamp of approval is still required where a reform is undertaken with a view to obtaining structural adjustment loans. Adamolekun furnishes empirical data on the reform measures adopted in a number of countries and concludes that the impact of these measures would depend on how effectively the collaborating agencies played their part and what mechanism exists at the national level to coordinate the activities of external donors.

In chapter 5, David Fasholé-Luke traces the influence of neoclassical economic thinking on contemporary policy in Africa. The emerging trends in the reorganization of the executive branch of government and of aid coordination agencies is part of the effort to remove the constraints imposed by excessive centralization, and promote managerial efficiency. According to him, the features of the current reform drives are the integration of planning with budgeting, flexibility in organization structure, cost consciousness, and performance monitoring.

The impact of the various reform measures is the subject taken up in part 3. In chapter 6, William N. Wamalwa discusses the impact of structural adjustment programs on the performance of Africa's public services. James Nti, in chapter 7, focuses on the impact of the crisis on public service personnel. The budgetary implications of the crisis are examined by Michael A. Bentil in chapter 8. It goes without saying that the socioeconomic crisis, as well as the measures that were adopted to tame it, contributed in no small measure to rapid deterioration in living conditions. The "austerity" and belt-tightening components of structural adjustment, in particular, brought about a steep decline in income and put the basic necessities of life (food, fuel, housing, and health facilities) beyond the reach of the mass of the people. In some countries, conditions became so unbearable as to threaten peace and stability. As a corporate entity, the public service felt the impact of structural adjustment directly and indirectly. Wamalwa begins with what he terms the positive impact. For a start the reform measures accomplished what would have been thought impossible a few years back. In particular, the measures succeeded in taking public officials from their bureaucratic fortresses to the marketplace. The immediate effect was to promote cost-consciousness at all levels. But while acknowledging the beneficial impact of the ongoing reform, Wamalwa believes that we should not lose sight of its immediate and long-term debilitating effects. First, the notion, whether valid or not, that the measures were externally imposed was not likely to endear the policymakers and their civil service advisers to the local populace. Second, and with particular reference to the public service, the rapid decrease in the resources available to governmental agencies constitutes a serious limitation on their goal-delivery capacity. The tendency toward cost cutting has also been responsible for the constant retrenchment of personnel, the decline in the "effective" or real value of public servants' remuneration, and the general deterioration in morale, motivation, and productivity.

The issue of motivation was taken a step further in chapter 7 by James Nti who quotes Douglas Macgregor's oft repeated proposition that "man lives by bread alone if there is no bread." As Nti notes, the supply of bread is becoming limited in Africa, and civil servants, like their compatriots, tend to spend the greater part of their time looking for this vital commodity. The increasing incidence of "moonlighting," bribery and corruption, abuse of office, and declining productivity are all symptoms of the rapid decay of public service values and are a direct outcome of the harsh conditions under which government officials have to operate. Nti questions the basis upon which the major decisions affecting the size and remuneration of the public service were based. He recommends that the arbitrary rule-of-thumb methods should be replaced with a systematic technique of performance analysis.

Michael Bentil in chapter 8 traces the impact of the economic crisis on budgetary allocations. He identifies a number of factors affecting the effectiveness of government financial operations, and apart from singling out the technical, managerial, and accounting constraints, he gives prominence to the paralyzing effects of corruption, indiscipline, and political instability.

Part 4 of the book provides empirical data on economic restructuring in a number of countries, as well as within a particular subregion, West Africa. In chapter 9, Asmelash Beyene looks at the situation in Ethiopia. He assesses the impact of the drought and internal strife on resource allocation. The Ethiopian government's approach to the perceived problems, according to Beyene, is based on the chosen ideological path and the government's interpretation of what was in the best interest of the country. The Ethiopian experience also shows that by mobilizing the bureaucracy and other production agencies behind an economic restructuring program, and with prudent management of domestic and external resources, it is possible to cushion the effects of the ongoing crisis. The fact remains, however, that unless a credible solution to Africa's problem is in sight, it will be difficult to resist external pressures for changes in policy direction.

The second country case study focuses on Senegal. Thus, in chapter

10, Amadou Sadio discusses Senegal's experience in economic management. He refers, in particular, to the New Agricultural Policy, the efforts made to restructure the banking system, the Re-integration Fund (designed to rehabilitate retrenched staff), and the reform of parastatals. The Senegalese initiatives in these areas (especially, regarding the establishment of a Re-integration Fund, and the introduction of performance contracts in parastatals) need to be carefully considered by other countries faced with similar problems.

Chapter 11, by B. Mulokozi, W. Shellukindo, and R. Baguma, examines the series of measures undertaken in Tanzania with a view to rectifying internal and external resource imbalances and to reversing the negative trends in the economy. While focussing on external barriers to growth, the authors also cite internal policy and institutional and managerial constraints that need to be removed to guarantee economic recovery and self-sustained growth. The Tanzanian case study reinforces Nti's argument that large-scale economic deprivation constitutes a serious threat to integrity and accountability in the public service. As the authors point out, public servants in Tanzania spend more time looking for commodities in short supply than they do on the public service jobs for which they were recruited. They also refer to the thriving parallel economy and the cases of boarding and profiteering.

The situation in Zimbabwe has not been as desperate as in many other sub-Saharan African countries. However, as S. Mahlahla notes in chapter 12, budget and trade deficits are becoming a serious issue in economic management largely because of the rapid expansion in the scope of government and the foreign exchange leakages occasioned by the repatriation of capital by multinational corporations. Zimbabwe, however, offers some important lessons in how creativity at the policy and managerial levels could prove useful in dealing with otherwise intractable problems—notably, external debt and foreign exchange management problems. Thus, by aligning the Zimbabwean dollar to a "basket" of foreign currencies and ensuring that external loans were denominated in the currencies that appreciated least, the managers of the country's economy ensured that Zimbabwe met its external obligations as and when due, and that the debt service ratios were not adversely affected by sudden and steep depreciation of the local currency. Moreover, Zimbabwe's policy on the repatriation of dividends might not go over well with multinational corporations, but in the long run, it is in everyone's interest that the national economy remain in good health. Finally, Zimbabwe is one of the few countries with a grains storage policy. Officials in other countries that are interested in tackling food security problems would be well advised to compare notes with their Zimbabwe counterparts on approaches to grain stock and exchange of surplus food items with those in short supply. This raises issues of economic cooperation.

As a subregional grouping, ECOWAS offers a wide scope for economic cooperation. This is brought out by Momodu Munu in chapter 13. Under normal conditions, regional or subregional bodies are expected to focus on broad and long-term development issues while leaving the immediate problems to the national governments. In a period of economic emergency, however, all hands are supposed to be on deck. This, according to Munu, is the justification for ECOWAS's formulation of a short-term economic recovery strategy for the West African subregion. It should also be noted that while ECOWAS was addressing the problem of the moment—that concerning the survival of its member countries—it did not overlook the medium- and long-term perspectives in subregional economic integration. In particular, the governing authority of ECOWAS has made far-reaching decisions in the areas of interterritorial trade, immigration, currency and monetary reform, and vehicle insurance. Munu reports that there is now greater awareness of the need to achieve monetary cooperation. It is hoped, however, that the barriers that Efange and Balogun referred to in chapter 3 would not frustrate efforts in this direction. Certainly, the proposal to introduce a common currency in West Africa ought to have gone beyond the drawing board by now.

The final chapter, part 5 of the book, examines the training and institution development implications of economic restructuring. Unlike the other chapters, M. Jide Balogun's contribution was not presented at the AAPAM's Roundtable meeting in Gaborone. The chapter is based on a paper presented at the Workshop for Heads of Management Training Institutions held at the Administrative Staff College of Nigeria (ASCON) in November 1987 under the auspices of the Management Development Programme of the Commonwealth Secretariat. The rationale for including the paper lies in Balogun's contention that the challenge of economic recovery and growth necessitates a novel approach to manpower development and capacity building in training institutions. While recognizing the limitations imposed on the performance of these institutions, Balogun suggests ways of removing the constraints and advocates a balanced capacity-building strategy. He also outlines a procedure for evaluating the contributions of training institutions during this critical period in Africa's history.

There is no doubt that a lot more needs to be done to put Africa firmly on a course of recovery and self-sustained growth. The various contributions to this volume represent a modest effort in this direction. It is the editors' hope that policymakers and managers operating at national and regional levels, as well as decision-makers in technical assistance and/or cooperation agencies will consider the issues raised and the recommendations made in this book. This volume should also be of interest to students of development administration, development economics, and public finance.

The editors wish to express their appreciation to all those who made the publication of this book possible. They wish to thank, in particular, all the donor agencies that provided generous financial assistance toward the organization of the Gaborone Roundtable and the printing and publication of this volume.

Jide Balogun
Gelase Mutahaba
Addis Ababa

Keynote Address

by His Honour, P. S. Mmusi
The Vice President and Minister of Finance and Development Planning,
Government of Botswana

I have great pleasure, on behalf of the President, the Government, and people of the Republic of Botswana, in extending to you all a warm welcome to Botswana, and to this Ninth Roundtable of the African Association for Public Administration and Management. I hope the delegates and observers coming from afar had a pleasant journey to Gaborone and are comfortably accommodated. I also hope, that the roundtable work program is so arranged that the visitors would have an opportunity of seeing parts of our country and meeting our people. You are most welcome to Botswana.

I note that Botswana's association with AAPAM has been long and close. Botswana has been a regular and prompt contributor to AAPAM's membership and I am happy to note further that our Minister of Presidential Affairs and Public Administration, Hon. P. H. K. Kedikilwe is second Vice President in the governing body of AAPAM for which I congratulate him. I can only interpret this as a reflection of the level of closeness, recognition, and esteem AAPAM enjoys in Botswana.

This is a very special occasion, special both for AAPAM and for Botswana. At this Roundtable, AAPAM is celebrating its twenty-fifth year of existence—a silver jubilee celebration. A review of AAPAM's activities over the period of a quarter century reflects a record of considerable achievement. This calls for celebration. We all join in extending our joy and felicitations to this continental organization of administrators.

This occasion is also special for Botswana as it is hosting this very important event. Indeed, the very conception of this Association took place in Botswana during the Inter-African Public Administration Seminar held here between 3 and 9 October 1970. It is a matter for joy that the bond of seventeen years between AAPAM and Botswana has flourished and matured fully, culminating in this historic roundtable. Botswana is almost AAPAM's second home. We are proud of this association and rejoice in its growth and achievements. The fact that this roundtable takes place in this southern African country, in the midst of many other turbulences, adds significance to the special relationship between AAPAM and Botswana.

As we celebrate the Silver Jubilee of AAPAM and deliberate on the theme of this roundtable, it is opportune to pause and reflect on the goals and objectives of AAPAM and assess their relevance to our current needs. The constitution of AAPAM, in its preamble, recognizes the importance of cooperation among African states and institutions in the effort to mobilize resources for the achievement of national socioeconomic development objectives. AAPAM is engaged in wide range of programs and activities to achieve, among others, the objective of mobilizing national resources (particularly human resources) for sustained and rapid national socioeconomic development.

I consider this objective of AAPAM as the most vital element and the key to solving some of the current development problems facing all African countries. If practical measures, appropriate and relevant to our local needs and priorities, are developed and effectively applied, a great deal can be achieved in a relatively short time to mobilize resources for development. Central to this effort of resource mobilization is the role of public administration in our respective countries. It is my earnest hope that AAPAM in general, and this roundtable in particular, will adequately address this subject and come forward with implementable proposals for our public administration authorities to consider.

AAPAM also reflects the continental image. Its constitution and membership, its range and scope of activities, and its specific concerns as highlighted in the theme of this roundtable, and in the range of topics to be deliberated, reflect the African concerns and aspirations. This I consider to be a most commendable foresight on the part of the Association. In that sense, AAPAM serves as an agent for uniting the nations of Africa and underscores the fact that the countries of Africa share a common past, a rich cultural heritage, and varied experience in the field of public administration. Our shared experience is a great and dynamic force and the basis of our strength as a people. Institutions such as OAU, SADCC and PTA are evidence of that strength. There is much to be gained by maintaining awareness of this commonality in all sectors and phases of our development.

AAPAM itself is a shining example of African unity, and this, in spite of the fact that forces of division are fully at work.

It is appropriate to emphasize that by hosting the banner of Public Administration and Management, AAPAM has a particular role to play in regional development efforts. I am aware that AAPAM is encouraging regional development efforts, particularly in the field of human resource development. As current Chairman of the Council of Ministers of SADCC, I welcome and encourage more active and close linkages between efforts of SADCC and AAPAM, particularly in the field of human resource development.

One of the very pertinent topics for discussion at this roundtable is the current economic crisis in Africa. A great deal of research and discussion has taken place, and continues to take place, on this highly volatile, and explosive problem—a problem of unprecedented magnitude. Many a resolution has been passed, and indeed much is being done at the national, regional, and international levels to overcome this problem. Unfortunately, the more the problem is discussed and the greater the number of action plans developed, the more elusive the solution seems to be.

This certainly is not the right forum and time for me to discuss in detail the causes, effects of, and remedial measures for the economic maladies of Africa. The crisis has a global perspective, a continental and regional dimension, as well as a national viewpoint. The crisis also can be seen from various sectoral angles such as communication, agriculture, water, mining, etc. The ideological and intellectual aspects are equally worthy of note. For purposes of this roundtable, however, the economic crisis in Africa should be seen from the public administrators' and managers' standpoint. The role of public administration, stated in terms of authority, institutions, policies, etc., or of management, stated in terms of capabilities, concepts, techniques, disciplines, etc., should be seen in light of whether it aggravates or stems the economic crisis of Africa. I have noticed from the schedule of papers to be discussed during this roundtable that the subject is to be addressed from the administrative/managerial dimension, among other things.

There is also the question of the structural adjustments to make to loosen the grip of the crisis and embark on a path of self-sustained development. This is one area which has fascinated me most. A leading question I would like to pose to the pundits and scholars of economic reconstruction is why the structural changes were made in the first instance, especially since the changes have led the economy to slow down or move in the reverse direction. Did those changes, when they were made, appear as most desirable and imperative, or did they appear to contain seeds of uncertainty and doubt? Were the designers of those structural changes oblivious of the realities of economic development and obsessed with their ideological and academic pursuits?

The reason I am posing these questions is that, as I see it, public administration has a direct role to play in structural adjustment and in the economic revitalization of Africa. I am aware that public administrators only carry out the decisions made by politicians and the government in power. But that is only half of the story. The role, ethics, competence, capabilities, discipline, authority, and a number of other factors relating to public administration need close examination in order to make it an instrument that the policymakers could rely on in their war against economic recession.

There is no question that the roundtable is taking place at the most opportune time. While on a global level a number of action programs are being contemplated to alleviate the debt burden and stem the economic crisis, on the continental level, specific proposals are being considered by the OAU and a number of regional bodies. For example, in the Southern African region, SADCC has a well-researched program of action to improve the economic situation. Implementation of this and other similar programs, is heavily dependent upon the capacity of our national institutions and the capabilities of our public administrators and managers. In a sense, therefore, public administration and management is one single critical factor in translating the well-prepared strategies and in channelling local and technical assistance resources to bring about the desired improvement in our economic situation.

At the national level, the Botswana Government is continuously aware of the need and importance of keeping public administration and management as efficient and effective as possible. We are aware of the dictum that "when public administration in a country fails, everything else fails." In view of the growing demand for more and better public services (as a result of the notable socioeconomic development achieved in this country), the need to keep public administration more relevant, efficient, and effective has become more pressing than ever before. In recognition of that need, the government has adopted, since 1984, a deliberate and bold strategy to systematically improve efficiency and effectiveness of the public service. The following are some of the components of this strategy:

A. A major organization and management review program has been launched; the exercise attempts to review and improve corporate objectives and functions of all government ministries and departments at all levels. Organizational structures, management practices and administrative systems are being thoroughly reviewed to make them simple, efficient, and relevant to the present-day needs and priorities. A number of ministries, among them the former Directorate of Personnel, have been fully reviewed and streamlined. For example, the control and directive role and the scope of the former Directorate of Personnel have been thoroughly reviewed and replaced by greater emphasis on its service, development, and facilitation role. A matrix organization structure has been introduced to provide faster and more effective services to ministries and the public.

B. An extensive job analysis exercise is in progress. This is likely to result in clarity of duties and performance standards which each job holder would strive to achieve. This, coupled with systematic development of accountability and supervisory role of managers, is likely to improve productivity standards in the public service.

C. The approach to public service training is being thoroughly revised, placing more emphasis on improving abilities, skills, and attitudes of individual staff in known areas of weakness thus improving output and efficiency of individual officers.

D. The traditional annual reporting system has been replaced by a development-oriented and open performance appraisal system. Annual increments are no longer automatic but have to be earned on the basis of the performance level attained.

E. A more pragmatic and need-related manpower planning and budgeting system is being introduced replacing the old "bargaining shop" budgeting system.

Let me hasten to add that in their wake all these changes have also created more problems of managing the change process. The government is determined to raise and keep the public service efficiency at the highest level attainable within our environmental and resource constraints. At the same time the government accepts the reality that all changes and their results cannot be achieved overnight.

Before I conclude my address, I would like to pose certain basic questions which I consider to be challenges to modern public administration concepts and practices. You, the participants at this conference, are professionals and specialists in your own disciplines. The purpose of the conference is to pool your experience and expertise to develop practical solutions to the economic crisis facing our continent. May I, therefore, venture to ask the following questions:

A. Are public administration and management concepts and practices, as applied in our national public services and parastatals, truly and realistically adapted to our national needs, priorities, and environment? Or are they legacies of past administrations and laboratories where management scholars and researchers test out their theories? How do we make public administration and management serve our socioeconomic development goals and objectives?

B. Much has been discussed, written, and published about public administration and management inadequacies in Africa, their causes, effects, and possible remedial measures. AAPAM, in its twenty-five years of existence, has continuously raised this subject. How much real practical improvement has been achieved in the public administration of our respective countries? You are ideally placed to assess the situation. Is it really not time to do some soul-searching on this dilemma?

C. Public administration as a profession or as an institution consists of administrators, the people. It is often observed, particularly in the rural areas, that an efficient, capable, and motivated worker will deliver very effective services to the public in spite of grossly inadequate facilities, systems, and structures. It is also observed that organizations which have well-defined goals and functions, well-refined structural arrangements, sophisticated and modern administrative tools, techniques, and systems and other facilities, but manned by unmotivated and/or incapable staff often completely fail to deliver the quality of services expected. The key factor is the worker; his abilities, knowledge, attitudes, and motivation. Has this crucial factor been adequately addressed in the search for making our public administration and management more relevant and effective?

These are some of the challenges which, I think, face our public administration today, and this is the ideal forum to raise the questions.

The business of this conference is most serious. The theme that has been selected and the titles of discussion topics confirm this. I am confident that deliberations on these topics will be equally serious and pragmatic. Our national governments, regional institutions, and international organizations will be waiting in great expectation.

I wish this Ninth Roundtable Conference of AAPAM every success in its deliberations and formally declare the conference open.

An Address

by the President of AAPAM W. N. Wamalwa

Your Excellency, Mr. Peter S. Mmusi, the Vice and Acting President of the Republic of Botswana, Honorable Ministers, Your Excellencies, Members of the Diplomatic Corps, AAPAM Fellows, Ladies and Gentlemen.

This week, AAPAM members, together with our friends and well-wishers, meet in the capital of this great Republic to discuss, as we have done over the last twenty-five years, momentous issues affecting Africa's development. For AAPAM, this is not the first time we are meeting in this country and in this city. The Ninth Inter-African Public Administration Seminar was held in Gaborone from 3 to 9 October 1970. We were fortunate to have in our midst the late President of the Republic, Sir Seretse Khama, who declared the seminar open. For me, as an individual, Botswana is even more of a home, because I have been accorded so many welcomes, and I share so many friendships, that I feel I belong here.

On behalf of all the members of the Association and on my own behalf, I would like to express our profound appreciation to the Government of the Republic of Botswana for agreeing to host this Ninth AAPAM Roundtable on the critical theme: Economic Crisis, Structural Adjustment, and Public Administration and Management in Africa. By accepting to host this conference, the Government of Botswana has once again demonstrated its support for the ideals of our Association and acknowledged the seriousness of the crisis facing our continent.

Ever since it became obvious that Africa's socioeconomic condition was likely to worsen rather than improve, many conferences, seminars, and workshops have been organized to discuss the nature and character of the crisis as well as measures for reversing the downward trend. The conferences have taken place at the national, subregional, continental, and global levels. African heads of states have met to discuss the issue. First, in 1980, they met in Lagos and out of their meeting, the Lagos Plan of Action emerged. The Lagos Plan of Action enjoined African countries to take concerted action at regional, subregional, and national levels to accelerate the pace of development. Emphasis was placed on adopting strategies that would promote collective self-reliance as well as the improvement of the capacities and capabilities of each country. Two years ago the OAU Summit adopted APPER (Africa's Priority Programme for Economic Recovery, 1986–90) which also outlined a number of actions to be taken at different levels to see Africa out of her present impasse. In addition, and for the first time in the history of the United Nations, the General Assembly met to discuss the social and economic problems of a single region—Africa—and in June 1986 adopted the UNPAERD, i.e. United Nations Priority Programme for African Economic Recovery and Development.

In spite of these reviews and action programs adopted globally, continentally, and at the national level, the situation shows no signs of improvement. There must be some missing link either in the analysis of the nature and character of the problem, or in the solutions suggested and adopted or both.

One wonders whether in much of the discussions taking place, there has been adequate attention devoted to one important aspect, that is, the extent to which public administration/management has defined the scope and intensity of the crisis.

It is our belief that in searching for causes of this crisis, and therefore, measures for resolving it, serious attention ought to be given to examining the extent to which Africa's public administration systems are adequate for the tasks of recovery and rejuvenation and what ought to be done to give them that capacity and capability. That is why we consider the decision by the Executive Committee of AAPAM to devote this year's roundtable to the subject to be timely.

As we focus on the theme during the next five days, however, we should avoid bemoaning what has not happened and rather suggest what should be done in the future. The aide-mémoire for this conference indicate the areas warranting in-depth treatment, viz.: A Review of the Role and Scope of Government in Society; Impact of the Crisis on Organization, Structure, and Size of Public Administration and Management; and Measures for Improving the Capacity of the Public Administration Systems. In respect to the first topic, we may wish to acknowledge the increasingly loud and strident demands from different corners of the world that the state ought to scale down its activities and to retain only what it has the capacity for. We might want to examine what, in the African context, is legitimate state activity, and whether in Africa the state can divest as rapidly as some states of the industrialized world are doing. The questions we should be asking at this roundtable are: how effective are the divestiture programs being adopted, in respect to their ability and potential to contribute to both the short-term recovery and the long-term economic development and transformation of Africa? Is there an optimal strategy that African countries should adopt?

In focusing on the second topic, i.e., the question of structure, size, and capacity of the public administrative system, we should also be raising seriously a number of questions. What is the appropriate division of responsibilities and authority between the center, the provinces and localities? In other words what constitutes appropriate balance between centralization and decentralization? And how should we approach the problems of headquarters organization? How can new approaches to decentralization contribute to the economic recovery efforts? To what extent are African governments willing to share power with intermediate and local governments, and if they seem unwilling, as some people have suggested, what is it that ought to happen to make them be more positive towards power sharing?

Pertinent to the foregoing issues is that of the goal delivery capacity of government agencies, and the constraints posed to that capacity by the economic crisis. A review of capacity in governance would include the range of skills of the human resource within the systems, the motivation, attitudes, and values of the work force; the data and information at the disposal of the policy-making bodies, appropriateness of organization structures, processes, and policies. Others are the strength and credibility of formal authority structures, the qualities of leadership, etc. Included also is the financial and technological resources at the disposal of the decision-makers. There is general agreement that African administrative systems need to overcome their weaknesses in all these areas. We should not lose sight of this when discussing factors mediating the operational efficiency of Africa's administrative systems.

I make no attempt to catalogue all the issues we should be discussing, nor do I claim to have all the answers. All I have done is to give an indication of what our main concerns should be, and in doing so, my intention was to enjoin us to be more forward-looking and avoid the temptation to spend precious time cataloguing the past ills of Africa. We have done enough by way of diagnosis. What we now need is action—action geared toward economic recovery and self-sustained development.

Today AAPAM commemorates its Silver Jubilee. As we do so, it is important to reflect on the factors that led to its founding and assess its performance over the last twenty-five years of its existence.

Twenty-five years ago, a group of senior administrators from what was then newly independent Africa met in Dar es Salaam in the first Inter-African Public Administration Seminar. For us in AAPAM, that was an occasion of historic significance. It was the first time that top civil servants from different English-speaking African countries got together to exchange ideas and share experiences in the area of public administration, and thereby set in motion the events that culminated in the formal inauguration of AAPAM.

As the literature from those early seminars will confirm, the greatest issue confronting civil services in independent African nations was Africanization—that is, the replacement of colonial civil servants with nationals. Senior African administrators sought to achieve the goal of Africanization while at the same time maintaining acceptable standards of efficiency upon which they believed the legitimacy of the new African regimes depended.

Those were the good times. The 1960s seemed to have been the decade of faith, hope, and confidence about the future. It was not surprising, therefore, that among the initiatives taken in that decade was the inauguration of the Inter-African Public Administration Seminars, the first in the series taking place in Dar es Salaam. Those were the times when much was expected from the public services—they were to be vanguards of economic development, engineers of technological revolution, the wheels of progress. If Africa was to become a full-fledged member of the international community, the public service had to play a key role.

The Inter-African Public Administration Seminar consistently took place each year in a different country and focussed on topics that were considered relevant to the socioeconomic and political development of Africa. From Dar es Salaam the seminar moved to Enugu, Nigeria in 1963, Kampala in 1964, Lusaka in 1965, Cairo in 1966, Accra in 1967, Nairobi in 1968, Monrovia in 1969, Gaborone in 1970, and Freetown in 1971 when AAPAM was launched as a professional association of practising administrators and managers, academicians and institutions undertaking studies and training in the two disciplines. The spread of venues indicated the Pan-African character of the seminars.

As I have already said, throughout most of the 1960s the main concern was with the Africanization of the civil services. However, attention soon shifted to a related issue, i.e., the adequacy of the civil services as regards their general orientation and methods of operation to meet the new challenges of nationhood. It was held that colonial civil services were primarily established to exercise control over the colonial subjects and that it was therefore essential to change this orientation in order to equip the civil services for the developmental tasks of the newly elected governments. In this connection it was the view at that time that the developmental role of government demanded not merely Africanization but much more.

By the end of the 1960s, however, the spirit of optimism and hope began to wane. The sense of commitment and dedication in civil services so evident during the early years of independence could no longer be taken for granted. The fire of nationalism among the political leaders which had burned so fiercely during those heady days of nationalism was beginning to flicker. Many senior administrators attending the Inter-African Public Administration Seminars thus started to wonder whether their earlier premises on how to create new civil services were valid. As a result, there was a significant shift in the nature of themes and topics from 1967 showing new concerns. It was becoming clear that the Africanized civil services were not meeting the new challenges. It was therefore not an accident that the theme for 1971 Seminar was "Professionalization of Public Administration and Management." It was a logical development. As a professional association, AAPAM was born at a time when new initiatives directed at administrative reform were gaining ground. Africanization, supported by training, appeared to have produced less than optimal results. It was now considered that the reform of inherited structures and procedures needed an added impetus. However, the founding fathers of AAPAM who assembled in Freetown, Sierra Leone, in 1971 believed that administrative reform measures were not enough to transform civil services to meet the new challenges. In order to achieve this, civil servants had to acquire professionalism, that is, specific knowledge and skills, and appropriate ethical standards for public servants.

A new mood of optimism seemed to be germinating. The new message that went out from Freetown in 1971 to the rest of Africa was the necessity for administrators and other public managers to shed the traditional amateurish approach to their tasks and to seek to become professionals. It was only in this way that they could be effective engineers of economic and social development. Reinforcing the spirit and climate of optimism at AAPAM's inauguration, the late President Siaka Stevens said, "The formation of such an association could not have come at a more opportune moment, for if there is anything that Africa is short of, it is administrative and managerial capacity for present-day tasks."

As I have already indicated, the First AAPAM Roundtable Conference was organized in 1978 in Freetown out of the realization that the downward trend in Africa's socioeconomic indicators could not continue without resulting in chaos. The Roundtable series was intended to create a new sense of urgency in responding to Africa's socioeconomic crisis. For its own part, AAPAM has diversified its own activities with a view to highlighting in a practical manner the areas where we believe concentrated action is required. In this regard there are four projects approved in Maseru in 1986 by AAPAM's Executive Committee for implementation during 1988, and I hope that our governments will respond with enthusiasm to take advantage of the opportunities offered.

Our achievements, modest as they are, would have been difficult to realize without the generous contribution of a number of people and institutions. I shall have another occasion to thank them, but here it suffices just to mention them. We want to thank the founding fathers of AAPAM for giving us a beginning and showing us the light. Some of them are here with us. They deserve a big thank you.

Second, we want to thank our African governments, which have in the course of the past twenty-five years shouldered much of the financial burden of keeping us going. Lastly, I wish to thank a number of foundations and donor agencies which have actively and generously supported our activities. Some, like the Ford Foundation, started with us twenty-five years ago and they are still with us. Others, such as the Commonwealth Secretariat, IDRC, the Fredrich Ebert Stiftung, CIDA, and now lately NORAD, came in later and we hope that they will be with us for a long time to come. We thank all of them.

I took too much of your time. The excitement of being twenty-five years as an association was such that I had to tell you a little about how the trail was blazed. And now, of course, the Government of Your Excellency and the people of this great Republic have made yet another contribution: to host us in 1987. To you, Mr. President, I thank you once again, and through you I thank my compatriots, the citizens of this great Republic.

PART I

Origin, Scope, and Responses to Crisis

CHAPTER ONE

The African Economic Crisis: Origins and Impact on Society

Eshetu Chole

INTRODUCTION

So much—perhaps too much—has been said and written on the African economic crisis that yet another contribution on this topic may impose an excess burden on the reader, with the consequence that, in a manner reminiscent of the opening scene of Shakespeare's *Twelfth Night*, "the appetite may sicken and so die." It is not only that this problem has caused much ink to flow; more to the point is that the facts of the African predicament are so well-known and the controversies regarding its causes so sharply defined that the writer risks treading on a beaten path. The writing of this chapter is, therefore, a task undertaken with considerable modesty. The only saving grace is that the chapter, while making no pretense to originality, may nevertheless serve the limited purpose of providing background reading to a roundtable convened to discuss not the economic crisis *per se*, but how the public administration and management system can best cope with it.

If there is one point of unanimity in the voluminous writing on Africa of recent years, it is that the continent finds itself in a deep economic malaise. This malaise has commonly been diagnosed as a crisis, but the crisis has been so pervasive and so persistent that it has become the norm, not an aberration as the word suggests. In this sense, therefore, the term may no longer adequately express the alarming state of the conditions in Africa, for in many countries what is threatened is the very capacity of societies to reproduce themselves as viable entities. If, all the same, we continue to use the word "crisis," it is more out of conformity with customary usage than out of conviction regarding its expressive capacity.

The prevailing mood in Africa today is one of widespread despondency, and this stands in marked contrast to the exuberance of the 1960s, the so-called Decade of Africa. The immediate post-independence period was characterized by considerable euphoria, not only because of political gains, but because of a pervasive optimism that it was indeed possible to bring about the so-called revolution of rising expectations. Nor was the optimism wholly unjustified. While the continent did, in fact, have to contend with formidable problems, it also registered respectable, even if percent in 1984, with a preliminary estimate of 1.2 percent for 1985. This record is distinctly inferior to that of developing countries as whole as well as that of low-income countries.[7]

The picture is even bleaker when viewed in per capita terms. While per capita GDP has been declining for sub-Saharan Africa as a whole since 1981, the decline in the low-income countries covers even the earlier decade of 1970–80. In fact, for the latter group of countries, GDP per capita had declined by 0.2 percent during 1965–83.[8] According to ECA, "it is now estimated that the output of developing Africa fell in 1984 by 0.5 per cent, whereas an increase of 3.2 per cent had been forecast in 1983. Given such a fall, per capita output would have decreased by at least 10 per cent since 1980."[9] In fact, based on more recent evidence, the World Bank states that "since 1980, this region's per capita GDP has fallen by 16.6 per cent."[10] In other words, *this is not even growth without development; it is neither growth nor development.*

Nor are the prospects brighter. The projections for 1985–1995 made by the World Bank under both the "low case" and the "high case" scenarios hold no bright prospects for sub-Saharan Africa. In the low case, "per capita income in low-income Africa would decline" by 0.5 percent, and in the high case, it "would still do badly"—i.e., per capita GDP would decline by 0.1 percent.[11] What is even more striking is that it is only low-income Africa for which negative growth rates are foreseen.

And what do these prospects imply? "On this basis, real African incomes in 1995 will be so low that between 65 and 80 per cent of the people will be living below the poverty line compared with roughly 60 per cent today."[12] In other words, the situation, which is distressing enough today, threatens to be even more distressing tomorrow.

Any attempt to understand this crisis of declining per capita incomes must begin with an examination of the agricultural sector, for this is indeed the villain of the piece. This brings us to the problem of the structure of production to which we alluded earlier. If we take the low-income economies of sub-Saharan Africa, which are the most vulnerable victims of the crisis, the share of agriculture in GDP in 1983 was a sizeable 40 percent. Perhaps even more revealing is the fact that this figure was 43 percent in 1965, thus suggesting very little structural transformation within a period of almost twenty years.[13] The upshot of all this is that stagnation in African economies can, to a large extent, be explained by a stagnating agriculture, whose most revealing manifestation is the series of recent famines.

The widespread famines in Africa, which have caused and are causing unprecedented devastation of human lives, are well known. The phrase "food crisis" is no doubt inadequate to describe this human tragedy because it does not capture the acuteness and multi-dimensional nature of the catastrophe. But to the extent that it portrays the inability of the African continent to meet the most elementary requirement of feeding itself, there is some merit in talking about a "food crisis."

Just what are the dimensions of the crisis? To be sure, not all African countries have been hit by famine. But it is equally certain that an increasing number are being threatened by the spectre of mass starvation. As of 1984, twenty-seven countries were characterized as "most seriously affected by drought," and these represented 182 million people, or about one-third of the region's population.[14]

The consequences of food shortages have meant an increasing dependence on food aid, rising food imports, a lowering of already low standards of labor productivity, and social and political instability. According to the Executive Secretary of ECA, at the end of 1984, twenty-four countries were declared "abnormally dependent on food aid."[15]

This increased dependence on international charity has gone hand in hand with rising food imports and the consequent diversion of foreign exchange resources from long-term development needs to emergency relief operations. We are told that "Africa had to double its volume of food imports between 1975 and 1980 by which year the average food self-sufficiency ratio for the continent had dropped to 86 percent from its level of 98 percent during the 1960s implying that, on average, each African had around 12 percent less homegrown food in 1980 than 20 years previously."[16] Food shortages and the hunger, poor health, and malnutrition that they cause inevitably lead to a decline in labor productivity, one of the prime reasons for the poor performance of agriculture in Africa. One must also take into account the economic and social instability that food shortage generates, especially the creation of massive numbers of refugees and displaced persons. And there is of course incalculable damage to morale and human dignity.

While it is true that the recent and recurrent droughts have served to dramatize the African food crisis, it must be recognized that the history of the continent's dismal agricultural performance is a much longer one. As many students of the problem have pointed out, to blame the crisis on the weather, while correct up to a point, is to miss the fact that "Africa's current food crisis is long term in nature and (that) it has been building up for two decades."[17] As Eicher has pointed out, the immediate problems of famine and the feeding and resettling of refugees can be alleviated through crash food production projects or a doubling of aid.[18] "But since the food and hunger crisis has been in the making for 10 to 20 years, viable solutions to the crisis cannot be found without facing up to a number of difficult political, structural and technical problems over the next several decades."[19]

The major problem is that in the last two decades or so food production in Africa as a whole has failed to keep pace with population growth. In other words, per capita food production has been declining. The average annual growth rate of food production per capita in sub-Saharan Africa, which was 0.2 percent in 1960–70, had plummeted to −0.9 percent during 1970–82. The corresponding figures for total agricultural production per capita are 0.2 percent and −1.1 percent, respectively.[20] Or, to quote an alternative set of figures, "the continent's per capita food production which fell by 7 per cent during the 1960s declined by 15 per cent during 1970s."[21] And it must be added that only in sub-Saharan Africa did per capita food production decline over the past two decades.[22]

In seeking the roots of the crisis, therefore, not much illumination can be obtained by focusing on the recent droughts alone. A full answer demands a critical appraisal of Africa's agrarian framework, institutions, and policies, as inherited from the colonial past and as they have evolved during the postindependence period. To quote Eicher again, "the crisis stems from a seamless web of political, technical and structural constraints which are a product of colonial surplus extraction strategies, misguided development plans and priorities of African states since independence, and faulty advice from many expatriate planning advisers. These complex, deep-rooted constraints can only be understood in historical perspective."[23]

Declining per capita output and declining per capita food production are intimately related phenomena, because "at the root of economic backwardness, stagnation and decline in many African countries is the poor performance of the agricultural sector, which is also the most dominant sector."[24]

Why has per capita output in Africa been declining? While it is possible to list various causes, it would be more fruitful to identify the most important variables. According to the World Bank, the major determinants of growth in per capita income are (a) the rate of growth of population, (b) the proportion of GDP allocated to investment, and (c) the additional income generated per unit of investment, i.e., efficiency of resource use.[25] Since "sub-Saharan Africa in the 1970s was not short of investment, as indicated by the investment income ratio, whether in comparison with the 1960s or with the 1970s average of low-income countries of South Asia," says the Bank, "declining availability of resources for development (as indicated by investment as percentage of GDP) was not a major contributory factor, at least not until 1982" to declining per capita output.[26]

The key factors according to this analysis are an accelerating rate of population growth and declining returns from investment. Take population growth first. The conventional wisdom views Africa as a vast, underpopulated continent. While there are countries for which this characterization is correct and while there is the usual danger of overgeneralization, the myth of an underpopulated Africa must be debunked. For Adebayo Adedeji, demographic phenomena "constitute the heart of the African development problematique."[27] We are also told that "Africa is the only region of the world where the rate of growth of population actually increased in the 1970s."[28] In other words, "the population of sub-Saharan Africa is growing faster than that of any other continent."[29] According to the World Bank's calculations, the growth rate of GDP in sub-Saharan Africa, which averaged 1.4 percent per year in the 1960s decelerated to 0.4 percent during 1970–81, the corresponding figures for population being 2.4 percent and 2.8 percent. In other words, about half the deceleration in GDP growth was due to an increase in the population growth rate.[30]

The rest of the burden is placed on "the failure of capital investment to generate income growth comparable to the previous decade."[31] The Bank attributes the low returns to investment to (a) basic constraints, and (b) inappropriate policies and programs.[32] The former includes poor climate and soil; rapid population growth; poor standards of health, education, and institutional development; technical and social constraints; and deteriorating economic management, while the latter includes, among others, "emergence of large macro-economic imbalances; erosion of incentives in agriculture; and overprotection of industry."[33] In other words, part of the problem is due to the constraints within which production takes place and part of it due to defective policies and programs.

As was pointed out earlier, the dismal performance of the agricultural sector, in particular with respect to food production, imposes considerable limits on expansion in other sectors of the economy. The origin of the food crisis antedates the drought and is, therefore, of a long-term nature. Based on FAO data, the World Bank has drawn a trend line for annual grain production per capita for the twenty-four countries most seriously affected by drought for the period from 1970–84.

> The trend line shows a fall of about 2 per cent a year. It passed below what might be considered a minimum for a healthy diet . . . in about 1975 and has continued falling since then. . . . It is difficult to avoid the conclusion that Africa's food production does not deviate dramatically from the trend line; the declines of the past provide a depressing foretaste of what lies ahead.[34]

In making much the same point about the long-term nature of the food crisis, Eicher says that "blanketing the entire subcontinent are its two inter-related components—a food production gap and hunger."[35] What generates these phenomena?

> The food production gap results from an alarming deterioration in food production in the face of a steady increase in the rate of growth of population over the past two decades. The hunger and malnutrition problem is caused by poverty—i.e., even in areas where per capita food production is not declining the poor do not have the income or resources to cope with hunger and malnutrition.[36]

In effect, therefore, one cannot view the food crisis outside the context of underdevelopment. This becomes more evident when one examines the factors behind the poor performance of African agriculture. Much has been written on this topic, and what is attempted here is no more than a highly compressed listing of the most salient factors.

There is, to begin with, the very organization of agricultural production itself. According to one report, "it is probably safe to say that over three-quarters of food consumed in rural households is self-produced."[37] What is the significance of this fact?

> As producers . . . , many rural households operate under very precarious conditions. They are frequently located in marginal production areas, their holdings are small, their techniques antiquated with a minimum use of modern farm tools and inputs. Their yields are, therefore, low and level of production highly susceptible to the vagaries of nature including in particular droughts, pests and diseases. As consumers, these households, being usually remotely located and given Africa's weak infrastructural system, are usually out of reach of centralized food security reserves and food imports. This situation is aggravated by their frequent lack of political organization and influence in comparison to their urban compatriots. This subsistence orientation of production and its inherently precarious nature sets a low ceiling on the extent to which domestic production can meet the food requirements not only of the rural people, but also of Africa's rapidly expanding urban populations. The situation is worsened by changes in life-styles and shifts of food preferences particularly of urban dwellers away from traditional staples.[38]

Second, African agriculture has for long played the role of stepchild in government policies:

> Throughout much of the post-independence period, most states have viewed agriculture as a backward and low-priority sector, have perpetuated colonial policies of pumping the economic surplus out of agriculture, and have failed to give priority to achieving a reliable food surplus as a prerequisite for national, social and economic goals. The failure of most African states to develop an effective set of agricultural policies to deal with the technical, structural, industrial, institutional and human resource constraints is at the heart of the present food crisis.[39]

One manifestation of this failure is the low priority given to investment in agriculture. "Available FAO statistical data on regional and subregional bases for 1978–1982 indicate that per capita total capital expenditure on agriculture has been declining as have per capita total public expenditure, and per capita total recurrent public expenditure on the sector."[40]

Related to this is what Eicher calls "colonial approaches to development," i.e., "the production and extraction of surpluses . . . for external markets while paying little attention to investments in human capital, research on food crops, and strengthening of internal market linkages."[41] The same point is made in a joint report by ADB, ECA, and OAU.[42] Neglect of the physical and institutional infrastructure indispensable for agricultural development (e.g., transport, distribution, extension services, etc.) must be viewed in conjunction with this point.

Especially noteworthy is the question of incentives to agricultural producers. The price and tax policies followed by many African governments are designed to provide cheap food to urban dwellers and cheap raw materials for industries. The effect of this on incentives has been detrimental as it "has translated itself into severely eroded terms of trade between rural communities and urban dwellers resulting in many instances in inadequate production of both food and other products and worsening rural-urban exodus."[43]

African agriculture is characterized by very low productivity, owing, in large measure, to the low level of technology. The green revolution, which has brought about spectacular increases in crop yields elsewhere in the Third World (albeit with built-in problem), seems to have bypassed Africa. And even where there have been some advances in technology, they "have tended to be concentrated on large-scale commercial production and therefore miss the mainstay of the continent's food economy—the small-holder sector."[44]

All these factors, together with the environmental constraints within which African agriculture operates and the neglect and bad management of environmental resources, as well as the well-known droughts, account for the sector's stagnation and the food crisis. Since many of these factors are inherent in the state of underdevelopment, it is pertinent to view the food crisis as a derivative of the crisis of underdevelopment.

For this reason is it dangerous to indulge in facile optimism as soon as nature decides to be more generous with rains. In this regard, consider the opening statement of the 1985 end-of-year message of the Executive Secretary of the Economic Commission for Africa:

> This time last year, when I made the 1984 end-of-year statement, Africa was still in the grip of the worst drought in decades. From the Sahel to southern Africa a belt of drought stretched across 27 countries, threatening the very survival of almost 200 million people. Now thankfully, the indications are that the intensity of the great 1983–85 drought has broken. Over most of the continent the rains returned to normal—in some areas, above normal. According to our information, . . . the 1985 crop will be a bumper one. . . . Even more encouragingly, some countries of Eastern and Southern Africa . . . will be able to resume the export of grains. And in such hard-hit countries as Ethiopia and the Sudan the harvest will be 1 million tons higher than in 1984. In West Africa the harvest will be 50 per cent higher.[45]

The sense of relief and the spirit of optimism that pervade this statement are understandable, but the weather is only one element of Africa's problem. Contrast the tone of the quotation above with ECA's assessment of the situation one year later:

> After the drought ended in 1985, it was hoped that 1986 would witness the start of a steady recovery of the economies of developing Africa. It did not happen.[46]

Why not? The reasons are not far to seek. Although "the 1986 season was generally good for agriculture,"

> external demand conditions turned for the worse, despite the exceptional case of coffee, the price of which rose because of drought in Brazil. Even the coffee boom was short-lived. . . . On other markets, demand was poor and over-supply a general condition. Oil prices in particular literally collapsed. . . . Inevitably, these developments had a profound impact on the fortunes of the region as a whole.[47]

The Crisis of Dependence

The crisis of underdevelopment manifests itself not only in the sphere of production but in the sphere of exchange as well. Hence the importance of the external economic environment. A quarter of a century after political independence, African countries are economically even more dependent on the international economic system than ever before. Their chronic balance of payments crises and their worsening external debt problems are an expression of this fundamental reality.

Africa's economies are dependent on the world market for their exports, imports, technology, and capital flows. The consequences of this dependence are not uniform, depending as they do on whether the country concerned is oil-importing, oil-exporting, least-developed, landlocked, etc. But the impact is there, and all African economies are sensitive to the vagaries of the world market. It is in this sense that one is justified in talking about a crisis of dependence, of which the balance of payments crisis is but one component.

This point is dramatically brought out by the impact of the 1980–83 world recession. This recession meant the stagnation of world trade, a decline in commodity prices and increased protectionism in the industrialized countries.[48] According to ECA, "the decline in Africa's share in world trade has continued in recent years. . . . The period 1981–1982 was one of serious recession, but the decline continued in 1983–1984. . . ."[49] According to the World Bank, for most of Africa's export crops "the fall in the world market shares that started in the 1970s continued in the 1980s. These declines have occurred in commodities in which Africa has a comparative advantage and which are likely to remain its main potential source of foreign exchange earnings."[50] These include oilseeds, tea, bananas, cotton, and coffee. To appreciate the proper magnitude of the problem, it is necessary to realize that "the structure of African exports is characterized by the predominance of primary commodities, concentration on a small number of commodities, and concentration of the leading commodities in a limited number of countries."[51] Twelve commodities accounted for 84.7 percent of total African exports in 1980.[52] Not only is this proportion inordinately high, but it has also been steadily rising since the 1960s. Moreover, in most African countries a large proportion of exports is accounted for by one or two commodities, a fact which makes them more vulnerable to the erratic behavior of the international market.

The problem is not only one of declining exports but also one of declining prices. According to the World Bank, "between 1980 and 1982, prices of non-oil primary commodities declined by 27 per cent in current dollar terms. The loss of income due to deterioration in the terms of trade was 1.2 per cent of GDP for sub-Saharan Africa; middle-income oil importers suffered the biggest loss (3 percent of GDP), oil exporters had a slight gain (0.5 per cent of GDP), and low-income countries a loss of 2.4 per cent of GDP."[53] The situation was much the same during the next two years.[54]

This has inevitably meant recurrent trade and current account deficits. "The aggregate account deficit during 1970s increased at the alarming average rate of 38.2 per cent per year, reaching a peak of 18,319 million SDRs in 1981.[55] However, the situation improved in subsequent years, the current account deficit, which had been more than 49 million dollars in 1981–1982, (having) decreased to 27.3 billion dollars in 1983–1984."[56] It ought to be pointed out, however, that while some of this improvement was due to an improvement in the export position, it was largely caused by "import cuts in the face of a growing gap between the availability of external finance and the deficits to be covered."[57]

What the last point suggests is that African countries have had to make adjustments in order to cope with the effects of the world recession. One consequence is a contraction of imports "either through currency devaluation . . . or by direct limitation of current categories of imports and of import-generating expenditure."[58] With the exception of the oil-exporting countries, the burden of import retrenchment has fallen on capital goods, whose relative share in total imports has been decreasing while that of food and fuel has been increasing.[59] The declining share of capital goods imports places obvious constraints on long-term development, and increasing dependence on imported fuel and food makes African economies even more vulnerable to external factors.

The picture with respect to exports and imports has important implications for capital flows. Traditionally, external capital flows to sub-Saharan Africa have been substantial. For example, "between 1970 and

1982, official development assistance (ODA) per capita increased in real terms by 5 per cent a year, much faster than for other developing countries."[60] But the picture has changed since then. We are told that ODA levels stagnated during 1980–82 and that "net flows from private sources declined sharply (by about 50 per cent) with the decline particularly marked for oil-importing countries."[61] This decline in net capital inflows continued into 1982–84 and was accompanied by a fall in foreign exchange reserves, which at the end of 1984 were only enough to finance two months of imports.[62]

The 1980–83 recession sent shock waves into both developed and developing economies. However, the recovery that began in 1984 and from which other regions benefited seems to have bypassed Africa, where "most commodity prices fell, including those of crude oil, and demand for the related African exports was sluggish."[63]

What this suggests is that Africa's balance of payments crisis is not a creation of recent world economic history, although this has certainly intensified it, but that it has underlying causes. A partial list of these would include a strategy of reliance on primary goods exports inherited from the colonial past, indiscriminately applied strategies of import substitution, and defective structures of production. In other words, while recognizing the importance of external factors in aggravating the situation, one must take a close look at the various policies of African governments themselves, whose policies have for the most part tended to perpetuate Africa's dependence on the world economy.

A corollary of the balance of payments crisis is the debt crisis. One must be cautious in talking about a debt crisis in Africa, because it is possible to exaggerate the magnitude of the problem. The phenomenon is by no means pervasive, concentrated as it is in relatively few countries. According to ECA, "in 1982, for example, six countries accounted for 55.8 per cent of the total debt in sub-Saharan developing countries, Nigeria alone accounting for 20.2 per cent."[64] This is not to belittle the seriousness of the problem for the countries concerned, because in some of them "notably the Sudan, Zaire and Côte d'Ivoire—debt has become a crushing burden on the balance of payments, practically choking off growth."[65] It is merely to emphasize the need for looking at the problem in the right perspective.

By the middle of 1987, public debt for Africa was 200 billion dollars which is not unduly alarming by, say, Latin American standards. But, when viewed in the African context, "it is . . . a very heavy burden for the fragile economies of Africa to bear."[66] In the words of the World Bank, "debt servicing has surfaced as a major problem in sub-Saharan Africa in the 1980's."[67]

In 1983 total external debt was 50 percent of GDP, and we are told that "no other part of the world has such a high proportion."[68] In the same year, external debt represented 20.3 percent of the value of exports of goods and services.[69] These are no small magnitudes, and they have important implications for debt servicing. "In 1984 debt-service payments by developing Africa reached 19.5 billion dollars and the ratio to exports increased to 22.3 per cent. The ECA secretariat had expected a decline to 21 per cent . . . and now forecasts the very high of 25 per cent for 1985."[70]

The consequences of increasing debt servicing difficulties include a reduction of import capacity and a reduced inflow of capital resources due to inability to meet past obligations—in general, reduced capability to find resources for long-term development. It remains to be seen, however, whether recent Latin American history with respect to debt servicing will be Africa's fate tomorrow.

The debt service problem is caused by interacting endogenous and exogenous forces. According to the World Bank, "Africa's debt servicing difficulties reflect the underlying weakness of its economy and particularly its inefficient use of investment."[71] As much is admitted by the ECA's Executive Secretary. He argues that "the rapid accumulation of external debt is in itself due to disequilibrium between resource needs and resources domestically available. In other words, external debt has been used to supplement declining domestic savings, augment foreign exchange receipts and smoothen the consumption path over time."[72]

But the problem is also due to a hostile international economic environment. According to Adedeji, the exogenous factors that exacerbate Africa's debt servicing problems include "the slow growth in world demand for primary commodities, aggressiveness of foreign banks in their lending behaviour to African countries . . . , structural changes in the flow of financial resources to Africa, the hardening of terms of external borrowing, and the appreciation of currencies in which external debt is contracted and serviced."[73] The relative role of domestic and external factors can be debated, but without getting into this debate, it is important to affirm that the African debt crisis emanates from and is intensified by the interaction of both sets of factors.

On the face of it, Africa's debt service and balance of payments problems, which are interrelated, are caused by external factors. While the role of such factors should not be minimized, neither should that of domestic ones. Debt and balance of payments questions are after all issues of foreign exchange, and a country's foreign exchange needs are to a large extent determined by the state of its economy. It is a well-established procedure in the literature on development to calculate a country's foreign exchange requirements by estimating the savings gap (i.e., the difference between planned investment and planned savings) and/or the foreign exchange gap (i.e., the difference between anticipated imports and anticipated exports). In other words, foreign resources are meant to make good the shortfall in domestic savings or to cover the difference between imports and exports. There can be no doubt that in a healthy economy these gaps cannot be substantial.

As was pointed out earlier, Africa's economies are highly dependent on the world market, the rhetoric about self-reliance notwithstanding. It is from this fundamental reality that any attempt at understanding the debt and balance of payments crises (i.e., the crisis of dependence) must start. The genesis of such dependence goes back to colonial days, but it has unfortunately been carried over into the postindependence era.

One element of the colonial heritage is a strategy of development based on the expansion of primary goods exports. The pitfalls of such a strategy are well known and need not be repeated here. Its harvest has been increased dependence, and hence increased vulnerability of African economies.

At a later stage, a redress was sought through policies of import substitution, both as strategies of industrialization and as means of alleviating balance of payments problems. But on neither score has import substitution proved effective. While it has been largely successful in meeting domestic demand for a number of consumption goods (e.g., textiles, shoes, etc.), it has a sorry record in producing intermediate and capital goods for local industry and manufactures for export. "Developing Africa accounts for less than 0.5 per cent of the world's exports of manufactures, a share which has declined in recent years and seems likely to decrease even further in the second half of the 1980s."[74] This is how an ECA study sums up the record:

> In a large number of countries import substitution was attempted via direct private foreign investment, which was offered substantial and indiscriminate protection, local investible funds at low rates of interest, and excessive concessions such as tax holidays and accelerated depreciation allowances. Despite these generous incentives, however, such policies have not resulted in the self-reliant utilization of African resources and capabilities mainly because they were attempted under the inherited colonial economic structure: instead a large number of developing African countries have become heavily dependent on their import-substitution industries on externally derived inputs. . . . Furthermore, since these industries operate in sheltered markets, investors have been able to maximize profits without rationalizing uneconomic business structures. In brief, far from alleviating the balance-of-payments problem, the pursuit of import substitution has tended to make it worse."[75]

Balance of payment problems are also built into the structure of African exports and imports. The items that dominate Africa's exports are cocoa, coffee, cotton, copper, and petroleum products,[76] all of which are primary commodities. With the exception of the last item, which is exported by only a handful of countries, the others have not done well in the world market either in terms of volume or in terms of prices. Moreover, the direction of Africa's exports is very narrowly oriented, thereby aggravating their vulnerability. In 1978, for example, 88.3 percent of Africa's exports went to the developed market economies while the share of the centrally planned economies was only 4.8 percent.

With regard to imports, the rising share of food and fuel has already been mentioned. The former is a direct result of the food crisis, a point which lends additional force to the argument that all the specific crises are not only interrelated but also derivatives of the crisis of underdevelopment. The impact of rising oil prices has been considerable for African countries that are not oil producers. "Their oil import bill rose from 0.8 billion dollars in 1973 to about 8.4 billion dollars in 1980, an average annual rate of growth of about 40 per cent. As a proportion of their total export proceeds, it increased from 8.2 per cent in 1973 to 29.2 per cent in 1980, when it was equivalent to 25.5 per cent of their expenditure on imports, 5.1 per cent of their GDP and 27.4 per cent of their fixed capital formation."[77] The special problem that fuel poses is that any attempt at curbing its consumption is bound to constrain growth. Hence it represents a delicate dilemma for the non-oil-producing countries. Nor is this the entire story. The increasing share of food and fuel in the total import bill has been accompanied by a decline in the share of capital goods, again with obvious implications for growth.

It is against this background that Africa's current account deficits must be considered. Lagging export volumes, declining export prices, and rising import prices must inevitably lead to deficits, as indeed they have done. In other words, the deficits are basically determined by the structure of exports and imports, which is but a reflection of the structure of production.

These balance of payments deficits, together with the domestic savings gap, represent the immediate causes of the debt crisis. As the ECA has observed,

> Aid has tended to supplant domestic savings and dilute efforts to mobilize domestic resources. Most African governments that have easy access to resources from abroad . . . step up consumption and refrain from raising taxes. If efforts had been made to mobilize domestic resources instead of relying so heavily on foreign capital, high levels of investment in African countries would not have put so much of a strain on their balance of payments.[78]

Although the debt crisis has domestic roots, there is no question that the international economic environment has exacerbated it. "For instance, the interest charged to sub-Saharan African countries increased from 3.7 per cent in 1970 to 10.1 per cent in 1981; at the same time average maturity periods declined from 25.2 years to 16.0 years; grace periods declined from 6.6 years to 4.4 years, and grant element in loans was reduced from 46 percent to 6 percent."[79]

The costs of dependence have, therefore, been quite high. It is in recognition of this reality that African leaders in a number of declarations, most notably the Lagos Plan of Action, have articulated a strategy based on self-reliance. There is of course more to the problem than mere statements of intentions. Africa today is more dependent than ever before on the international economy, and the task of building truly self-reliant economies has yet to begin in earnest.

Impact of the Crisis

While dealing with the character of the African crisis above we have, *en passant*, made references to different aspects of its impact on society. Therefore, what is attempted here is not so much a novel treatment of the problem as a more systematic articulation.

The most obvious impact of the crisis is the deterioration in the quality of life, which had never been high to begin with. To return to a point that was made at the beginning of the paper, after a generation of political independence, low-income Africa is poorer today than twenty-five years ago. This is no mere abstract fact, but manifests itself dramatically in the day-to-day life of the ordinary African. Thus, "about 70 per cent of the total African population is now destitute (seriously below the poverty line) or is on the verge of poverty."[80] Under such circumstances it is the very survival of millions of human beings that is at stake:

> The review of the social conditions and trends over the past decade, and especially over the past four years, gives cause to much alarm and dismay. As a result of the rapid escalation of the socio-economic crisis, Africa finds itself in the grip of a human tragedy and social and economic difficulties of unprecedented proportions. Serious losses of human life, widespread famine and hunger, increased and massive displacements of populations have become the order of the day. . . . Overall, the impact of the current economic and social crisis on African countries has been so severe to the extent that for many of those countries, the main issue at stake has not been one of economic and social development, but one of sheer survival.[81]

Moreover, the retrenchment programs that many African governments have been forced to implement on account of the crisis have seriously limited the resources at their disposal, with obvious implications for their capacity to finance such vital activities as nutrition, health, education, transportation, housing, etc. Declining export earnings have meant reduced availability of foreign exchange and, together with reduced imports, significant loss of government revenues in the form of taxes on the foreign trade sector, to say nothing about the multiplier effect on domestic incomes and hence taxes. Unfortunately, in times of retrenchment it is on the social services that the axe falls first. We are told that in Africa, "as a result of the deteriorating economic conditions, the social development sector has had to suffer. Governments have had to make severe cuts in social services and programmes which meant further setbacks to living standards and accentuation of the widespread impoverishment."[82] While thus depicting the precarious existence of the living we should of course not forget that their lot is better than that of the hundreds of thousands whose lives have been claimed by famine. It remains to add, however, that there is no guarantee that the famines of recent memory will not repeat themselves with the same or intensified fury.

In considering the social implications of the crisis a question that should not be lost sight of is the problem of unemployment, serious even in "normal" times, but exacerbated by the crisis. Declining rates of economic growth in the face of a constantly expanding labor force have inevitably meant more unemployment. In Africa this takes mostly the form of urban, educated, youth unemployment. We are told that "unemployment in urban areas would work out to a startling rate of between 30 per cent and 40 per cent of the urban labour force."[83] According to another source, "ECA calculates that unemployment and underemployment in developing Africa has now risen to about 45 per cent of the labour force and the trend will continue if present economic conditions persist."[84] This represents a staggering waste of human resources as well as a breeding ground for a host of social problems usually associated with widespread unemployment.

While the negative impact of the crisis on contemporary living standards is thus considerable, perhaps even more significant from a long-term perspective is that it has seriously eroded Africa's capacity to create a viable, autonomously propelled economy. It is a cruel paradox that the crisis, generated in no small part by Africa's dependence on the international economy, has in turn pushed the continent into greater dependence on this economy. And the costs of dependence are prohibitive. Greater reliance on food aid, apart from the "image" problem it has created, has tended to undermine local initiatives and to perpetuate a dependent mentality. Where food aid has not been enough to close the gap between demand and supply, resort has had to be made to imports, thus drawing scarce foreign exchange away from the tasks of financing long-run development to meeting today's subsistence needs. And, as shown earlier, the balance of payments and debt crises have put Africa increasingly at the mercy of the international economy. Consequently, the prospects for independent development are dimmer, the destiny of future generations is mortgaged and, inevitably, political independence—never really substantive—seriously compromised.

The crisis has also generated a massive displacement of persons and widespread social and political instability. Famines, in particular, have forced millions of people to abandon their homes in search of food, and coupled with other factors, they have given rise to the intractable refugee problem with which the continent is burdened today. And the crisis has also destabilized regimes or otherwise provoked political unrest.

Such, in brief, are the major effects of the crisis on African societies. One should hasten to add, however, that the impact has not been uniform with respect to countries or with respect to classes. The efficacy with which countries have been able to cope with the crisis has varied; in general, it is the more fragile economies that have received the brunt of the burden. Likewise, it is the poorer segments of society that have proved most vulnerable to the deleterious effects of the crisis. Therefore, if the ordinary African feels cheated by a generation of so-called independence, he will be entirely correct.

ORIGINS OF THE CRISIS: THE NEOCLASSICAL/RADICAL CONTROVERSY

While the facts regarding the African crisis brook no debate, there is little agreement with respect to its causes. To be sure, there can be no dispute that, for example, the food crisis is related to drought, that the debt crisis cannot be viewed in isolation from a hostile economic environment, and that adverse terms of trade contribute to the balance of payments crisis. But this is only looking at the problem superficially. Every crisis has its proximate and underlying causes, and the task of analysis is, while recognizing the former, to go beyond them and articulate the latter. What is required, therefore, is a "grand theory," and it is at this level that controversies arise and become meaningful.

At the risk of oversimplification one can say that there are two clearly defined and opposed interpretations of the African crisis. One is what has variously been described as the neoclassical, monetarist, pragmatic, orthodox school, whose most effective champion is the IMF-World Bank fraternity. The other, which may be dubbed the radical or political economy approach, finds expression in Marxist or neo-Marxist writings. The "official" African position (e.g., the Lagos Plan of Action and the Recovery Programme) is less well-defined and it seems to be an eclectic amalgam of certain aspects of each of the first two.

Shorn of its embellishments, the IMF-World Bank position is predicated on the supremacy of the free market and on the inefficiency of state intervention in the economy. According to this school, the malaise of African economies stems from the fact that the role of prices, markets, and the private sector is too little while that of the state is too large. In other words, the problem is one of faulty policies pursued by African governments. Such policies, it is argued, discriminate against agriculture, give rise to inordinately high urban wages, lead to inflated state expenditures, promote inefficiency, undermine producer prices, and lead to an overvaluation of currency.

The prescription that follows from such diagnosis is obvious. It advocates greater reliance on the market and minimum state intervention in the economy. Whether in the form of the conditionalities package on the IMF's short-term stabilization measures, or the "structural adjustment" programs of the World Bank, the medicine recommended is fairly standard. It involves reduced government spending, restrictions on credit creation, currency devaluation, a reduction of imports, and a greater role for prices, markets, and the private sector. For example, the World Bank's "adjustment with growth" strategy for sub-Saharan Africa involves raising more resources for investment, using new and existing resources efficiently, and curbing population growth.[85]

It is the second element, the efficiency question, that lies at the heart of the strategy. It involves devaluation (the stated objective being to reduce balance of payments deficits and to shift "the internal terms of trade in favour of those who produce for export . . . and away from those who consume imports"),[86] correcting the urban-rural bias and rationalizing the public sector (which is characterized by "inefficient management and over-ambitious investment programmes").[87] Thus, the pragmatic thesis is that, since the crisis is largely a product of misguided policies, a determined and speedy rectification of these policies (preferably with the firm guidance of the IMF and the World Bank) is the only sure way out of the crisis.

The radical school, on the contrary, attributes the crisis to *structural* causes. It is argued, to begin with, that the current crisis cannot be understood unless put in broad historical perspective. Thus the point of departure for examining Africa's economic malaise is the history of colonialism. Colonialism not only exploited Africa (underdeveloped Africa, to use Walter Rodney's language) but it also denied it an opportunity of autonomous development, having relegated it to the status of a mere appendage of the world capitalist economy. At independence, therefore, the economies inherited by African countries were essentially incorporated into the capitalist framework. The economic structures were largely colonial.

Further, the postcolonial state in Africa is a neocolonial one, meaning it is incapable of dismantling the inherited economic structures and bringing about structural transformation, all claims to the contrary notwithstanding. What exists in these countries is thus a capitalism that is incomplete and has no chance of full-blown development. It is also extroverted, its dependence on the "center" even greater in the postindependence era, and therefore its chances of autocentric development effectively blocked. Being dominated by foreign capital, it inevitably gravitates to the distortions produced by undue reliance on export and the preponderance of light industries and the so-called informal sector. Whatever "development" takes place in this context is therefore dependent "development."

According to this analysis, there is little to be gained by lamenting the policy failures of African governments, because such failures are not accidental but a logical outcome of the structure of dependence. After all, the neocolonial ruling classes are beneficiaries of the neocolonial economy. The state, in other words, being part of the problem, cannot be part of the solution. What is prescribed, therefore, is the replacement of the neocolonial state by a revolutionary state, which alone is capable of providing the leadership for disengaging from dependency and embarking on autonomous development.

What do we make of these divergent positions? If the accuracy of a diagnosis is judged by the effectiveness of prescriptions based on it, the record is a mixed one in both cases. As far as the IMF-World Bank prescription is concerned, it seems to have raised more problems than it has solved in most of the countries where it has been applied. This is not the place to go into a detailed examination of the record, but IMF and World Bank reports support our contention.[88] That results have not turned out as envisaged is usually attributed to not enough of the medicine being applied or to unforeseen developments. It is especially noteworthy that adjustment programs have had social implications which have on a number of occasions threatened the very stability of societies which have attempted to implement them. At any rate, it is difficult to cite a case which can be called an unqualified success.

With respect to the political economy approach, it must be said that the fortunes of what might be called "radical states" have not been particularly enviable either. In fact, some of them (e.g., Tanzania,[89] Mozambique) have been forced to swallow the IMF-World Bank medicine. Of course, the advocates of this school can argue that none of these countries has brought about the required amount of structural transformation, or that there are extenuating circumstances that explain their dismal performances. But the dividing line between theorizing and casuistry becomes uncomfortably thin here.

Still, this (radical) approach gives a more accurate perspective or vision of the problem than the neoclassical stance, although the latter has more appeal for practical day-to-day "crisis management."

What is clear is that the African crisis did not emerge, although it became acute, in the last five or ten years. It is rooted in the very structure of African economies and exacerbated by policies which can only be described as misguided and short-sighted. In fact, *the African crisis is a crisis of underdevelopment.*

What is this crisis of underdevelopment? The best way to demonstrate that it is the root of all the other crises is to take each one of them in turn and show that they have roots in the very phenomenon of African underdevelopment. To do so is not to deny the magnitude of, say, the famine or balance of payments crisis in Africa, but to focus on the underlying causes of these crises. Take famine, for example. It has now become axiomatic to attribute this scourge to the successive droughts that have hit the continent. But droughts, being aberrations of nature, are not peculiar to Africa. Why is it that droughts do occur in certain countries but that their peoples do not experience mass starvation? Why is it that one does not talk about a debt crisis in the developed countries? Why are many countries that bore the brunt of the world recession now beginning to recover from it while sub-Saharan Africa has not managed to do so? Or why is it that certain countries which have had successive merchandise trade deficits are not threatened with the spectre of depleted foreign exchange reserves? To raise these questions is in effect to redress the imbalance of much writing on the African predicament, which has largely tended to view each "crisis" on its own, as though it were independently generated and only peripherally related to the deeper crisis of underdevelopment.

In seeking the roots of the crisis, it is tempting but erroneous to settle for one-dimensional explanations. There is no doubt, for example, that the colonial past has had an important impact on Africa's subsequent development, but it cannot be held to account for the policy failures of independent African governments during the last twenty-five years. Similarly, while there is no doubt that the world economic environment is hostile to Africa's development, it should not always be conjured to explain away failures to remove constraints on the domestic front. The roots of the problem should rather be sought in a dynamic interaction between internal and external factors, with the accent on the former, because (a) they are more decisive in the long run, and (b) there is in any case little that African countries can do to change the world economic environment. To quote the ECA Conference of Ministers:

> At the root cause of Africa's economic and social crisis and Africa's underdevelopment in general are the internal structural imbalances of African economies and their excessive outward orientation and overt dependence—an unenviable legacy of our colonial past. Regrettably, post-independence development policies have not brought about significant changes in this colonially-inherited, lopsided production structure which is heavily dominated by export-oriented agriculture, a small industrial base—factured and only minimally linked with the region's natural resource base—and a mining sector which is not only dependent on external finance, technology and management but whose output is also predominantly destined for export.[90]

The tragedy is that such analysis finds little reflection in the conduct of Africa's rulers, who are loud in proclaiming their commitment to self-reliance and structural transformation but are even louder in their appeals to the international community to pull them out of the quagmire.

NOTES

1. OAU, *Lagos Plan of Action for the Economic Development of Africa 1980–2000* (Addis Ababa: OAU, 1981), 5.

2. *Ibid.*, 7–8.

3. OAU, *Africa's Priority Programme for Economic Recovery 1986–1990* (Rome: Food and Agricultural Organisation, for the OAU, 1985), 4.

4. *Declaration on the Economic Situation in Africa Adopted by the Twenty-first Ordinary Session of the Assembly of Heads of State and Government of the Organization of African Unity* (Addis Ababa, 18–20 July 1985), 1.

5. ECA, *ECA and Africa's Development 1983–2008* (Addis Ababa, 1983), 2.

6. The World Bank, *Financing Adjustment with Growth in Sub-Saharan Africa, 1986–90* (Washington, D.C.: The World Bank, 1986), 1.

7. The World Bank, *Annual Report 1986* (Washington, D.C.: The World Bank, 1986), 40.

8. The World Bank, *World Development Report 1985* (Washington, D.C.: The World Bank, 1985), 174.

9. ECA, *Survey of Economic and Social Conditions in Africa 1983–84* (Addis Ababa: ECA, 1984), 1.

10. The World Bank, *Annual Report 1986* (Washington, D.C.: The World Bank, 1986), 39.

11. The World Bank, *World Development Report 1984* (Washington, D.C.: The World Bank, 1984), 35–37.

12. The World Bank, *Toward Sustained Development in Sub-Saharan Africa: A Joint Programme of Action* (Washington, D.C.: The World Bank, 1984), 9.

13. The World Bank, *Financing Adjustment with Growth*, 69.

14. ECA, *Survey, 1983–84*, 44.

15. *Ibid.*, 4.

16. African Development Bank, Economic Commission for Africa, and Organization of African Unity, "The African Food Crisis and the Role of the African Development Bank in Tackling the Problem," 1984, 2.

17. Carl K. Eicher, "Facing up to Africa's Crisis," *Foreign Affairs* (Fall 1982): 151.

18. *Ibid.*

19. *Ibid.*, 152.

20. The World Bank, *Toward Sustained Development*, 77.

21. ADB, ECA, OAU, *op. cit.*, 2.

22. Eicher, *op. cit.*, 154; ADB, ECA, OAU, *op. cit.*, 4.

23. Eicher, *op. cit.*, 157.

24. Adebayo Adedeji, *The African Development Problematique: Demography, Drought and Desertification, Dependency, Disequilibrium, Debt and Destabilization or The Paralysis of Multiple Debilitating Crises* (Addis Ababa: ECA, 1985), 6.

25. The World Bank, *Toward Sustained Development*, 21.

26. *Ibid.*

27. Adedeji, *op. cit.*, 10.

28. Eicher, *op. cit.*, 155.

29. The World Bank, *Toward Sustained Development*, 26.

30. *Ibid.*, 26.

31. *Ibid.*, 21.

32. *Ibid.*, 24–25.

33. *Ibid.*, 25.

34. *Ibid.*, 13–14.

35. Eicher, *op. cit.*, 151.

36. *Ibid.*

37. ADB, ECA, OAU, *op. cit.*, 5.

38. *Ibid.*

39. Eicher, *op. cit.*, 163.

40. ADB, ECA, OAU, *op. cit.*, 8.

41. Eicher, *op. cit.*, 157.

42. ADB, ECA, OAU, *op. cit.*, 4–5.

43. *Ibid.*, 4.

44. *Ibid.*, 6.

45. ECA, *Survey of Economic and Social Conditions in Africa, 1984–85* (Addis Ababa, 1986), 2.

46. ECA, *Survey of Economic and Social Conditions in Africa, 1985–86* (Addis Ababa, 1987), 3.

47. *Ibid.*

48. The World Bank, *Toward Sustained Development*, 11–12.

49. ECA, *Survey, 1983–84*, 113–14.

50. The World Bank, *Toward Sustained Development*, 11.
51. ECA, *The Balance of Payments Problems of Developing Africa—A Reassessment*, August 1984, 7.
52. *Ibid.*
53. The World Bank, *Toward Sustained Development*, 12.
54. ECA, *Survey, 1983–84*, 18.
55. ECA, *The Balance of Payments*, introduction.
56. ECA, *Survey, 1983–84*, 120.
57. *Ibid.*
58. *Ibid.*, 7.
59. ECA, *The Balance of Payments*, 39.
60. The World Bank, *Toward Sustained Development*, 13.
61. *Ibid.*
62. ECA, *Survey, 1983–84*, 121.
63. *Ibid.*, 7.
64. ECA, *Survey, 1983–84*, 9.
65. Adedeji, *op. cit.*, 16.
66. *Ibid.*
67. The World Bank, *Toward Sustained Development*, 12.
68. ECA, *Survey, 1983–84*, 127.
69. *Ibid.*
70. *Ibid.*, 128.
71. The World Bank, *Toward Sustained Development*, 46.
72. Adedeji, *op. cit.*, 17.
73. *Ibid.*
74. ECA, *Survey, 1983–84*, 105.
75. ECA, *The Balance of Payments*, 2–3.
76. *Ibid.*, 7.
77. ECA, *Survey, 1983–84*, 115.
78. ECA, *The Balance of Payments*, 1.
79. *Ibid.*

80. ECA, OAU, *Social Trends and Major Social Development Problems in Africa* (Addis Ababa, 1985), 1–2.

81. *Ibid.*, 42.

82. *Ibid.*, 11.

83. ILO/JASPA, *Impact of Recession in African Countries: Effects on the Poor* (Addis Ababa, 1985), 74.

84. ECA, OAU, *Social Trends*, 29.

85. The World Bank, *Financing Adjustment with Growth*, 11.

86. *Ibid.*, 16.

87. *Ibid.*, 21.

88. See The World Bank, *Financing Adjustment with Growth;* J. B. Zula and M. Saleh, "Adjustment Programs in Africa: The Recent Experience," IMF Occasional Paper no. 34 (1985); B. Balassa and F. D. McCarthy, *Adjustment Policies and Developing Countries, 1979–1983: An Update* (Washington, D.C.: World Bank Staff Working Paper no. 675, 1984).

89. See H. Campbell, "The IMF Debate and the Politics of Demobilisation in Tanzania," *Eastern Africa Social Science Research Review*, vol. 2, no. 2 (June 1986).

90. *Second Special Memorandum by the ECA Conference of Ministers; International Action for Relaunching the Initiative for Long-term Development and Economic Growth in Africa* (Addis Ababa, 1985), 6.

CHAPTER TWO

The Adaptation of Government to Economic Crisis: Philosophical and Practical Considerations on the Role and Scope of the State in Society

Ibbo Mandaza

INTRODUCTION

The purpose of this chapter is to outline broadly the parameters and main elements of the debate about the state in Africa and its capacity (or the lack of it) to adjust to economic crisis. The Zimbabwe situation is used to illustrate the point. Our intention is to highlight the postcolonial state as one essentially dependent and integrated into an international economy in which it has extremely limited initiative and little independence with which to determine economic policy. This is not to suggest that the postcolonial state is forever hamstrung, precluded and preempted from breaking out of the parameters so defined by the nature of the unequal relationship between developed and underdeveloped countries. It need not be forever a neocolonial state. Indeed the whole problem about development and economic self-reliance is how best the postcolonial state can be liberated from the neocolonial chains. The point, however, is to emphasize the historical conjuncture of which the postcolonial state is part: constrained by the legacy of the colonial past, and faced with the challenge of developing an economy which is linked with those of the developed countries. All this raises important questions about the conception of the problem itself, let alone the methods with which to overcome it.

In the context of our subject, there is the likelihood that "adjustment to economic crisis" is merely adjustment within this structure of dependence. Not surprisingly, this type of adjustment has become synonymous with the initiatives of those international financial institutions that control and police our economies. No doubt many of our countries in Africa are currently more concerned about this type of adjustment than with an economic transformative process that would strengthen the economies against the vagaries of dependence. There are obvious dangers in such a trend, even if we acknowledge that this is in itself a reflection of the weakness of African economies. It has tended to undermine the credibility of African governments vis-à-vis the mass of the people; threatening thereby the postcolonial state itself as it is caught between the demands of the International Monetary Fund (IMF) and the World Bank, on the one hand, and those of the mass of the people, on the other.

I want to believe that we are not yet so economically destitute and ideologically bankrupt as to accept our current economic condition as both inevitable and irredeemable. For even the Lagos Plan of Action and Africa's Priority Programme for Economic Recovery (APPER) acknowledge that the current economic crisis in Africa is fundamentally structural. To quote the words of APPER:

> Nothing short of radical measures will be necessary to ensure the fundamental restructuring and re-orientation of the economies to lead Africa on the road to self-sustained recovery and development. Bold steps must be taken to change these structures and establish more dynamic self-reliant and self-sustaining economies in which economic growth would be more dependent on internal demand stimuli. This will be achieved by adopting an integrated approach to development that takes into account the effective interdependence of sectoral economic activities and by increasing the substitution of factor input from outside, by strengthening regional and sub-regional cooperation and encouraging the coordinated exploration and utilisation of the vast resources of the continent for the benefit of the continent.[1]

It is acknowledged that inappropriate strategies and policies of the African governments themselves have tended to aggravate the crisis. There are two main reasons for this. First, those who are directly responsible for policy, the public administrators and managers, are largely a reflection of the malaise of the neocolonial, postcolonial state. As has already been pointed out, these policymakers design and implement policies within the parameters of the neocolonial situation. This is largely because they have vested class interests in that status quo; but also because the orientation of African public administration, like all public administration systems, is so conservative that it is almost heresy to expect that such bureaucrats could be the agents of socioeconomic change and development.

This leads to the second reason, namely that most public administrators and/or state bureaucrats are, by their very discipline, largely precluded from an understanding of the nature and function of the postcolonial state. In fact, this is the first time in the history of the African Association for Public Administration and Management (AAPAM) that the theme of the Annual Roundtable has fortuitously led us to the discussion of such a subject. And happily so. For it is, perhaps, a reflection of both the growing diversity of opinion in AAPAM, and the fact that twenty years of independence has at last compelled African administrators to begin to realize that no mere platitudes can resolve the economic and social problems that afflict our countries. In any case, it would be useful for this conference to outline briefly the philosophical and practical considerations on the role and scope of the postcolonial state in Africa. This will, perhaps, in turn indicate the enormity of the task before us as we discuss the real possibilities for our governments to adapt to the current economic crisis.

THE POSTCOLONIAL STATE

This discussion flows out of the Leninist conception of the state as a specifically organized and coercive force, "a machine for holding in obedience to one class other subordinated classes."[2] Also politically and ideologically, the state seeks to disorganize and demobilize the exploited classes through the threat of repression as well as through the granting of limited actual or expected benefits and promoting and sustaining ideological illusions. The discussion also takes into account the current debate among African Third World scholars on the nature of the postcolonial state. It emphasizes:

> the historical specificity of post-colonial societies, a specificity which arises from structural changes brought about by the colonial experience and alignments of classes and by the superstructure of political and administrative institutions which were established in that context, and secondly from radical re-alignments of class forces which have been brought about in the post-colonial situation."[3]

The postcolonial state in Africa reveals essential structural similarities with those of the postcolonial states that are referred to in the foregoing quotation. This is particularly so with regard to the dominant role of international finance capital in these states:

> The post-colonial state may foster or frustrate its national bourgeoisie or its landed classes or both, but short of a revolution which puts the direct producers into power it cannot escape its servitude to the metropolitan bourgeoisie.[4]

In the postcolonial situation, the state plays an important and somewhat new role of concealing, for a time, the full and direct impact of international finance capital as it (foreign capital) continues to exploit the human and material resources. In general, therefore, this postcolonial state seeks to reconcile, on the one hand, the pursuit of the developmental objectives of independence in response to the popular aspirations and expectations of the masses; and on the other, the sheer weight—economic and political—of the imperialist force of international finance capital:

> Herein lies the contradictory character of the post-colonial state. It is at the best of times a state split in two—a schizophrenic state, a state torn apart between, on the one hand, the democratic forces of the

people, and, on the other hand, the imperialist forces of the international financial oligarchy. This split is evidenced right through all the institutions of the state—the army, the police, the court system, the parliament and even the government itself (including the cabinet), and we might add, even the political leaders sometimes display schizophrenic tendencies when they feel impelled on the one hand to respond to the democratic demands of the people, and on the other hand feel the pressure of international capital on them which impels them to suppress those very demands they could want to respond to but cannot.[5]

Initially, therefore, the postcolonial state might be able to conceal the ongoing exploitative role of international capital through the political and ideological paraphernalia that accompany the arrival of national independence. In the African situation, in particular, nothing is more enthralling and lulling to the masses—and to the African petite bourgeoisie itself—than the arrival of black majority rule, especially when, in the mind of the average person, this event immediately offers the promise of total (political and economic) liberation. Gradually, however, the postcolonial state, and particularly that component of it that comprises the African petite bourgeoisie, begins to develop an ideological superstructure within which to explain the ever growing disparity between these popular demands and the economic and social realities of the neocolonial situation. It might at first try to enhance, through both ideological expression and social development programs (e.g., education reform, democratization of the employment system, etc.), the myth of equality of opportunity and mobility in a capitalist society; make available and distribute resources in such a way as to mobilize and maintain national support for the governing class; or develop a populist ideology that is imbued "with a harmonistic dream" of a society in which the interests of the African petite bourgeoisie "might be reconciled with the interests of all the other non-capitalist classes and the more enlightened sectors of the metropolitan bourgeoisie."[6] As Mkandawire observes:

> The ruling class must harp more on the myth of homogeneous nationalist cause and movement to conceal the profound division engendered by the adopted model of accumulation which has demanded the historical social alliance that sustained the independence struggle.[7]

However, like all states, the postcolonial state in the final analysis depends on the repressive apparatus which invariably expands and strengthens. It will use this, if necessary, against any action by the exploited and disgruntled masses that may unduly undermine the neocolonial status quo of which the postcolonial state itself is an expression.

The metropolitan bourgeoisie needs activist states on the periphery, states that are strong enough to suppress, by whatever means, growing social contradictions and states that can make foreign investments profitable and profits secure despite various unfavourable circumstances within the national and world economy.[8]

THE POST-WHITE SETTLER COLONIAL STATE IN ZIMBABWE

Elsewhere, I have in the context of the Zimbabwean situation referred to the post-white settler colonial state as a special form of the postcolonial situation in Africa.[9] This is precisely because of the historical legacy of white settler colonialism, the inherited economic and social structures associated with it, and its persistent and pervasive role within both the state itself and the society at large as a viable conduit through which the imperialist forces of international finance capital can compromise and control the new state. But it is a state which, in the circumstances of post-independence Zimbabwe, provides a framework within which the leading sections of the African petite bourgeoisie can also find fulfillment of their class aspirations as they enter the arena that was hitherto restricted largely to the white classes.

As the Lancaster House Agreement of Zimbabwe illustrates, the transitional phase is an important one as far as imperialism (and international capital) is concerned. Its value to the white settler factor is unquestionable. But it has also turned out to be immensely useful to a significant section of the African petite bourgeoisie, including those elements of it who had either actively collaborated with the white settler colonial regime, or feared that the arrival of national independence might threaten their existence and class aspirations. The subject categories of the African petite bourgeoisie are:

A. The governing class: i.e., the ministers, permanent secretaries, and other senior personnel and directors of the administrative apparatus, the general managers of the large parastatals (not including the university and other higher institutions of learning and training), the heads of the appointed party bureaucracy at the different levels, the heads of repressive apparatuses—the army, air force, police, prisons, and state security

B. The comprador elements for whom Zimbabwe's political independence has meant an increase in both their numbers and scope with regard to their link with international capital as either the general managers and chief executives of the major multinational corporations, or mere business "front men" and "public relations" troubleshooters in the intermediary role between these large corporations and elements of the state apparatus

C. The emergent business people—the middle-level merchants, transport operators, and landowners—for whom national independence has meant an increase in opportunities and access to capital accumulation

D. All other sections of the African petite bourgeoisie who, through either the fact of national independence or the accompanying democratization (and Africanization) of the society, find themselves in better employment, with a higher standard of living, and as is the case with students and trainee professionals, are generally in a potentially better position to partake of the "fruits of independence."

The post-white settler colonial state became, therefore, the agency through which international capital hoped to maintain Zimbabwe under imperialist hegemony. But unlike the white settler colonial state, which depended primarily on coercion and repression to control and exploit the wage earners and peasants, the post-white settler colonial state had to develop a new ideology with which to contain popular demands for economic and social change in the period after independence. Like all other postcolonial states, it is caught in a "serious contradiction within itself."[10] On the one hand, it has to seek to complete the mandate and momentum of the armed struggle beyond political independence, in particular, to begin to resolve the land question, which is a burning one for the peasants, and to attend to the equally popular demands of the working people for more jobs, more pay, and better conditions of service. All this was, of course, compounded by the fact that the peasants and workers attributed the land hunger, the exploitation, and the inequalities in general to the white settlers, a great number of whom were still in the country, and in the same positions of economic and social privilege as they had been before independence. It is true that national independence is a great achievement for all the classes among the African people. It ushers in democracy, a sense of security and real peace, and raises new hopes for a qualitative change in the lives of a people the majority of whom had been dehumanized by the weight of colonial oppression and exploitation. Yet the mass of these people expected that national independence would totally liberate them from oppression and exploitation: the end of white rule, the end of racism, the end of imperialism! The African national struggle had mobilized the masses precisely on the basis of these promises. But independence would fulfill the promise only for a few more of the African petite bourgeoisie, leaving the mass of the people with mere promises which, even with the best will on the part of the leadership, could not be fulfilled under the prevailing economic order. The post-white settler colonial state was inherently unable to fulfill the popular demands. At the end of the day, the new state has become an apparent mediator between capital and labor, between the aspirations of the mass of the people for genuine independence and the role of international capital in its quest for more profit. With time, however, this state should become weighted in favor of the latter, inclined toward controlling these popular demands, if only to appease capital in the name of "stability," peace and security.

For the post-white settler colonial state is more than just a neocolonial state. It is a state born fettered and constrained by the midwife, imperialism, and in growing, it has to contend with the former white settlers who, by their economic and political existence, also influence the nature and direction of the state, in league with imperialism and international finance capital. There is also the threat of a South African state on which the new Zimbabwe state finds itself economically dependent mainly for transport and trade links; but also one that could, either on its own initiative or as part of the imperialist strategy in the Southern Africa subregion, quite easily inflict terror on the new state. All these factors have to be considered in relation to the role of the African petite bourgeoisie which, as has already been indicated, had developed a vested interest in this new order. Both the imperative of this transitional phase (that we have just described) and the class interests of the African petite bourgeoisie would gradually undermine the mass political mobilization and momentum that might have served as a countervailing force. Indeed, it became increasingly necessary as an act of survival for the new state to put a rein on mass movements. In turn, this began the process of demobilizing a mass political base through which political independence had been won and without which no petite bourgeoisie, no matter how progressive its leadership, could effectively contain imperialist and white settler machinations or wage the struggle for genuine economic and social progress. In general, therefore, change in the economic sphere meant essentially the gradual entrenchment of the African petite bourgeoisie.

It was expected that there would be conflict between the African petite bourgeoisie and the former white settlers. But as the African petite bourgeoisie began gradually to find access to the same economic and social status as their white counterparts so, too, did it become increasingly unable to dismantle the bastions of privilege or to respond effectively to the aspirations of the workers and peasants.

There was more than a symbolic commitment to the capitalist order as the members of the African petite bourgeoisie variously bought houses, farms, and businesses. Political principles and ideological commitments appeared mortgaged on the altar of private property!

There had never been a clearly articulated ideology in the Zimbabwean national liberation movement, and whatever commitment there was to socialist transformation became increasingly isolated as the capitalists have proved irresistible to the leaders. The increased access to the markets for the peasantry, the increase in minimum wages for the workers, the feeling of a new democratization process all helped to reinforce rather than weaken this capitalist thrust.

As a concept, "development" became confused between, on the one hand, the tendency to translate it in terms of making capitalism accessible to the masses, and on the other, the social democratic view of "bridging the gap" between the rich and the poor. Therein lay the hope for the transformation of the capitalist system and for the transition to socialism. At the same time, foreign aid was viewed as an important component in this "development" strategy. If it was impossible now to institute a development process from a mass base, it was necessary to institute a framework for the very difficult exercise of ensuring an equitable distribution of very scarce development resources. This became the major focus of the provincial administration policy that was inaugurated by the government in 1984.[11]

The party lost the momentum that it had developed in the period leading to independence, a momentum that had been based more on the popular response to the struggle for national independence than on an organized party structure throughout the country. The latter task became the major objective in the period leading to the next general election in 1985. But the political and ideological content did not change. The declared goal of socialist construction could not be translated into the organizational political framework of the party without creating a fundamental contradiction with the post-white settler colonial state. With time, therefore, the party became an agency for the leadership to try and explain the slowness of change, to plead for patience, to highlight the achievement of the postindependence period in contrast to the deprivation of the colonial past, to listen to general as well as parochial complaints, to promise change, to emphasize the goal of national unity, and so on and so forth.

Ideologically, the party became immobile, divested of innovativeness by the apparent supremacy of the affairs of the state and the economy. It was caught in the same trap as that in which other parties in the postcolonial situation had found themselves once the excitement of independence had waned. The level of depoliticization began to show in the reports that people were now being forced (by youths) to attend party meetings which, in the words of the ZANU (PF) Secretary for Administration and Acting Secretary of the Commissariat for Culture, Maurice Nyagumbo were "only sloganeering and singing party songs."[12] He added:

> Such people are destroying the party and not building it. People are not interested in chanting slogans and singing party songs when there is nothing big that is to be said. Such acts are unbecoming of the party and the Government. We can send them (youths) to jail for that. It is not difficult to do. . . . On complaints the senior (officials) in both

the public and private sector were reluctant to attend party meetings, he said they might be busy with other issues but urged people to persuade them (officials) to attend progressive meetings.[13]

THE LIMITS OF ECONOMIC POLICY INITIATIVES

All these aspects of the post-white settler colonial state determine and influence the arena of domestic and external policies.[14] But further illustrations from the Zimbabwe case might assist in highlighting the limits of economic adjustment and adaptation within the context of the postcolonial state. We will then conclude the discussion with some suggestions as to what could be done to begin to rectify the situation.

Zimbabwe's current economic dilemma originates from the Lancaster House Agreement, and from the consequent contradiction between what is viewed as the imperative to maintain white and international confidence in the economy, on the one hand, and satisfying the expectations and aspirations of the mass of the people, on the other hand. This is reflected quite clearly in the first economic policy document, *Growth with Equity*.[15] In such postcolonial situations, economic policies are likely to reflect these contradictions and constraints. The three-year Transitional National Development Plan[16] in turn expresses and reveals the nature of the post-white settler colonial state. The contradictions are complicated rather than resolved by the belief that capitalism, whether inherited from colonial regimes or acquired through neocolonial links and foreign aid, can be mobilized toward the fulfilment of the popular demands of the masses.

In the final analysis, the government finds itself increasingly having to follow the broad guidelines of international finance capital, although those directly responsible for economic policy would want to think that their policies are "homegrown" and independent of external influence. Such was the controversy when the government announced the 1983 austerity measures designed to improve the economy.[17] Were these homegrown or a reflection of the influence of the international finance capital? Thandika Mkandawire[18] argues:

> Whatever is the true story, we shall give the government of Zimbabwe the benefit of doubt and simply assume that the austerity programme is indeed 'home-grown'. We note, in passing, however, that the controversy does illustrate the problems of reconciling the exigencies of capitalist accumulation and the quest for political legitimacy. Having decided that accumulation in Zimbabwe would need a large dose of private capital—local and foreign—the state had to enjoy the 'confidence' of capital and the IMF stamp of approval which is often considered crucial. This in turn, demanded a set of policy measures that would tilt the scales in favour of capital and against the popular

classes so central in the struggle for independence and the political legitimacy of the state.[19]

Controversy will, for the foreseeable future, linger on as to the possible reasons why foreign aid became an important—if not central—component of state policies in the period since the attainment of national independence. There can be no doubt that there was such international goodwill toward a new nation that had been the victim of a long war and therefore required massive reconstruction in the economic sphere. Equally however, such aid and assistance as did come were not entirely politically disinterested and therefore tended to be premised on the need to develop a "stable" Zimbabwe. It was a continuation of a theme already established at Lancaster. In turn, it was predictable that the government would be "too anxious to establish its credentials with the financial world."[20]

Indeed, it is of little consequence now to consider what might have been the alternative economic policy were it not for the various "wrong-headed" and "high-risk" policies that the government introduced in the months following independence, in the hope of liberalizing the economy and thereby attracting foreign investment.[21] Nor is it important now to consider what might have been the alternative scenario had the new state adopted a cautious approach toward foreign capital, relying mainly on the available local resources in a development program. The latter would have been much slower in its implementation but dependent largely on people who, just emerging from the huge sacrifices of war, would have been quite patient and motivated toward such a self-reliant program. The point is, however, that international finance capital has, since the Lancaster House Agreement, been the major factor in the formation of the international and external policies of Zimbabwe.

The role of the former settlers is important only in as far as it tends to coincide with and reinforce the overall interests of international finance capital and those of imperialism. The African petite bourgeoisie remains quite weak and is forced, in the interests of both its class and the need to maintain the state, to make compromises with both the former white settlers and international finance capital, not to mention the fact that there would be a significant and influential section within the African petite bourgeoisie class that would rather see Zimbabwe's destiny closely tied to the West than have it move toward socialism. Likewise, both the dominance of international finance capital and the directions of imperialist policy in Southern Africa tend to define the broad parameters of state action on the external front. Obviously there is a close correlation between domestic and external policies within any state. But it is in the field of foreign policy that the government is most keen to project the impression of independence of action, even though it should be obvious that international relations by definition prescribe and proscribe the limits of that "independent" action on the part of the individual state. Such a conception of international relations raises the question of hierarchy in global politics, with the major powers not only defining the arena of international politics, but also controlling it; and the small state, in their "foreign policies," merely reflecting, or at best, just responding or dancing to the tune of the giants. Small states, in any event, have to behave accordingly if they are to survive and not fall victim to the vengeful wrath of the big powers. Moreover, dependent states will tend to exhibit external policies that are a reflection of that condition of dependence.

With respect to Zimbabwe, both Britain and the United States have tended to adopt preemptive and aggressive postures, all designed to ensure that the new state does not unlock itself from the grip that imperialism incorporated in the Lancaster House Agreement. The role of the former white settlers has, therefore, a direct bearing in the field of external relations. This is illustrated in the attempt of the white leadership to highlight the role (and threat) of South Africa as an additional insurance against any action by the African petite bourgeoisie that might undermine white confidence. This stance is quite integral to that which views white interests as dependent on the prevailing influence of the West in Zimbabwe. Not surprisingly, therefore, the British and the United States, from time to time, utilize key white politicians within Zimbabwean society in the pursuit of their neocolonial policies. There is no question that the whites—particularly the barons of industry and commerce are represented by the Confederation of Zimbabwe Industries (CZI) and the Zimbabwe National Chamber of Commerce (ZNCC) respectively—obviously favored a pragmatic policy toward South Africa and would therefore be opposed to sanctions against that country. Such a position was greatly reinforced by the attitude of the United States and Britain. In the end, whatever decision the Zimbabwean state would take with regard to the question of sanctions, for example, would depend to a large extent on how far it could take the private sector with it and on how far the governing class was agreed on the wisdom of such a decision. But, as has been pointed out elsewhere,[22] the issue of sanctions against South Africa rests more on the role of the Western countries than on that of the African states.

No doubt some of the white leaders still have tried to project the view that the white presence in Zimbabwe is a guarantee that South Africa will not harm Zimbabwe. As a columnist of the *Herald* wrote in reply to some of the white leaders during the 1985 election campaign:

> It was offensive (for the white leaders like Ian Smith of CAZ and Bill Irvine of IZG) to claim that post-independence Zimbabwe is living off the fat of UDI; and that for the last five years the (white) parliamentarians—jointly or individually—have been the custodians of good government and financial management. . . .

> Lastly, it was rather unfortunate that Mr. Irvine's interview should have been screened on the very day the South African Army invaded another Frontline State, Botswana. For Mr. Irvine had the temerity to tell us that South Africa would not invade or destabilize Zimbabwe.
>
> My question is: What do the likes of Mr. Smith or Mr. Irvine know that we do not know? Is this another attempt to hold Zimbabwe to ransom, implying that unless the 'white community's' interests are sustained and maintained, South Africa will be a threat to Zimbabwe?[23]

Whether or not the government of Zimbabwe considered this in terms of a conscious policy is difficult to determine, but there would appear to be some relation between the presence of a sizeable number of whites in Zimbabwe and the limited (in comparison, for example, to those suffered by Mozambique and Angola) physical and economic attacks that Zimbabwe has had to endure at the hands of South Africa in the period since independence. But this would not, in itself, displace the more fundamental reason for the white presence in Zimbabwe, namely, that Zimbabwe has neither threatened South Africa, the former white settlers, nor the strategic and economic interests of imperialism. Any South African attack on Zimbabwe will therefore be viewed as uncalled for and unreasonable, subject to the strongest condemnation by both Britain and the United States. Such was the case when South Africa attacked Zimbabwe on 19 May 1986. It is interesting that similar attacks on Angola and Mozambique have not always met with the same kind of disapproval on the part of the United States, Britain, and other Western countries.

There is, therefore, the implied threat that Zimbabwe might find herself in circumstances similar to those in Mozambique and Angola if she does not "behave" herself. The code of good behavior requires that Zimbabwe condemn terrorism; (and, with regard to South Africa, that it does not offer rear base support to the freedom fighters); pursue a pragmatic course; shun Marxist ideology and keep the socialist bloc at arm's length; and in general, not fundamentally run counter to the broad objectives of imperialist policy in Southern Africa. On 25 January 1985, Mr. David Charles Miller, the U.S. Ambassador, expressed the theme of U.S. policy toward Zimbabwe. (It should be noted from this statement that the United States expected African countries to be "nonaligned" with the socialist bloc and, therefore, by implication, aligned with the United States itself.)

> For those of us who are optimists and who believe that constructive engagement will work, we see a number of exciting and positive changes in Southern Africa which are only halfway to fruition. These would include the return of Mozambique to a truly non-aligned status—and hopefully, domestic tranquility; a dialogue with the Angolan Government which however difficult is much improved over

our position of no dialogue a few years ago; and a great deal of what is required to implement Resolution 435 is in place. The final elusive steps remain precisely that—elusive. . . .

All of this has important bearing on Zimbabwe. If the mainly liberal community in the United States succeeds in crippling foreign policy objectives of drawing South Africans into the world, I am confident that the conservative community will see to it that aid and diplomatic outreach to Marxist governments in Southern Africa will be adversely affected. If the policy of constructive engagement comes unravelled, I am confident that it will mean not only less engagement with South Africa, but also with Zimbabwe, Mozambique and our budding relationship (sic) Angola.

While bilateral relations between the United States and Zimbabwe are in an acceptable state today, they could easily become the victim of a domestic political fight in the United States with the Prime Minister's occasional Marxist speeches being used as the rationale for reducing our presence here. Rarely have your personal interests been so directly at stake in our legislative process. If we in effect withdraw from South Africa and retreat down a conservative road, while at the same time we withdraw support for Zimbabwe and Mozambique— and possibly Angola—my guess is that the region has the possibility of taking a large and distinct step backward.[24]

It is difficult to believe that the United States would ever consider withdrawing from Southern Africa, let alone Zimbabwe. The threat is therefore perhaps based on the confidence that imperialist policy in the subregion, and in Zimbabwe, has been so largely successful that even the African governments would find a U.S. withdrawal very much to the detriment of the security and prosperity of their countries. As has been outlined elsewhere,[25] the frontline and SADCC states themselves tend to give credence to this position. In terms of their reliance on the imperialist powers to pressure South Africa, and in the light of a SADCC that is dependent for its existence and operations largely on the Western countries, the African states of Southern Africa have tended to act within the ambit of imperialist policy (and hegemony) in Southern Africa.

They will invariably complain about aspects of US policy—particularly with regard to South Africa. But, as a US diplomat explained, No one is saying to us, get out of the region. . . . No one has [told] to us to pack our bags and go. . . . They want the US to be constructively engaged in Southern Africa.[26]

It is, accordingly, a curious aspect of this situation that it is precisely on this basis that the Frontline and SADCC states have been able to mobilize Western support for the cause of African political liberation and thereby enhance the process of isolating South Africa internationally.

Furthermore, the Zimbabwean experience so far would suggest that it is the kind of model that the Western countries would like to project in terms of an overall Southern Africa of tomorrow. But it is also a model that provokes a lynchpin for the maintenance of imperialist interests in the subregion. It is, therefore, appropriate to quote at length the "Zimbabwe Testimony"[27] given by the U.S. Deputy Assistant Secretary of State for African Affairs, Frank Wisner. Addressing the Sub-Committee on Africa of the Foreign Affairs Committee of the House of Representatives on 24 May 1984, he said:

> In the four years of its independence, Zimbabwe has captured the interest of many Americans. It is only right that it should. Zimbabwe's coming to independence—via the 1979 negotiations at Lancaster House between the British Government and the Zimbabwean parties—was a triumph of diplomacy and one in which the US played an important supporting role. We have watched Zimbabwe emerge from a bloody civil war and begin the construction of a new nation, committed to national reconciliation, non-racialism, democratic procedures, the rule of law, social justice, and economic development. There have been no war crime trials. Instead, opposition parties have taken seats in Parliament, from which they freely criticized the government of Prime Minister Mugabe. Zimbabwe inherited a reasonably strong economy, with an active private sector. While buffeted heavily by world recession, transportation difficulties, drought, and a certain amount of Socialist rhetoric, it has been managed by the new leadership with a respect of market principles and international economic realities and in cooperation with international economic institutions.
> . . . Flatly stated, *Zimbabwe is critical to our policy in Southern Africa* . . . (my emphasis).

Zimbabwe, quite obviously, is a model to the region and the world "about the prospects of lasting negotiated settlements" and "of reconciliation among the region's strife-torn peoples"; and the Zimbabwean economy was evidence of the successful "mix" between a vibrant private sector (of commercial agriculture, private-owned business, communal farms, state-provided infrastructure) and a "commitment to public welfare." In turn, both as a model and as an engine of development, the Zimbabwean economy could, with the support of the United States and other Western countries, "grow, and stimulate growth elsewhere in the region."

The "Zimbabwe Testimony" concluded with an outline of five regional policy objectives, designed to consolidate the U.S. policy in the subregion, with particular regard to Zimbabwe and to ensure that Zimbabwe itself remains firmly in line:

> First, we want to see Zimbabwe succeed. . . . Second, we want to see Zimbabwe continue to enjoy the benefits of an economic infrastructure and potential that would be the envy of any other developing country, and turn that economy to the task of stimulating growth elsewhere in the region. The United States has contributed generously to

Zimbabwe's reconstruction and development—in fact, the US is Zimbabwe's largest aid donor, bar none—and we are committed to helping Zimbabwe avoid the economic tarpits into which some of its less fortunate neighbors have fallen. Zimbabwe will recover from present economic adversity if it maintains social and economic policies, works closely with the IMF during the time of adjustment, offers incentives to the private sector, provides a favorable climate for foreign investment, and manages its budget prudently. Third, we want to see Zimbabwe complete the transition from liberation movement to responsible government. . . . Fourth, we have engaged the Zimbabweans as a partner in the work of bringing about peaceful change in the region . . . its pragmatic policy toward South Africa and its influence among the Frontline states makes Zimbabwe a crucial element in our search for regional stability—fifth, we want to develop a more mature relationship with Zimbabwe in international affairs. . . . We have *a lot at stake at Zimbabwe's success* . . . (my emphasis).

Against this very favorable assessment, it would have been expected that the United States might have dismissed as insignificant the differences with Zimbabwe on the latter's decision to abstain on the resolution condemning the Soviet downing of the Korean airliner, and for cosponsoring a resolution condemning the U.S. action in Grenada. On the contrary, the United States cut aid to Zimbabwe as punishment for these actions, a threat to be repeated in July 1986, following the Zimbabwean foreign minister's condemnation of the U.S. position on South Africa. As Prime Minister Mugabe retorted in response to these threats:

> There have been these threats and I understand some aid which was due to be signed has not been signed for. This is the behaviour of a country which in one vein would want us to believe that it does not ever want to impose sanctions (against South Africa) and in another it is imposing sanctions against us for saying it refused to impose sanctions against South Africa. I find that quite ironical, but what I find quite objectionable is the fact that the United States, of all countries, tends to use its aid as a weapon to coerce or impel countries which are the beneficiaries to toe a certain political line, even contrary to their own political and ideological persuasion. Perhaps, it is their tradition but of course such aid comes to us generously, if the donor decides to withdraw we still say thank you for what you gave us in the past. But let it be known that when we fought for our independence and sovereignty, we never meant to sell it at all, and so what I give you for the future is independent Zimbabwe with resources and a determined population to exploit these resources and become their own masters and not beggars and beneficiaries.[28]

Yet the United States did not cut the aid completely nor did it do anything to contradict the main import of the "Zimbabwe Testimony" cited above. Some might dismiss these threats as a mere token, the bullying tactics of a superpower, designed more to flaunt Reaganism than a trend towards disengagement. More seriously, however, it could be indicative of a lingering nervousness on the part of the imperialist center, the fear that this Zimbabwe might still break out of the Lancaster cage and return to the revolutionary course that it appeared so far to have rejected. If so, then these threats should be taken seriously, indicating the U.S. resolve not only to keep Zimbabwe in line but even to resort to more drastic action should Zimbabwe decide to "break away" altogether.

A closer analysis of British policy towards Zimbabwe in the years since Lancaster reveals acute suspicion that the country might just "degenerate" into the kind of anarchy that Lancaster was designed to avoid. It is, as yet, not possible for us to determine precisely whether the British Foreign Office policy on Zimbabwe is as sensational in its assessment as some of the British media, or that it relies more on a careful and concrete analysis that would show that Zimbabwe has, in the words of Lord Soames on his last visit to the country in 1986, confounded the prophets of doom. There is also evidence to suggest that the Foreign Office is kept appraised of the Zimbabwe situation by a team that includes notable liberal academicians who are viewed as "experts" on Zimbabwe within the tradition of "Western democracy."

At any rate, the occasional benedictions by such people as Lord Soames would tend to confirm the view in British official circles that Zimbabwe is firmly following the letter and spirit of the Lancaster House Agreement. In the words of another observer of the Zimbabwean situation:

> This document remains largely intact. Following independence a new dynamic has evolved in Zimbabwe in which the government has sought to demonstrate adherence to the Lancaster House Agreement as a means of maintaining the support of the economically critical domestic white community and of those Western governments and international agencies that have supplied high levels of financial assistance.[29]

CONCLUSION

This chapter has sought to outline a theory of the postcolonial state in Africa, with particular reference to the Zimbabwe situation. The subject of the postcolonial state is, perhaps, a new and controversial one in the annals of the African Association of Public Administration (AAPAM). But we have introduced it intentionally in the context of this year's Roundtable theme, which seeks to expose African public administrators to the concrete realities and challenges of economic policy in the postindependence situation. In doing so, we wish to emphasize the need to continue the search for solutions to our problems. For it behoves progressive public administrators and political activists to identify, within the broad framework of the principal contradictions in our society, the possibilities for the development of a progressive development policy. As Samir Amin suggests,[30] such a policy must seek to "de-link" with the structures of dependence and must rely on effective planning. It is a difficult and long-drawn task but one that has to be attempted, beginning with a clear perception of the causes of underdevelopment. As Samir Amin suggests in his repudiation of a unilinear view of society, socialism has to be planned for[31] rather than developing countries having to wait, as Kitching suggests, for the arrival of full-fledged capitalism and its "sophisticated working class." Accordingly, a start can be made:[32]

> The perception of underdevelopment naturally shapes the strategies for its transcendence. At one level, there must be a development policy, which must be based, on another level, on a social structure capable of sustaining it. The policy must aim at achieving three objectives. First it must create a homogenous national economy, progressively transferring the working population from low productivity, mainly agricultural, sectors into high productivity sectors.
>
> Second, it must aim at the overall cohesion missing from the underdeveloped economy by deliberately creating integrated industrial groups made up of complementary activities. Third, it must aim at imparting to the economy its own 'dynamism', freeing it from dependence on the outside economy. On the technical level this strategy demands, according to Amin, the use of modern techniques for the immediate improvement of productivity and of the condition of the masses. This, he maintains, necessarily goes with the spread of 'specific forms of democracy' at every stage and at every level, village, region and state, making real development at once 'national, socialist, and popular, democratic'. The strategy also demands autonomous scientific and technological research in the Third World, an undertaking that precludes the limitation of the technology of developed countries and entails the use of rather elementary levels of technology. These objectives depend on effective planning for their realisation, and effective planning itself depends on a break with the world market. 'The failure of planning in the Third World . . . is essentially due to (the) refusal to break with the world market'.[33]

This raises the question about the need to develop not only appropriate planning skills in the state sector but also the correct orientation—and political will—to plan for socialism.

NOTES

1. "Aide-Mémoire: Economic Crisis, Structural Adjustments and Public Administration and Management in Africa," Document of the AAPAM Ninth Roundtable (1987), 5.

2. V. I. Lenin, *The State: A Lecture Delivered at the Sverdlov University, July 11, 1919* (Peking: Foreign Languages Press, 1973), 14.

3. Hamza Alari, "The State in Post-Colonial Societies: Pakistan and Bangladesh," *New Left Review* 74 (July-August, 1972): 59–81.

4. Michaela Von Freyhold, "The Post-Colonial State and Its Tanzanian Version: Contribution to a Debate," *The State in Tanzania: Who controls it and whose interest does it serve?* ed. Othman and Haroub (Dar es Salaam: Dar es Salaam University Press, 1980), 88.

5. Yash Tandon, "The Post-Colonial State," *Social Change and Development*, no. 8 (1984), 2–4.

6. Michaela Von Freyhold, *op. cit.*, 100.

7. Thandika Mkandawire, "State Policy Responses to Economic Crisis in Africa," *Eastern Africa Social Science Research Review*, vol. 1, no. 2 (June 1985), 31–51.

8. Michaela Von Freyhold, *op. cit.*, 87.

9. Ibbo Mandaza, ed., *Zimbabwe: The Political Economy of Transition, 1980–1986* (Dakar: CODESRIA Book Series, 1986).

10. Yash Tandon, "The Post-Colonial State," *Social Change and Development*, no. 8 (1984). See also his monograph, *The People Versus the IMF: The Struggle of the Poor in Zimbabwe*.

11. See the Prime Minister's "Statement of Policy and a Directive on Provincial Councils and Administration in Zimbabwe," Harare, 27 February 1984.

12. *The Herald*, 21 July 1986.

13. *Ibid.*

14. For an elaboration of this, see Ibbo Mandaza, "The State and Foreign Powers: The Case of Zimbabwe," (Dakar: CODESRIA publication, 1987).

15. Government Printers, Harare, February 1981.

16. Government Printers, Harare, November 1982.

17. Government Printers, Harare, April 1986.

18. Thandika Mkandawire, "Home-grown (?) Austerity Measures: The Case of Zimbabwe," *Africa Development*, vol. 10, no. 1/2 (1985): 236–63.

19. *Ibid.*, 237.

20. *Ibid.*, 259.

21. *Ibid.*

22. Ibbo Mandaza, "Perspectives of Economic Cooperation and Autonomous Development in Southern Africa." (Paper prepared for the United Nations University's Project on African Regional Perspectives, Dakar, 1986.)

23. The Scrutator, in *The Herald*, 22 June 1985.

24. Text of an address to the National Forum at the Park Lane Hotel, Harare.

25. Ibbo Mandaza, "Southern Africa: US Policy and the Struggle for National Independence," *op. cit.*

26. *Ibid.*

27. Frank Wisner, "Zimbabwe Testimony" USIS, SR. 51/5/29/84. Unless otherwise stated, the following references are from this document.

28. Hansard, vol. 13, no. 11, 16 July 1986.

29. Jeffrey Davidow, *A Peace in Southern Africa: The Lancaster House Conference on Rhodesia* (London: Westview Press, 1979), 94.

30. Kweku G. Folson, "Samir Amin as a Neo-Marxist," *Africa Development*, vol. 10, no. 3 (1985): 112–35.

31. *Ibid.*

32. Gavin Kitching, "Politics, Method and Evidence in the 'Kenya Debate,'" *Contradictions of Accumulation in Africa: Studies in Economy and State*, ed. Henry Bernstein and Bonnie K. Campbell (London: Sage Publications, 1985), 144–45.

33. Kweku G. Folson, *op. cit.*, 122–23.

PART II

Policy and Managerial Responses to Crisis

CHAPTER THREE

Economic Crisis, Organization, and Structure of Government for Recovery and Development: A Comparative Review of Experiences and New Perspectives

P. M. Efange and M. Jide Balogun

INTRODUCTION

Many African countries have been independent for over a quarter of a century. Within this period, rapid, and at times, traumatic changes have taken place in socioeconomic conditions and in political arrangements. The early years of independence were characterized by the launching of development plans aimed at transforming the predominantly agrarian societies into modern, industrial ones, and at improving the standard of living of the people. However, in spite of the fact that vast resources have been channelled into the development effort, real progress has continued to elude Africa. The severity of the ongoing socioeconomic crisis in fact poses a difficult challenge to policymakers and administrators. In specific terms, the crisis calls for a radical rethinking of development strategy and immediate restructuring of policy-planning and implementation institutions.

In this chapter, an attempt is made to examine the responses by African public services to the challenge of economic recovery and development. The chapter starts by discussing the magnitude of the socioeconomic crisis as well as the structural adjustment programs drawn up in response to the critical situation. The second part of the chapter makes use of empirical data to assess the progress attained in implementing the turn around programs. The third section looks at the future of African public administration with specific reference to the ongoing crisis and the reform of governmental institutions.

AFRICA'S SOCIOECONOMIC CRISIS: CAUSES, EFFECTS, AND TURN AROUND POSSIBILITIES

In recent years, virtually all African countries have seen their economies battered by unfavorable developments in the domestic and international environment. In almost every part of the continent, there is an air of frustration and a feeling of helplessness. The reasons are not difficult to fathom. Funds for the administration of development programs and the maintenance of infrastructural facilities have literally dried up. Some governments now find it extremely difficult to meet the monthly wage bills of their staff. Many of them are lagging behind in the payment of teachers' salaries. Health and medical institutions are short of drugs and essential supplies. Monies owed to local contractors take years and several trips to the ministry headquarters to be paid. Industrial production is on the decline because the raw materials and the spares required to keep the machines working are not available. The public and the private sectors are retrenching staff and/or are not recruiting new hands. Most serious of all, access to foreign credit is blocked partly because of the creditors' tougher lending policies and because of the African countries' failure/inability to settle long-standing debts. One thing is clear: the current economic crisis has not landed on Africa like a bolt from the blue. The signals of a serious economic depression have been flashing for a fairly long time. Unfortunately, it took the traumas of the recent months to drive the message home.

Granted, it was not always this bad. The early years of independence (the 1960s) were marked by a generous inflow of development finance to many African countries. The idealism of the period coupled with the goodwill enjoyed by the then newly independent societies within the community of nations provided a strong impetus for Africa's development. With the then prevailing belief in the interdependence of nations, and in an atmosphere characterized by widespread euphoria and optimism, the 1960s was declared the First Development Decade. Within this period, barriers to the movement of resources were limited. In return for Africa's export products, the rest of the world appeared willing to pay fairly good prices. In addition, loans and grants were made available to Africa by the economically developed societies. Then began an era of institutional expansion, particularly in the public sector. New ministries and departments were created as part of the civil service, and the parastatal sector was characterized by institutional proliferation. The evidence of the rapid—some would say unbridled—expansion in the scope of government was provided by the increase in the number of agencies that were created between the 60s and 70s, the constant rise in the number on the government payroll, and the growth in recurrent and capital spending.

However, the foundation upon which a government led development strategy rested appeared fragile. Certainly the trend in economic growth between the early 60s and the late 70s was not such as to warrant wholesale expansion of institutions. Thus, from a modest average annual rate of growth of 3.5 percent within the period from 1960–73, sub-Saharan

Africa recorded a negative rate of growth (-0.1) in 1983, and this at a time when other "developing" regions (Asia, the Middle East, and North Africa) were reporting impressive growth rates.

Development Crisis: Analysis of Causes

What are the possible causes of Africa's perpetual underdevelopment? While an increasingly hostile international environment has been implicated along with inadequate or misdirected policy responses, the objective factor in Africa's development crisis is structural rigidity. This was acknowledged by the 21st Assembly of Heads of State and Government of the OAU in July 1985. According to the African leaders, the region's persistent depression was attributable to "the lack of structural transformation and the pervasive low level of productivity, aggravated by exogenous and endogenous factors."[1]

It is structural rigidity more than anything else that accounts for Africa's unbroken dependence on a narrow range of export commodities over the years. As of 1971, eleven African countries were heavily dependent on one major export product, ten on two major export products, and another ten on three products. As of today, only a few have succeeded in diversifying their economies and exporting new products. What of the figures recently published in the United Nations *Yearbook of International Trade Statistics*? Certainly, many African countries are reported to be earning increasing sums from the export of nonagricultural products (mainly industrial manufacturing). If the conventional "rule of origin" is rigorously applied, many of these so-called export products would not feature on the international trade accounts of the African countries concerned. This is simply because the bulk of the inputs into the products (technical know-how, raw materials, tools, spares, and CKDs (or completely knocked down parts) originate from outside Africa. The exportation of such products should at best appear on the debit side of Africa's trade accounts since the proceeds would ultimately be claimed by the real manufacturers, be they in Europe, North America, Japan, or Taiwan.

Effects/Symptoms of Crisis

It goes without saying that a monocultural economy, which appears typical in Africa, is highly vulnerable to the vicissitudes of the international environment. Such an economy is powerless when confronted with unfavorable external forces. The worsening terms of trade provide an illustration of the intrinsic weakness of the African economy. Even in the area of agriculture, where one would have expected the economy to hold its own, the evidence available suggests that the contrary is the case. Between 1970 and 1981, Africa was a net importer of food and agricultural items. And while Africa was paying high prices for its imports, it received relatively little for its exports. In fact, it has been reported that overall, Africa lost not less than U.S. $2.2 billion between 1979 and 1981 as a result of the continuous decline in the value of its export commodities. Between 1980 and 1983, the total loss from declining export prices was approximately U.S. $13.5 billion. In 1986 alone, the value of Africa's exports dropped by 28.7 percent.

The effects of the decline in commodity prices were worsened by the protective barriers imposed by Africa's trade partners. Hence, Africa's increasing trade deficit. In 1982, the deficit rose to $24.7 billion. The situation improved but only slightly in 1986 when the deficit was reduced to $21.5 billion.

Another price which Africa has had to pay for its dependence on a narrow range of export products (and by implication, for institutional rigidity) is the continued dependence on other (mostly the advanced) regions of the world for the supply of basic economic requirements. Not just agricultural inputs but also raw materials for industrial production, tools, equipment, and machinery for manufacturing operations, and CKDs for assembly plants. These and many other items have to be imported at exorbitant prices. The consequent surge in import bills automatically worsens the balance of payments position. And to plug the current account deficits, many African countries have had to resort to borrowing from external sources. In 1985, Africa's external debt amounted to $175 billion. The figure for 1986 is not yet available, but it is not likely to be lower than $200 billion.[2]

The debt situation has been exacerbated by the rising interest rates and the backbreaking debt-servicing obligations. In the early 70s, interest rates were in the neighborhood of 4.2 percent; in the 80s, the figure rose to 10.1 percent. Consequently, Africa's total external debt (in relation to exports and GDP) more than doubled between 1974 and 1984 and accounted for almost 50 percent of the continent's GDP. The increasing debt service obligations have constituted yet another barrier to economic recovery. It has been estimated that not less than $30 billion is required for annual debt servicing. But as the debt service ratios have risen, so has the rate of default in debt repayment. At least twenty African countries reported payment areas as at the end of 1984.[3] And as an increasing number of African countries sought to reschedule their debts, what appeared as a resource embargo was placed on indebted nations generally. As of 1982, Africa began to feel the impact of the credit squeeze, and at about the same time, capital flow to Africa began to nose-dive.

With all these negative economic indicators, one begins to understand why a feeling of gloom pervades the length and breadth of Africa. It is one thing if a member of a family is down with the common cold, it is another when the entire family is struck by a plague.

Alternative Prescriptions for Recovery

The tragedy of the current situation lies not in the state of debility that Africa finds itself in, but in the lack of consensus on the appropriate medication. The affliction is not in the illness (of which there is no doubt) but in the cure. On the one hand are those who believe that Africa's malady is traceable to excessive government intervention in the economy and that the best remedy is rapid dismantling of government controls. In other words, Africa had been living beyond its means, and now that economic realities have finally caught up with the continent, each country should seize the opportunity to restructure the institutions responsible for allocative and investment decisions. In practical terms, "restructuring" means the "privatization" of public enterprises, reduction in the size of the public sector, reduction of budget deficits, imposition of ceilings on government borrowing from the banking system, removal of price subsidies, elimination of price controls, deregulation/liberalization of the economy, devaluation of currency, and improvement in production incentives. These are the major ingredients of the short-term structural adjustment programs which a number of African countries have introduced in agreement with the IMF and the World Bank.

On the other hand, it has been argued that the "conditionalities" which form part of the structural adjustment packages are more likely to perpetuate the depression than provide a lasting cure for Africa's ailment. The authors of the *African Priority Programme for Economic Recovery* (APPER) and the *United Nations Programme of Action for African Economic Recovery Development* (UN-PAAERD) attribute Africa's development crisis to lack of structural transformation, and that means if the obstacles to growth are to be removed, both the public and the private sectors must promote the versatility of policy-making and implementation institutions. In the next section, an attempt is made to assess the implementation of the structural adjustment and transformation programs.

IMPLEMENTATION OF TURN AROUND PROGRAMS: A PRELIMINARY ASSESSMENT

At least two-thirds of sub-Saharan African countries have implemented varieties of structural adjustment reform since 1982.[4] Table 3-1 indicates the countries that have formulated such programs as of the end of March 1987.

The twenty-two countries listed in Table 3–1 differ in their policy thrusts. Arranged in order of frequency, the following would appear as the policy priorities in the various countries:

1. Increase in producer prices (twenty-one countries or 95 percent of those implementing SAP)
2. Freezing of public service vacancies and reduction of public employment (twenty countries or 91 percent)
3. Realignment of exchange rates and devaluation of currency (sixteen countries or 73 percent)
4. Privatization of state enterprises (fourteen countries or 64 percent)
5. Reduction/elimination of agricultural input subsidies (fourteen countries or 64 percent)
6. Elimination of public agricultural marketing agencies or encouragement of private sector competition (thirteen countries or 59 percent)
7. Deregulation of producer prices (ten countries or 45 percent)
8. Reduction/elimination of food subsidies (eight countries or 36 percent)
9. Adoption of floating market rates for foreign exchange (seven countries or 32 percent)
10. Transfer of responsibility for importation of agricultural inputs to the private sector (seven countries or 32 percent).[5]

It is probably premature to assess the overall impact of these short-term measures. However, on the basis of available data, it would appear that they have not been effective in dealing with the root causes of Africa's development crisis. It is true that a few of the countries implementing structural adjustment programs have reported positive achievements in some areas. For example, the macroeconomic data recently published by Kenya gives an indication of progress. For one, the GDP at constant (1982) prices has risen steadily between 1983 and 1986 (see Table 3–2).

However, while Kenya's GDP is growing, its rising external debt and debt servicing obligations pose a serious threat to the long-term development of the economy. Table 3–3 shows how external debt service charges have substantially increased in relation to exports between 1974 and 1985.

If Kenya was able to show a redeeming face of structural adjustment, many other countries regard the prescription as more dangerous than the

TABLE 3–1
IDA-Eligible Sub-Saharan African Countries Implementing Structural Adjustment Programs
March 1987

Burundi	Mali
Central African Republic	Mauritania
Chad	Niger
Equatorial Guinea	Rwanda
The Gambia	Senegal
Ghana	Sierra Leone
Guinea	Somalia
Guinea Bissàu	Tanzania
Kenya	Togo
Madagascar	Zaire
Malawi	Zambia

Source: U.S. Overseas Development Council, "Should the IMF Withdraw from Africa?" *Policy Focus* no. 1 (1987): 6. See also David Fasholé-Luke, (note 4), *op. cit.*, 11.

TABLE 3–2
Annual Percentage Change in Kenya's GDP at Constant 1982 Prices

1983	1984	1985	1986[a]
3.1	0.9	4.1	5.7

[a] 1986 figure obtained from *New African*, 239 (August 1987): 31.
Source: Central Bank of Kenya, *Twentieth Annual Report*, 30 June 1986 (Table 4).

TABLE 3–3
External Public Debt Service Charge and External Debt Service Ratios: Kenya, 1974–85

As at End December	Total Annual Debt Service (Shs. m)	Export of Goods and Services (Shs. m)	External Debt Charges as Percentage of Exports
1974	279	7,144	3.9
1975	388	7,138	5.4
1976	506	9,434	5.4
1977	959	13,004	7.4
1978	1,146	11,862	9.7
1979	1,472	12,002	12.3
1980	1,849	15,066	12.3
1981	2,788	15,474	18.0
1982	4,105	16,940	24.2
1983	5,328	19,592	27.2
1984	6,354	22,874	27.8
1985	7,697	24,226	31.8

Source: Central Bank of Kenya, *Twentieth Annual Report*, 30 June 1986 (Table 9).

malady. It is a question of which kills first—the medicine or the illness. Zambia is one of the countries which decided that it had had more than enough dosage of "conditionalities." Having started with the structural adjustment formula as far back as 1977, the country did not notice any significant improvement in its economic health over the years. Between 1980 and 1984, revenue from copper fell by 23 percent (even though 95 percent of export revenue still came from this source). By 1986, its external debt had grown to $4 billion, representing 84 percent of GNP. Between 1983 and 1986, the purchasing power of the Kwacha dropped by two-thirds. When new IMF prescriptions were announced shortly before the Christmas of 1986, Zambia witnessed unprecedented civil disturbances, leading to the immediate withdrawal of the increase in the price of maize. From then on, the country resolved to tackle its problems its own way. Medical doctors would call this self-medication, but, at least, Zambia has a precedent elsewhere.

Homemade Structural Adjustment

Nigeria provides an example of local initiative in structural adjustment. After a highly publicized national debate on the IMF, the government announced that the current public opinion was against approaching the Fund for credit facilities. The government subsequently introduced its own structural adjustment program in 1986. The major elements of the program are:

1. The establishment of the Second-tier Foreign Exchange Market (to assist in the search for a more realistic naira exchange rate and the simplification of administrative rules and regulations for resource allocation)

2. The abolition of import licensing system (as another step towards the deregulation of the economy)

3. The phased withdrawal of petroleum subsidies

4. The gradual privatization of ailing enterprises and

5. Promulgation of enactments on the local "sourcing" of raw materials.

While untying the invisible hand of private enterprise to enable it to lend support to the government's recovery program, the government extended its own (highly visible) hand in directions in which it considered the private sector deficient. For example, it introduced an integrated rural development program, and set up a Directorate of Food, Roads, and Rural Infrastructures. This Directorate has since invested approximately ₦3 billion in various rural projects and has commissioned scientists in universities as well as research institutes to work on not less than one hundred rural projects and produce improved designs. Second, the government formulated a national employment policy, the main thrusts of which are agricultural development, small-scale business and entrepreneurial development, skills acquisition and apprenticeship, and public works programs. Third, the government pegged the settlement of external debt obligations at 30 percent of foreign exchange earnings. Fourth, it came out with a new import tariff structure to reflect, among other things, the new exchange rate, protect local "infant" industries, promote fair and healthy competition among local industries, and guarantee the customer value for money.

How has the Nigerian economy performed since the introduction of the structural reforms? According to the president, the signs are encouraging. In his 1987 budget speech, he noted that:

> it is becoming increasingly evident that some desirable changes are already taking place in our basic national attitudes, life-style and consumption behaviour. Contrary to many predictions, fears and anxieties, the operation of the second-tier Foreign Exchange Market has neither led to capital flight nor to frivolous imports.[6]

The report from the Central Bank of Nigeria is less cheering than the president's assessment. In its appraisal, the bank stated that:

> The various economic policies adopted in 1986 appeared not to have significantly improved the economic situation during the year. Output declined in most sectors except agriculture where it rose by 2.1 per cent.[7]

In contrast to an increase of 1.2 percent recorded in 1985, the GDP fell by 3.3 percent in 1986. The unemployment problem worsened consequent upon the influx of school leavers and the saturation of the labor market.

The balance of payments situation appears slightly perplexing. In naira terms, the external surplus for 1986 is ₦1,946.3 million as against ₦561.1 million for 1985. But what looks like an improvement is nothing but a notional gain made possible by the substantial devaluation of the naira. In U.S. dollar terms, the balance of payments showed an overall deficit of $560.2 million in 1986 in contrast to a surplus of $768.9 million in 1985. By the same reasoning, the increase of the external reserves (from ₦1,816.6 million in 1985 to ₦5,022.6 million in 1986) is notional. In U.S. dollar terms, external reserves fell from $1,817.5 million in 1985 to $1,514.3 million in 1986.

The latest figures from the Central Bank (based on an appraisal of the first half of 1987) show little signs of improvement. While petroleum earnings increased substantially (as a result of the improvement in oil prices) and in spite of a significant (205 percent) increase in the value of earnings from non-oil sectors, the external reserves dropped to $791.4 million.[8] The industrial sector of the domestic economy recorded a slight improvement, but agricultural production dropped by 2.7 percent. One must concede that it is too early to assess the overall and long-term impact of the "home-made" structural adjustment program. In particular, it would take not less than five years for the rural development, employment, and raw materials "sourcing" policies to begin to bear fruit. It should also be emphasized that whatever little achievement is recorded since the introduction of the measures could not be totally credited to the laissez-faire doctrine under-pinning the IMF formula. The government's "hand" looms large at every critical stage of the reform program. An illustration of this is the government's recent decision to deploy soldiers to strategic points at airports and seaports with a view to dealing with smuggling and other activities likely to cancel out the gains of the past few months.

The assessment of the reform would not be complete if we fail to mention its impact on the generality of the people. The continuous rise in the domestic prices of import-dependent products imposes severe hardships on individuals with a fixed income. The government acknowledges this fact, but maintains that high prices of imports are precisely what Africa needs to discourage frivolous consumption and promote the spirit of self-reliance. The philosophy of self-reliance is indeed the one underpinning the latest concerted efforts toward recovery and development.

APPER/UN-PAAERD and Structural Transformation

Perhaps in realization of the danger which externally imposed solutions constituted to national sovereignty and to the philosophy of self-reliance, the African countries collectively adopted a program of action in 1985 titled *Africa's Priority Programme for Economic Recovery* (APPER). The program is based on the Lagos Plan of Action and it seeks to reverse the negative trends in Africa's development and place the continent on a course of self-sustained growth. It places food and agriculture at the center of action in the belief that improvements in the (food and agriculture) sector would foster linkages with industry and the economic infrastructure, and promote all around development. But the most crucial aspect of the new program is the recurring emphasis on structural transformation or institutional reform. In specific terms, the program stresses the need to:

1. Strengthen incentive schemes

2. Review investment policies

3. Improve the management of the economy (through optimal allocation of resources and improved management of state enterprises)

4. Formulate effective human resource development and utilization policy and

5. Encourage citizen participation in plan formulation and implementation.

Interim Report on Structural Transformation

In April 1987, barely five months after the launching of APPER, the ECA dispatched questionnaires to its member states with a view to assessing the progress attained in implementation. Thirty member states (sixty percent of the total) responded to the questionnaires. Table 3–4 summarizes aspects of the responses having a bearing on institutional reform.

Apart from the measures identified in Table 3–4, a number of African countries have reported significant changes in decentralized administration and rural development. Examples are Botswana, Cameroun, The Gambia, Kenya, Tanzania, Zambia, and Zimbabwe. However, whatever gains might have resulted from the reforms have been offset by the tendency, in some of the countries, to subject local institutions to increasing central government control.

In general, Africa's policymakers are becoming increasingly flexible and innovative, thanks to the pressures of the environment. Policies

TABLE 3–4
Summary of Policies/Decisions Reported To Have Been Taken by Selected African States on the Launching of APPER

Decision/Policy Measures Taken	Percentage of Respondents Taking Decision or Implementing Policy
1. Attainment of the investment target of 20-25 percent in agriculture	63
2. Formulation, with the support of the World Bank and IMF, of SAP	70
3. Encouragement of the private sector and active involvement of the sector in investment activities	80
4. Measures to increase domestic savings	83
5. Measures to ensure efficient utilization of domestic resources	93
6. Contemplating adoption of measures indicated in (5) above by 1990	7
7. Export promotion measures	70
8. Improved project identification and preparation, recruitment of competent local counterparts, and the restructuring of technical assistance and aid coordination agencies	80
9. Formulation and implementation of skills acquisition and manpower development programs	87

which fail to work quickly get thrown out and others explored instead. The question is whether the career officials are equally versatile and enterprising. Africa's development crisis has reached a stage that warrants discarding old management styles and operating new ones. The next section discusses the administrative/managerial priorities in Africa's economic recovery and development effort.

ADMINISTRATIVE/MANAGERIAL RESPONSE TO ECONOMIC CRISIS

In pursuance of the objective of structural transformation, the ECA has advocated the implementation of an administrative revitalization and re-equipment strategy the main elements of which are:

1. The restructuring of policy-making institutions
2. The reinvigoration of policy implementation agencies (in both the public and private sectors)
3. Entrepreneurial development
4. Improvement of economic and financial management practices
5. Improvement of aid coordination and debt management
6. Human resource development, management, and utilization
7. Dissemination of information about the goals, strategies, and tactics of collective self-reliance.[9]

In addition to the measures proposed above, it is advisable to stress the need for a policy agenda focusing specifically on the ongoing socio-economic crisis. High on the agenda would be issues directly related to recovery in the short run, and development in the long run. APPER and UN-PAAERD have identified a number of priority sectors, among them, food and agriculture, other sectors in support of agriculture, drought and desertification, and human resources development. The policy agenda referred to earlier should indicate what each public service in Africa proposes to do within the priority sectors over the next few years, how it intends to approach the problems, and the type of resources it requires to accomplish its objectives. The establishment of early warning systems should form part of the issues to be resolved in each sector.

Perhaps more important than anything else is the subject of how to overcome the current liquidity constraint. If Africa finds an answer to this question, it is more than half way to stemming the socioeconomic crisis. As of now, the shortage of hard currency has virtually paralyzed normal economic activities. In order to stimulate production all over again and motivate the latent inventive spirit in Africa, an interim measure should be worked out by policy-making institutions to facilitate the circulation of an African Currency/Exchange Unit. This would promote inter-African trade and generate employment in the short run, while putting Africa in a position of strength in its relations with the outside world. The details of such an arrangement should receive the immediate attention of policy-makers at the national, subregional (e.g., ECOWAS/PTA), and regional (OAU/ECA) levels. We anticipate that the proposal would run into a number of obstacles. There are, for a start, the non-African vested interests which would want a perpetuation of the existing arrangements. But these are not as formidable as the opposition that is expected from within Africa itself. National political elites would hesitate to lend their support for fear of losing vital political/strategic advantages. The bureaucratic and empire-protection instincts of the career officials would most likely upset any plan directed at the introduction of a common exchange system for Africa. However, the alternatives to regional cooperation are perpetual economic backwardness and continued dependence on external (non-African) institutions for the resolution of Africa's financial and economic problems. In the spirit of independence and self-reliance, and within the prevailing atmosphere of policy flexibility, Africans should give themselves a break at this critical stage. Action on monetary reform has been postponed for too long, but the events of today dictate that before we discuss any other strategy of economic recovery, an African common denominator for the exchange of goods and services should be the first item on our agenda. The badly devalued currencies of Africa have been held captive by the world's major currencies. To liberate Africa's productive forces, we should start by having a currency that is capable of stimulating production and facilitating exchange of raw materials, finished products, commodities, and services. It goes without saying that monetary reform should go hand in hand with the reform of national statutes constituting barriers to the movement of labor, goods, and services.[10]

If, however, it is not possible in the foreseeable future to reform Africa's monetary and immigration systems—and we do not see any logical reasons for delaying the reforms—then, at the very least, the on-going counter-trade arrangements existing among a few African countries should be strengthened and extended to as many countries as have products to exchange. After all, before the advent of money economy, Africa lived on trade by barter. The policy planning units should now explore the possibility of getting this ancient economic mechanism to tackle the problems of a modern age.

Need for Bureaucratic Flexibility

Africa's problems, like all human problems, are not insurmountable. If they appear to have defied solutions, it is mainly because while some institutions are trying out new formulae, others are working diligently on the side of forces opposed to change. As a social institution, the bureaucracy can make or un-make Africa's economic recovery plans. If it emphasizes hierarchy and protocol over production and results, the bureaucracy would have played into the hands of the agents of recession. If its operational code dethrones *purpose* and elevates *procedures*, it would be easier for the camel to pass through the eye of a needle than for Africa's material condition to improve.[11] Unfortunately, in a number of countries today, methods and procedures have taken over from achievement and productivity. Rules and regulations are applied without regard for the problems of our time. Heaps of forms and documents are kept which no auditor finds time to audit. Recently, market women (mostly nonliterate) in an African city were interviewed by news reporters on the reason for conducting their foreign exchange transactions on the black (or parallel) market rather than in banks. Their reply was unanimous, spontaneous, and highly educative: in the banks you fill out forms, you make declarations, you indicate the sources of foreign exchange. On the black market, there are no forms, no questions, and no standing in a queue. We hope that the O & M and management services experts have got the message.

Motivation and Administrative Ethics

Perhaps the bureaucracy needs to be adequately motivated to effect the necessary reforms in work-flow patterns. After all, "lost" and otherwise "untraceable" files have been known to resurface after the client has taken "appropriate" steps. Complex tendering procedures have been "simplified" where it is in the interest of tendering committee members to speed up action. The economic conditions of the recent years might have contributed in no small measure to large-scale deprivation, and therefore, to the temptation to abuse procedures. The answer lies in the supervisors showing greater interest than before in the welfare of their subordinates, and in constant reform and simplification of operational methods.

NOTES

1. OAU/ECA, *Africa's Submission to the Special Session of the United Nations General Assembly on Africa's Economic and Social Crisis* (OAU/ECM/2XV/Rev. 2, E/ECA/ECM. 1/Rev. 2, 1986).

2. Sadig Rasheed and Makha D. N. Sarr, "The African Response: From the Lagos Plan of Action to the Thirteenth Special Session of the United Nations General Assembly," *International Conference on Africa: The Challenge of Economic Recovery and Accelerated Development* (Abuja, Nigeria, 15–19 June 1987).

3. *Africa's Submission to the U.N., op. cit.*

4. David Fasholé-Luke, "African Development Management Reform: Political and Sociocultural Constraints vs. the Neo-classical Imperative," Abuja Conference, *op. cit.*

5. The percentages are calculated by the authors of this paper on the basis of data supplied in David Fasholé-Luke's paper, *ibid.*

6. *Address to the Nation on Consolidating Budget 1987,* by Major-General Ibrahim Babagida, President of the Federal Republic of Nigeria.

7. Central Bank of Nigeria, *Annual Report and Statement of Account,* 31 December 1986, 12.

8. Central Bank of Nigeria, *First Half Year Report for 1987.*

9. ECA, "Re-dynamising Africa's Administrative/Managerial Systems and Institutions for Economic Recovery and Development," ECA/EDI Senior Policy Seminar on Development Management (Addis Ababa, 6–10 July 1987) (Ref. ECA/PAMM/PAM/87/1).

10. The ability to engineer socioeconomic change is one of the attributes emphasized by Adebayo Adedeji. Africa's monetary and trade reforms provide a litmus test of this ability. See Adebayo Adedeji, "Administrative Adjustments and Responses to Changes in the Economic Environment," in *The Ecology of Public Administration and Management in Africa* (Addis Ababa: AAPAM, 1986), 116.

11. See M. J. Balogun, "The Role of Management Training Institutions in Developing the Capacity for Economic Recovery and Long-term Growth in Africa," (Paper presented at the Commonwealth Secretariat's Workshop for Heads of Management Training Institutions in West Africa, ASCON, Badagry, 2–6 November 1987.)

CHAPTER FOUR

Public Sector Management Improvement in Sub-Saharan Africa: The World Bank Experience

Ladipo Adamolekun

INTRODUCTION

This chapter seeks to achieve three objectives. The first is to provide a brief survey of the World Bank's involvement in public sector management (PSM) improvement in sub-Saharan African (SSA) countries during the past six years. SSA countries have been selected as the focus of the study because the Bank's experience in the preparation and implementation of development activities relating to both project-based and policy-based lending since the late 1970s has revealed the serious weakness of the administrative systems in these countries.[1] The second objective is to assess the Bank's efforts against the backdrop of the public service reform agenda articulated in the *World Development Report 1983* (WDR 1983) and the Bank's stated goal of using such interventions to improve the chances of success of structural adjustment loans (SALs). The third objective is to evaluate the impact of the Bank's interventions on the SSA countries involved. The survey of the Bank's interventions will examine the source of reform initiative, the methods of the Bank's interventions and the extent of involvement of other donor agencies, in addition to an overview of the actual and proposed reform measures. The assessment of the Bank's interventions and the discussion of their impact on SSA countries will be very tentative. This is partly because actual implementation of reform measures has covered less than three years in the majority of cases (and institutional reform everywhere takes time to produce results) and partly because the fieldwork necessary for both performance measurement and impact study have not yet been undertaken. The penultimate section to the chapter highlights some issues that deserve the attention of both the Bank and the SSA countries concerned in the joint effort to promote PSM improvement. In the concluding section, some observations are made on the desirable directions for the Bank's involvement in promoting PSM improvement in SSA countries.

SURVEY OF THE BANK'S INVOLVEMENT IN PSM IMPROVEMENT

Out of seventeen Bank interventions in support of PSM improvement by the end of 1984, eight were in SSA: Central African Republic (CAR), Ghana, Guinea-Bissau, Liberia, Mali, Mauritius, Sierra Leone, and Uganda. For a variety of reasons, most often resulting in a slackening of country commitment, the Bank's involvement in PSM in four of the countries was aborted and no project funds were approved for these countries: Guinea-Bissau, Liberia, Sierra Leone, and Ghana. Table 4–1 shows the amounts approved to support the Bank's interventions in support of PSM in the CAR, Mali, Mauritius, and Uganda as of December 1983. Beginning from 1985, the Bank's support for PSM improvement increased tremendously both in number and scope and by April 1987, Bank-supported PSM activities were implemented or under preparation in about thirty SSA countries (see Tables 4–2 and 4–3). A checklist of specific PSM improvement measures, grouped under the two broad issues of civil service management and economic and financial management is provided in Table 4–4.

TABLE 4–1
Technical Assistance Loans and Credits for Administrative Reform, 1981–83

Country	Date of Approval	Amount
Central African Republic	May 1981	$700,000
Mali	December 1982	$800,000
Mauritius	December 1983	$100,000
Uganda	December 1983	$5,000,000

Source: Compiled from various internal documents of the World Bank.

Who determines the PSM reform agenda? On the face of it, the answer to this question should be either the Bank or a Bank member country in SSA. What happens in practice is usually more complicated. The following examples illustrate the variety of ways in which the content of a PSM improvement project is determined. In the CAR, it was the government that first expressed an interest in undertaking administrative reform as part of the economic recovery program that was embarked upon after the collapse of the Bokassa regime. The Bank's initial support consisted of accepting the government's administrative reform program as a component of a freestanding Technical Assistance (TA) project. The preparatory work was carried out by a French consultant. While the TA approval was based on the consultant's report, it was found necessary to use part of the TA to finance further study of the CAR's administrative problems. This task was

TABLE 4–2
PSM Components in Bank Operations
Implemented as of April 1987

Country	SAL Supporting Institutional Reforms[a]	TALs Supporting Institutional Reforms Focused on — Civil Service Management	TALs Supporting Institutional Reforms Focused on — Economic and Financial Management	Country Economic and Sector Work with Institutional Support Component
Comoros		X	X	
Benin		X	X	
Burundi	X		X	X
Cameroon			X	
CAR	X	X	X	X
Congo			X	
Côte d'Ivoire	X			X
Djibouti			X	
Ethiopia			X	
The Gambia	X			
Guinea	X		X	
Guinea-Bissau	X			
Kenya	X			
Liberia	X		X	
Madagascar				X
Malawi	X		X	X
Mali	X	X	X	X
Mauritania	X	X[b]	X	
Mauritius	X	X	X	
Niger	X		X	
Nigeria	X		X	X
Rwanda			X	X
Senegal	X	X[b]	X	X
Sierra Leone	X		X	
Sudan			X	X
Tanzania	X		X	X
Togo	X		X	X
Uganda		X	X	X
Zambia			X	X

[a] Institutional reforms supported by SALs include, in most cases, support for public enterprise management reforms.
[b] New PSM components under preparation.
Source: Compiled from various internal World Bank documents.

contracted to a team of Canadian consultants who eventually became the principal contractor for the project. By November 1984, contracts totalling $700,000 had been awarded to the National School of Public Administration (*Ecole Nationale d'Administration Publique*, ENAP) in Quebec, Canada.

TABLE 4-3
PSM Components in Bank Operations Under Preparation as of April 1987

Country	SAL Supporting Institutional Reforms	TALs Supporting Institutional Reforms Focused on Civil Service Management	TALs Supporting Institutional Reforms Focused on Economic and Financial Management
Ghana[a]	X	X	X
Madagascar	X		X
Sao Tome and Principe	X		X
Zaire	X		X

[a]Ghana's "Structural Adjustment and Institutional Support" IDA Technical Assistance Credit of $10.8M was approved in April 1987. The TA Credit is to support PSM improvement with a focus on both civil service management and economic and financial management. A separate public enterprise management project was under preparation as of April 1987.

Source: Compiled from various internal World Bank documents.

TABLE 4-4
Checklist of Bank-Supported Measures for the Improvement of Public Sector Management

Civil Service Management
- staff reduction and growth control (including census of civil servants)
- salary and compensation policies review
- job classification and evaluation
- documentation and records management (statistics/management information system)
- strengthening and reorganization of selected ministries and agencies, e.g., Office of the Head of Civil Service, Ministries of Public Service, Local Government/Interior
- promoting public service training through strengthening of national training institutions
- administrative decentralization

Economic and Financial Management
- strengthening and reorganization of economic planning and economic financial management institutions, notably Ministries of Planning and Finance
- improving formulation of economic policy, planning, and management
- public investment and expenditure planning
- reform of the budgetary system
- improving government accounting and auditing
- reform of tax administration and revenue mobilization
- external financial management (aid, debt management)
- training for staff of economic institutions

Source: Compiled from various internal World Bank documents.

The administrative reform agenda that was first elaborated by ENAP adopted something close to a comprehensive approach. Beginning with the establishment of a high-powered committee to be responsible for setting and reviewing national policies (the strategic function), it was proposed that the government should establish a budget committee that would direct and coordinate economic and financial planning and management. Other reform proposals included job classification and evaluation, study of civil service staff growth, and management training for government officials. Although the government agreed with these proposals, actual implementation had not started when the government invited ENAP for discussion over a redefinition of the terms of reference (TOR) in the contract. A new contract and TOR agreed to required ENAP to focus its attention first on assisting the government to achieve a significant reduction in the staff strength of the civil service and to propose measures for controlling staff growth. All this with a view to effecting a reduction in the annual wage bill.

What had happened was that toward the end of 1982, the CAR began negotiations with the International Monetary Fund (IMF), and one of the issues raised by the Fund was the absolute necessity for the government to effect an urgent and drastic reduction in the size of public employment and the civil service wage bill. By 1981, 86 percent of the CAR's budgetary receipts were being spent on the wage bill of 25,600 civil servants. Faced with this emergency, the CAR government decided to use the available ENAP assistance in meeting the IMF conditionality. Since the Bank had, on its part, expressed serious reservations about the 1982 the CAR-ENAP reform agenda, it readily participated in formulating the new TOR set out in the renegotiated 1983 contract. By 1984, the Bank was reasonably satisfied with what the CAR and ENAP had achieved in respect to staff reduction and growth control, and it played a more active role in determining the new TOR for ENAP. At this point, the Bank had begun discussions with the CAR on preparatory work for a possible SAL and the new issues raised in the administrative reform agenda more or less amounted to SAL conditionality. Thus, from 1985 onward, the content of administrative reform agenda in the CAR was largely determined by the imperatives of IMF conditionality and the Bank's SAL conditionality. Tables 4–5 and 4–6 show that almost every item on the checklist of Bank-supported PSM improvement measures (Table 4–4) was being implemented in the CAR. It will be shown later than in countries where the Bank's support for administrative reform is directly linked to an SAL, the tendency is for PSM improvement measures to include as many items on the checklist as possible.

The Ugandan experience is different from that of the CAR in some important areas. The $5 million TA credit approved for administrative reform in Uganda in December 1983 was based on the recommendation of a Bank mission with which the government had discussed its plans to re-

TABLE 4-5
Countries in Which Bank-Supported Civil Service Management Improvement Measures Were Being Implemented or Planned by April 1987

Staff Reduction and Growth Control	Salary and Compensation Policies Review	Job Classification and Evaluation	Strengthening and Reorganization of Selected Ministries	Government Procurement	Documentation and Records Management (Statistics)	Promoting Public Service Training	Administrative Decentralization
CAR	Benin	CAR	CAR		CAR		
Gambia	CAR		Gambia[a]			Gambia[a]	
Ghana	Gambia		Ghana		Ghana	Ghana	Ghana
Guinea	Ghana						
Mali	Guinea						
Mauritania	Mauritania						
Niger	Niger						
Senegal	Senegal			Senegal[a]	Senegal[a]		Rwanda
Sierra Leone[a]	Sierra Leone[a]						
	Togo						
Uganda[a]	Uganda	Uganda	Uganda		Uganda	Uganda	
						Zambia	
						Zimbabwe[a]	

[a] Countries in which PSM improvement measures were still being planned by April 1987.

Source: Compiled from various internal World Bank documents.

form the country's public administration system in October 1982. As a follow-up to this initial support, the Bank sponsored a full-scale diagnostic study of Uganda's administrative problems in February and March 1983. The five-member Public Administration mission was composed of three Bank staff members and two consultants. On the basis of the mission's report, a Public Service Performance Improvement Project was elaborated to be financed under a 1984 SAL. The broad objective of the project was to increase the managerial and administrative capacity of the Government.[2] A resident adviser financed under the Bank loan was recruited and his TOR enjoined him to strengthen the capacity of the Ministry of Public Service and Cabinet Affairs and that of the country's Institute of Public Administration. The resident adviser was made operationally responsible to the Ugandan government and he was to send periodic reports to both the DTCD/UNDP, the executing agency, and the Bank. In 1985, the Bank conducted further diagnostic study of the administrative problems in Uganda resulting in an internal document by a staff member on *The World Bank's Approach to Public Administration Assistance in Uganda*.[3] On the basis of this document and additional input from the Ugandan Government, a revised project was prepared in 1985–86: *Improvement of Public Service Performance in Uganda* (November 1986), for a two-year period, effective from January 1987.[4] Again DTCD is expected to serve as the implementing agency. Although the project outputs are more or less a continuation of those set out in the 1984 project, they are more sharply focused: improved organization and staffing structures to enhance the responsiveness of the public service machinery; optimum effectiveness in manpower development and utilization, and improved management systems, techniques and procedures.

One important difference between the CAR and Ugandan experiences deserves to be highlighted. This difference is with respect to the use of ENAP as contractor-executing agency in the CAR and UNDTCD in Uganda. These two implementing agencies are fundamentally different. In particular, UNDTCD was also at the same time the executing agency for a UNDP PSM project focused on more or less the same subjects as that of the Bank. Thus, a problem of donor coordination has featured prominently in the Ugandan case, a problem that is further complicated by the involvement of two other bilateral donors in the same activities—the Overseas Development Administrative (ODA) of the United Kingdom and the United States Agency for International Development (USAID).

The Bank involvement in PSM improvement in Zambia has been focused on economic and financial planning and management (see Table 4–2). In this case, the reform activities carried out were identified jointly by the Bank and the government, and the Bank's intervention has been almost exclusively through staff members serving as technical assistants.[5] Furthermore, while PSM improvement measures focused on economic

TABLE 4-6
Countries in Which Bank-Supported Economic and Financial Management Improvement Measures Were Being Implemented or Planned by April 1987

Strengthening and Reorganization of Planning and Financial Management	Improving Formulation of Economic Policy, Planning, and Management	Public Sector Investment Planning	Reform of Budgetary System	Improving Government Accounting and Audit	Reform of Tax Administration and Revenue Mobilization	External Financial Management (Aid and Debt)	Training for Staff of Economic Institutions
Benin							
Burundi[a]							
CAR	CAR	CAR			CAR	CAR	CAR
	Comoros[a]						
Ghana	Ghana	Ghana	Ghana	Ethiopia	Ghana	Ghana	Ghana
Liberia[a]							
Malawi	Malawi	Malawi					Malawi
Rwanda[a]							
Senegal[a]	Senegal[a]	Togo[a]					Senegal[a]
Uganda				Uganda			Uganda
Zaire[a]							
Zambia	Zambia		Zambia		Zambia		Zambia

[a]Countries in which PSM improvement measures were still being planned by April 1987.

Source: Compiled from various internal World Bank documents.

and financial management were part of SAL conditionality in the CAR, the prior adoption of such measures was regarded as a positive development when dialogue on a possible SAL for Zambia started in 1986.[6] The Gambia,[7] Ghana, Malawi, Senegal, and Sierra Leone provide additional illustrations of a combination of PSM improvement measures focused either on the economic and financial or civil service checklist or a combination of the two as prerequisites for SAL approval (The Gambia, Ghana, and Sierra Leone) or as companion measures to an ongoing series of SAL (Malawi and Senegal).

Although SAL conditionality now appears as the critical push for the Bank's involvement in PSM improvement in SSA countries, it must also be emphasized that the Bank's commitment to assisting its less developed member countries to strengthen their administrative capacity as set out in WDR 1983 has not been abandoned. This Bank commitment is underscored in its Operational Manual Statement (OMS) on institution building and development management capacity building: the Bank "expects significant institution-building and policy improvements to take place in connection with its loans" (OMS 1.19, para. 10) and the Bank is committed "to encourage and to foster the development of local capabilities to conceive, design and carry out development work on a sound basis" (OMS 2.18, para. 1).[8] All the first eight Bank-supported PSM improvement initiatives in SSA appear to have been largely influenced by this operational commitment to institution building and development management capacity building.

The determination of the content of administrative reform agenda, then, is attributable to several actors. The Bank's intervention derives from a commitment to managerial and administrative capacity building both as ends in themselves (hopefully resulting in more efficient, effective, productive, and responsive administrative systems) and as means to the end of well elaborated and successfully implemented SALs. The available evidence suggests that the governments of the member countries in SSA in which the Bank has been involved share these objectives. Obviously, the concrete results achieved will be a function of government commitment to the reforms, the effectiveness of the Bank's methods of intervention, and the contributions of other donor agencies. In the next section, we shall examine the results produced by the interplay of these various factors.

ASSESSMENT OF IMPACT OF PSM IMPROVEMENT PROGRAM

The diagram which follows is a representation of the major stakeholders whose actions and interactions influence the effectiveness and impact of PSM improvement measures: the government of the country concerned, the Administrative Reform Agency (where one exists), the government agencies to be reformed, the Bank, and other donor agencies. The role of the government of the country in which a Bank-supported PSM improvement project is being undertaken is crucial. At the minimum, the government must be committed to the initiation of the project. If at any point the government's commitment slackens to an extent that an agreed upon action plan is consistently ignored, whatever support the Bank has promised is withdrawn and expenses incurred are written off.[9] This was what happened in Ghana and Sierra Leone between 1982 and 1984. An important index of government commitment is its readiness to designate or establish a reform implementation institution which will serve as the focal center for further elaboration of agreed upon reform measures as well as the principal instrument for reform implementation. A strategic location

Major Stakeholders Involved in PSM Improvement

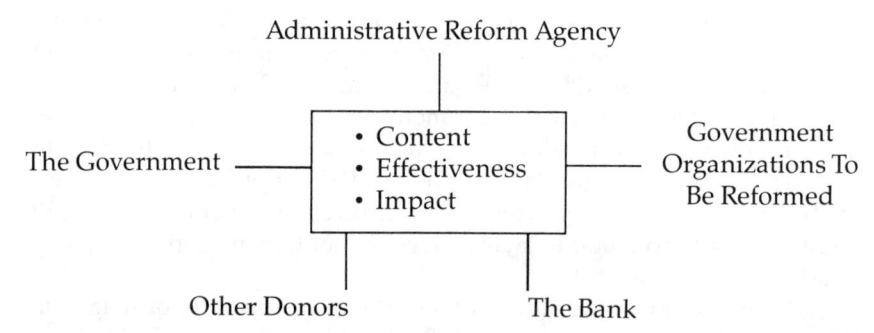

```
                    Administrative Reform Agency
                              │
                    ┌─────────────────────┐
                    │  • Content          │        Government
The Government ─────│  • Effectiveness    │──── Organizations To
                    │  • Impact           │        Be Reformed
                    └─────────────────────┘
                         │           │
                   Other Donors   The Bank
```

of the reform agency in the office of the president/office of the head of government or in a key ministry is considered essential to its effectiveness. The third set of stakeholders consists of government agencies that will be affected by the reform measures. These could be existing organizations which might need to be reorganized and strengthened or new ones to be assigned functions that are either newly established or taken away from existing agencies. What happens to these government agencies (both new and old) and their actual functioning have significant consequences for both the effectiveness and impact of reform measures. Although both the Bank and the other donors normally set out to assist governments in promoting PSM improvement, in practice, the coordination of efforts is not always achieved either because of inadequate consultation or because host governments are unable or unwilling to establish an effective framework for coordination. When this happens there is failure of donor coordination and this could limit both the effectiveness and impact of PSM measures.

Let us briefly review a few country cases. In the CAR,[10] the progress of reform from broad institutional capacity building through specific, sharply focused civil service management improvement measures to macroeconomic and financial policy management reform appears to have followed a sequence that was worked out jointly by the government (aided by the ENAP consultants) and the Bank (with the IMF push at the second phase). The establishment in 1984 of a Permanent Committee for the Reform of Administration of Central African Republic *(Conseil permanent pour la réforme de l'administration Centrafricaine, CPRAC)* appears to have played an important role in the implementation process. The Committee's location in the office of the president provided both visibility and political clout while the ENAP consulting team succeeded in establishing a good working relationship with the government. Significant results were achieved by the Committee in 1984 and 1985 with respect to staff reduction and growth: the civil service strength of 25,600 in 1981 had been reduced to 22,037 in 1985. This in turn resulted in a significant reduction in the wage bill: from 86 percent of the national budget in 1981 to 58 percent in 1985. Other reform measures undertaken included documentation and record management, and staff training. From 1985 through 1986 to 1987, the Permanent Committee continued to elaborate and implement specific PSM improvement measures including the computerization of personnel administration, the restructuring of government ministries, redefinition and reallocation of functions among ministries, manpower planning and utilization, and continuous training and retraining of civil servants. For example, by April 1987, six ministries had been reorganized: Agriculture, Rural Development, and Livestock; Public Works; Public Service; Education, Economy and Finance; Industry and Commerce. The role of other donors in all these reform efforts had consisted of supporting some of the specific activities, notably public service training, (UNDP, USAID, and France) and the structural reorganization of ministries (UNDP). In the circumstance, no serious problem of donor coordination has been experienced. In addition to the specificity of the PSM improvement activities, the "demonstration effect" of the successful operation of staff reduction achieved in 1984–85 and the credibility of the resident expert of the ENAP consulting group seem to have encouraged the cooperative effort of the donor agencies.

Although the point can be made that some progress has been recorded in strengthening the CAR governmental administration, the preceding overview of the reform measures carried out falls short of a full impact study. Indeed, several of the reform measures likely to have long-term consequences (restructuring of ministries, manpower planning and utilization, and public service training) still require a few more years before their real impact can be assessed. A critical factor that will determine the eventual balance sheet of reform efforts is whether or not government commitment is sustained. For example, while continuing to maintain the staff control measures introduced alongside the staff reduction exercise of

1983–85, the government has had to make some exception in 1986–87 by hiring 1,500 graduates as non-regular staff in order to accommodate social pressures. So, the question can still be posed as to whether or not effective staff control will continue to be maintained. Furthermore, will the government implement faithfully the proposed reforms on ministerial structures, manpower planning and utilization? Will civil servants continue to be trained and retrained in adequate numbers and in the relevant areas of expertise? What concrete improvements will be achieved in the actual performance of the CAR civil servants on the job, including such issues as the quality and regularity of delivery of goods and services and commitment to public service? It will take another three to five years before these important evaluative questions can be answered, and until then, one cannot reach reliable conclusions on the effectiveness and impact of PSM reform measures in the CAR.

In the Ugandan case, the progress made to date has been rather limited. Although the Bank succeeded in recruiting a resident adviser who is an experienced public administration expert with both African and international experience, continued political instability in Uganda together with some limitations of the executing agency, UNDTCD, have combined to limit the effectiveness of the project. This appears to be largely responsible for the six-month delay in obtaining final approval for the revised PSM project negotiated in November 1986. Furthermore, a real problem of donor coordination has emerged, clearly illustrated by the declared commitment of four different donors to the strengthening of Uganda's Institute of Public Administration: the Bank, the Overseas Development Administration of the United Kingdom (ODA/UK), United States Agency for International Development (USAID) and the UNDP. Although each donor has claimed that it assigns priority to the rehabilitation and strengthening of the IPA in successive PSM improvement proposals since 1983, very little progress had been made by April 1987. It has probably been a case of too many cooks.

To some extent, the Bank's support for PSM improvement in some other countries can also be said to have produced significant results. For example, civil service staff reduction and growth control have been successfully carried out in The Gambia,[11] Mali, and Senegal. These exercises have also had the corresponding effect of reducing the wage bills in the countries concerned. Two caveats are in order here. First, the reductions of both staff strength and wage bill have in almost every case been spurred in part by "IMF conditionality." Second, in spite of the control measures already introduced in some of these countries, notably Senegal, several aspects of the problems of staff strength and wage bill reduction remain unresolved.[12] On the reform of economic and financial management, the case study on Zambia suggests that the Bank's interventions have been effective, notwithstanding the hesitant approach of the Bank and the grudging cooperation of the Zambian government officials. And it is a measure of the impact achieved that the improved institutional and administrative capacity in macroeconomic management was acknowledged during the recently suspended discussion of a SAL for the country. Malawi is the other country where important economic and financial reform measures have been introduced: establishment of an Economic Planning and Development unit in the Office of the President and Cabinet, reform of public sector investment plan and training of staff operating in economic and financial institutions. An economic and public enterprise management project currently under preparation for the country includes proposals for further strengthening of macroeconomic and financial policy-making and management.

The above comments on the effectiveness and impact of PSM improvement measures introduced in some SSA countries must be regarded as tentative. However, the spread in the number of countries covered and the steady increase in the number of specific issues on the reform agenda adopted (more and more a combination of civil service management and economic and financial management) say something for the belief of both the Bank and the SSA countries in the need for these reform measures. Whether or not the results achieved will eventually justify the high expectations of all concerned remains to be seen.

ISSUES FOR THE CONSIDERATION OF THE BANK AND SSA COUNTRIES

There are four issues that are likely to be of continuing interest to both the Bank and the SSA countries in the joint effort to promote PSM improvement: content of reform agenda; methods of the Bank's intervention; effectiveness and impact of reform measures; and donor coordination.

Content of Reform Agenda

It is reasonable to assume that the two major justifications for the Bank's support for PSM improvement—institutional development (ID)[13] and SAL conditionality—will remain valid for another six years and probably a little longer. What needs to be emphasized is that there is really no fundamental contradiction between SAL-oriented and ID-oriented PSM improvement measures. The approaches adopted in determining the content of reform agendas in the CAR, Zambia, Ghana, and Senegal provide evidence in support of this assertion. In the CAR, the Bank began by supporting ID-oriented reform measures focused on civil service management. After some progress had been recorded, reform measures focusing on economic and financial management were introduced just before the elaboration of an SAL. In Zambia, the Bank's effort was at first focused on the improvement of economic and financial management, several years before the preparation of an SAL was embarked upon. The Zambia SAL was expected to include provisions on institutional development focused on both civil service management and economic and financial management. And in the two cases of Ghana and Senegal, the lessons of the CAR and Zambian experiences appear to have been combined, resulting in an integrated approach where ID focused on both civil service management and economic and financial management are combined. This integrated package of PSM improvement measures is aptly described in the Ghanaian case as "Structural Adjustment and Institutional Support."[14]

It is likely that the content of reform agenda in the different SSA countries will combine elements from the checklist (Table 4-4). More countries will probably adopt the integrated approach (combining both civil service management and economic and financial management) as macroeconomic policy issues occupy center stage within the context of SALs. In this connection, the emerging importance of policy planning and research is likely to concentrate attention on the policy function in public service training. Already, the development of policy analysis capacity and training for the policy function has been identified as a key area for PSM improvement.[15] A second issue that is likely to feature prominently in the content of reform agenda is administrative decentralization. This subject was highlighted in WDR 1983 and it is widely cited as a priority issue by most SSA countries and by several donor organizations that contribute to PSM improvement.[16]

Methods of Bank Intervention

The Bank's work in support of PSM has been carried out through five major instrumentalities: special Bank missions, country economic and sector work (CESW), technical assistance staff, the use of consultants, and "hiving off" (meaning contracting out) implementation to an executing agency. In most cases, especially in cases of sustained PSM support efforts, two or more methods are combined. The Bank's intervention can be broadly divided into two phases: the diagnostic (study) phase and the action (implementation) phase. At the diagnostic stage, the central concern is the study and diagnosis of the prevailing administrative problems in the different SSA countries in which PSM improvement projects are to be undertaken. To date this diagnostic work has been carried out either by special Bank missions or by consultants. Most often, a mission comprises three or more Bank staff with one or two consultants, with a Bank staff member as team leader. Consultants are normally brought in to provide expertise in management-related disciplines such as public administration, business administration, sociology, psychology, political science and organization analysis. In a few cases, diagnostic work has been entrusted entirely to consultants (for example, in the CAR in 1981 and 1982) but this method has more or less been discontinued.

While not setting out consciously to study the administrative problems of a country, the Bank's missions involved in CESW sometimes end up undertaking a PSM diagnostic work as a side concern. Whenever this happens, further study is undertaken, usually by a formally constituted diagnostic team, with the appropriate mix of expertise.[17] The obvious explanation is that the country economists involved in CESW are not normally fully equipped to undertake a full-scale PSM diagnostic work. As a result of the modest increase in the number of the Bank's staff with PSM-related expertise since 1983, reliance on consultants for diagnostic work has been reduced somewhat. If there is continued steady growth in the number of the Bank's staff involved in PSM, the reliance on consultants may be further reduced. But if this does not happen, increased demand from SSA countries (and other less developed countries) might lead to greater reliance on consultants. The fact that Bank preference in recent years is for diagnostic missions dominated by Bank staff suggests that the implied limited use of consultants is arguably more effective and certainly more cost effective. This should be interpreted to mean that the desirable direction is to strengthen the Bank's staff with PSM-related expertise while using consultants on a selective basis.

At the implementation stage, one or the other of the following three strategies is used: the Bank's staff members as technical assistants, short-term and long-term consultants as experts/advisers, and "hiving off" to an executing agency. The first two methods constitute the traditional approach to TA. Technical assistance staff are usually appointed with TORs which set out some specific PSM improvement activities that they are expected to undertake during a specified time frame ranging from a few weeks/months to one or more years. The Zambian case illustrates both the possibilities and limitations of a reliance on the Bank's staff serving as technical assistants to implement PSM improvement. Although some concrete results were achieved in the end, the difficulties encountered at both the Zambian and the Bank's end suggest that it might not have been particularly cost-effective. The use of both short-term and long-term consultants to undertake PSM activity is an established practice in the Bank. Although OED evaluation reports on the performance of consultants as technical assistants in project implementation has consistently pointed up inadequacies (notably with respect to skill transfer through on-the-job training of counterpart staff), no good substitute has been found. It appears that it will remain an important method for implementing PSM improvement measures. Both the Bank and the countries concerned will have to seek ways of increasing its effectiveness.

The practice of "hiving off" the implementation of a PSM reform package to an executing agency has been used by the Bank in the CAR and Uganda. As an alternative strategy to the direct intervention by the Bank through technical assistants, this method has the advantage of freeing the Bank from day-to-day management of operations. However, the usefulness of this strategy will depend on the quality of the executing agency and its ability to operate effectively in the country concerned. The Bank's experience with the ENAP as the executing agency in the CAR appears to have been moderately successful. The ENAP consulting group has a resident expert (financed under IDA credit) in Bangui who provides the overall technical leadership for the CAR reform effort on a continuous basis. Other ENAP experts provide periodic short-term interventions. Available evidence shows that the resident expert has benefited significantly from the fact that he can rely on both the technical and professional support of ENAP in guiding the work of the CAR's Permanent Committee on Administrative Reform. However, the absence of a corresponding technical and professional control from the Bank's side appears to have reduced the chances of introducing more innovative reform measures as the ENAP experts naturally seek to introduce only innovations with which they are familiar.

Effectiveness and Impact

As already mentioned, effectiveness measures performance against stated objectives. Evidence that the objective of reducing the staff strength of the civil service has been achieved in one country by, say, 10 percent can justify a verdict of effectiveness. Similarly, when a wage bill that was 70 percent of budgetary receipts is reduced to 60 percent, the action taken qualifies to be described as effective. It is in this sense that some of the actions taken with the Bank's support to reduce civil service staff strength and salaries in the CAR and The Gambia, among others, can be described as effective. However, beyond the immediate results which are used to judge effectiveness lies the more lasting goal of having a civil service of a size appropriate to its functions, taking a share of the national budget that is proportionate to its productive and efficient contribution to national growth. In this sense, not only are the reductions already achieved sustained, the "reformed" civil service is also able to make an impact on the progress of the country, an impact that can endure over several years. In other words, while effectiveness measurement refers to the short-term, impact measurement must be seen within a long-term perspective.

From the overview of the PSM improvement measures discussed earlier in the chapter, it is clear that for now, we can only meaningfully discuss the effectiveness of the Bank-supported reform measures in some SSA countries. In addition to the references already made to the areas of civil service staff strength, salaries, and staff training, some reorganization of selected government ministries has taken place in government institutions, and agencies have been established in the area of economic and financial policy-making and implementation (Malawi and Zambia). In particular, a few countries have established administrative reform agencies such as the Permanent Committee for the Reform of the Administration of Central African Republic (*Conseil permanent pour la réforme de l'administration Centrafricaine,* CPRAC) in the CAR and the Public Administration Restructuring and Decentralization Committee (PARDIC) in Ghana. Just as the long-term is a succession of short-terms, the impact of PSM improvement will also most certainly be the cumulative result of a series of effective reform measures. But the critical requirement is to sustain such effective improvements over time such that they become institutionalized. In other words, the yardsticks for measuring the impact of PSM improvements are their sustainability and institutionalization. And this should be the goal of both the Bank and the SSA countries.

Donor Coordination

In spite of the increasing use made of donor consultative meetings for SSA countries (a practice initiated by the U.N. for all the developing countries since the late 1970s), problems of donor coordination persist in many areas of technical assistance, including TA for PSM improvement. Ideally, the country undertaking PSM improvement measures is expected to coordinate whatever support is forthcoming from donor agencies. For obvious reasons, different countries approach donor coordination in different ways, depending on each country's local realities and the "policies" of specific donor agencies involved in providing support for PSM improvement. Sometimes, the "policies" of some donor agencies and their methods of interventions are such as to render coordination very difficult. For example, a bilateral donor agency might be seeking to relate its PSM improvement interventions in country X to what it is doing in some other countries thereby focusing more on the coordination of its interventions across countries than on coordination with other PSM improvement efforts in country X. At other times, it could be the country concerned that fails to provide leadership for coordination either because it lacks the capacity to do so or because it simply does not attach importance to the subject.

It must be admitted that despite formal commitment to the need for coordination, donor agencies sometimes concentrate on specific PSM improvement measures with a view to making a distinct visible impact and taking credit for same. Some SSA countries, for their part, sometimes take the view that the involvement of several donor agencies allows for more PSM improvement support while at the same time providing some degree of choice. Notwithstanding the immediate advantages derivable from the "strategies" of both the donor agencies and the host countries, it is only through effective coordination of the inputs from the different donors that a country committed to PSM improvement can achieve concrete results. Therefore, donor coordination deserves the serious attention of both SSA countries and the Bank.

CONCLUSIONS

The Bank's interventions in support of PSM improvement activities in SSA, which started around 1980, increased significantly during the past seven years. This expansion was partly in response to the internal impetus for administrative reform in some of the SSA countries and partly dictated by the Bank's own interest in strengthening the administrative capacity of SSA countries. Specifically, the Bank's support for PSM activities in SSA countries has two objectives: (i) to assist the countries concerned in strengthening their administrative institutions (this is sometimes referred to as institutional development and/or institution building), and (ii) to ensure the success of the development activities financed through its loans especially, the structural adjustment loans (SALs). It is in respect of the latter that the expression "SAL conditionality" is sometimes used. In practice, ID-oriented and SAL-oriented PSM improvement measures are complementary.

By mid-1987, the Bank was involved in supporting PSM improvement measures in more than thirty SSA countries including Benin, Côte d'Ivoire and Ghana in West Africa, the CAR and Zaire in Central Africa, and Malawi, Rwanda, Uganda, and Zambia in Eastern and Southern Africa (see Table 4–7). The PSM activities cover the two broad issues of civil service management and economic and financial management. The checklist of specific activities under the two broad issues is provided in Table 4–4. On civil service management, the reform measures include staff reduction and growth control, salary and compensation policies review, and public service training. With regard to economic and financial management, the activities include strengthening and reorganization of economic planning and financial management institutions, improving formulation of economic policy, planning and management, public investment and expenditure planning, and external financial management. The emerging dominant pattern of the Bank's support for PSM improvement is to include as many items on the checklist as possible especially in countries where a structural adjustment program has been adopted. Bank-supported PSM improvement activities in the CAR and Uganda are among the earliest (1981 and 1983, respectively) while the "Structural Adjustment and Institutional Support" project in Ghana (approved in April 1987) is the most comprehensive to date.

Because the actual implementation of PSM improvement measures has lasted for only about four years, it is rather too early to assess the effec-

TABLE 4-7
Selected Technical Assistance (TA) Projects Including Credits for Public Sector Management Improvement, 1980–87[a]

Country	Date of Approval	Amount	Remarks
Benin:			
TA	5/77	$1,700,000	PSM and PE
TA	2/82	$8,000,000	components
TA	12/84	$5,000,000	
Burundi:			
TA	2/76	$1,500,000	PSM and PE
TA	5/79	$2,500,000	components
TA	4/84	$5,100,000	
CAR:			
TA	5/81	$4,000,000	Important PSM
TA	4/85	$8,000,000	components
Ethiopia:			
TA	9/84	$4,000,000	PSM component
Gambia:			
Private sector development	Appraisal mission for July 1987		PSM and PE components
Ghana:			
SA Institutional support	4/14/87	$10,800,000	Important PSM component
Guinea:			
TA	3/85	$9,500,000	PSM and PE components
Guinea-Bissau:			
TA	9/84	$6,000,000	PSM and PE components
Madagascar:			
TA	12/80	$2,300,000	PSM and PE
Accounting and management training	2/86	$10,300,000	components
Malawi:			
TA	6/81	$1,000,000	PSM and PE
TA II	12/83	$1,500,000	components
ID, Ministry of Finance	Under preparation		
Mali:			
Economic management and training	12/82	$10,400,000	Important PSM component
ODIPAC TA	7/81	$6,500,000	PSM and PE components

[a]The remarks focus on the relative importance attached to PSM improvement and public enterprise (PE) management. In practically every case, some other specific sectoral activities are covered by the approved credits, usually in the agricultural, mining, manufacturing, and infrastructure (transportation, communication) sectors.

Source: Compiled by author from various internal World Bank documents.

TABLE 4-7, continued

Country	Date of Approval	Amount	Remarks
Mauritania:			
TA	11/76	$2,700,000	PSM component
TA II	9/82	$4,600,000	
TA for development management	Appraisal report being written		PSM activities only
Mauritius:			
TA	12/83	$5,000,000	Significant PSM component
Niger:			
Economic and financial management improvement	6/84	$11,700,000	PSM and PE components
Rwanda:			
TA	3/82	$5,000,000	Important PSM component
TA	3/85	$4,800,000	
PSM III		$7,400,000	
Senegal:			
TA	8/80	$5,300,000	PSM and PE components
Parapublic TA	7/83	$11,000,000	
Development management TA, equipment and training	Appraisal scheduled for 7/87		PSM activities only
Sudan:			
TA	2/76	$4,000,000	PSM and PE components
TA II	5/81	$6,000,000	
Public enterprise and economic management		$9,000,000	
Togo:			
Private enterprise development	Negotiations proceeding		
TA	6/79	$2,200,000	Largely PE components
TA II	6/82	$3,500,000	
TA III	5/85	$6,200,000	
Uganda:			
TA II	12/83	$15,000,000	Significant PSM component
PSM I	6/87	$20,000,000	PSM Only
Zaire:			
TA	5/81	$2,900,000	PSM and PE components PSM Only
Economic management TA	Scheduled for board approval 6/87		
Zambia:			
TA	12/78	$5,000,000	PSM activities are dominant
TA	4/86	$8,000,000	

tiveness and impact of the Bank's efforts. However, it is pointed out that whatever is achieved will result from the interplay of the following factors: government commitment to PSM reforms, the degree of effectiveness of the Bank's methods of intervention, and the contributions of other donor agencies. To date, modest achievements have been recorded in respect of civil service staff reduction and growth control (the CAR, Gambia), strengthening and reorganization of economic planning and financial management institutions (the CAR, Malawi, and Zambia), and public service training (several countries).

On the basis of available evidence on what has been happening in the different SSA countries in which the Bank supports PSM reform activities, four key issues that are likely to be of continuing interest to both the Bank and the SSA countries are: content of reform agenda; methods of the Bank's intervention; effectiveness and impact of reform measures; and donor coordination. With regard to the content of reform agenda, the trend toward a combination of PSM improvement activities focused on both civil service management and economic and financial management (the integrated approach) is likely to continue. Of the items on the checklist, two have emerged as deserving special attention: development of policy analysis capacity and administrative decentralization. On the methods of the Bank's intervention, the combination of approaches used to diagnose PSM problems can be maintained with greater emphasis on strengthening the Bank's staff with PSM-related expertise while consultants will continue to be used on a selective basis. The limited experience with actual implementation of PSM reform measures means that the Bank's strategies for implementation cannot be meaningfully assessed yet. However, the idea of "hiving off" (contracting out) implementation put in practice in the CAR (the ENAP of Quebec, Canada) and Uganda (DTCD/UNDP) will have to be studied carefully with a view to determining its usefulness and limitations. In the meantime, it appears that there is a strong case for designating a unit within the Bank to provide technical and professional backstopping for all the Bank-supported PSM improvement activities in SSA countries and elsewhere. (The obvious unit is the Public Sector Management and Private Sector Development Division of the Policy, Planning and Research, Senior Vice Presidency.) Finally, on donor coordination, the established principle that each SSA country concerned should assume the primary responsibility needs to be constantly emphasized and the Bank can provide some assistance in this regard through its central PSM agency.

NOTES

1. It is important to mention that several SSA countries had, on their own initiative, embarked on the reform of their administrative systems with a view to making them more

development-oriented. These reform efforts were first introduced tentatively in the late 1960s, increased in scope in the 1970s, and became widespread in the 1980s. Thus, in some SSA countries, the Bank's support for PSM improvement complemented an internal impetus for administrative reform.

2. Project Document UGA/84/009, *Enhancing Public Service Performance for Development*, September 1984.

3. G. Lamb, *The World Bank's Approach to Public Administration Assistance in Uganda*, 1985.

4. The implementation of the project was delayed for about six months.

5. For comprehensive study of Zambian experience, see T. Triche, *Institutional Development in Macro-economic and Financial Policy-making and Implementation: A Case Study of Zambia*, 1985.

6. Zambia-Bank discussions were suspended in early May 1987 because of domestic social and political problems in Zambia.

7. As in the CAR, IMF conditionality has also influenced the speed and content of PSM improvement measures in The Gambia.

8. Cited in Operations Evaluation Department, "Structural Adjustment Lending, A First Review of Experience," Report no. 6409, The World Bank, Washington, D.C., (1984).

9. Compared to other projects financed under Bank loans/IDA credits, the money committed at the preparation stage of PSM improvement projects is usually very small; even the funds approved for such projects are small compared to funds approved for projects in such sectors as agriculture, education, and transportation. Table 4-7 shows the credits approved for some TA projects with PSM improvement components. In most cases, the credits for PSM activities, excluding public enterprise management, constitute only a small proportion of the total. The notable exceptions are the CAR, Ghana, Mali, Mauritania, Senegal, Uganda, and Zambia.

10. This discussion of the Bank's support for PSM improvement in the CAR (paras. 12 and 13) benefits from findings made during a brief study visit to the CAR in May 1987. A full report on the Bank's support for public administration reform in the CAR is under preparation.

11. In 1986–87, The Gambia government achieved a 30 percent reduction in total government employment while the annual wage bill was reduced by about 15 percent.

12. See B. Nunberg, "Public Sector Pay and Employment Policy Issues in Bank Lending: An Interim Review of Experience," (April 1987).

13. Considerable overlap exists in the usage of the terms "institutional development," "institutional building," "public sector management," "public administration," and "development management," in the Bank's documents. The following useful clarification is provided in one internal Bank study: "Institutional development increases or creates capabilities for policy development, planning, organization design, programming, budgeting, scheduling, processing, staffing, training, personnel management, and financial management. Public sector management is a term that encompasses all these activities with specific reference to the public sector . . . it will be used as virtually synonymous with institutional development." In this study, PSM is used, as suggested, as synonymous with institutional development and it also subsumes both public administration and development management. See Public Sector Management Unit, "Bank Assistance for Public Sector Management," (December 1984).

14. The PSM improvement project under preparation for Senegal is called "Development Management Project." Public enterprise management is NOT included in both projects.

15. Within the Bank, both the PSMU and the Economic Development Institute (EDI) have already initiated activities in this area, and most of these activities are focused on SSA countries.

16. This is true, for example, of the United Nations whose new initiative in the PSM field (currently at the preparation stage) is called "Special Action Programme for Administration and Management in Africa" (SAPAM). It is significant that "policy advice" is another priority issue highlighted in SAPAM.

17. In The Gambia, after the Bank's CEM of 1985 had drawn attention to the need for public administration reform, the government succeeded in securing technical assistance from OAU/UK for both the diagnostic work and the follow-up reform activities.

CHAPTER FIVE

Economic Management in Africa: The Reform of Organization and Process

David Fasholé-Luke

INTRODUCTION

Future historians writing about development this decade will conclude that the 1980s represented a watershed in the reorientation of development management in Africa in response to persistent difficulties. In 1987, twenty-eight African countries implemented or planned major reform programs. The checklist in Table 5-1 identifies some of the reform measures. Table 5-2 identifies some of the countries. For many of them, such as Ghana, Senegal, Togo, Zaire, and Zambia, reform and adjustment measures have been pursued since the early 1980s (and in most of these cases, with growing despair over the political cost in the short term, and doubt over the benefits in the long term). For others, such as Chad, the Central African Republic, Guinea, Nigeria, Sierra Leone, and Tanzania, 1986 was the turning point. It was also the year when African governments took the case of their fragile economies to a Special Session of the United Nations General Assembly.

Building upon earlier declarations and pronouncements on economic diversification articulated in the Lagos Plan of Action[1] and Africa's Priority Programme for Economic Recovery,[2] African representatives at the Special Session declared a commitment "to undertake individually and collectively all measures and policy reforms necessary for the recovery of our economies."[3] They avowed that debt and debt service burdens, declining concessional flows, and the persistent downward spiral of the terms of trade of most countries in the region were severe constraints which result in an annual outflow of some U.S. $9 billion in 1985 prices.

This chapter examines emerging trends at the organizational level at the highest echelons of government, as Africa enters into the reformist era of the late 1980s and early 1990s. The term "reform" has a number of connotations, and in some social science theoretical perspectives, it is even used derogatorily. In this chapter, the term is employed in its ordinary usage to mean "the amendment or altering for the better, of some faulty state of things . . . the removal of some abuse or wrong."[4] Reform in this sense is predicated on Kantian voluntarism as the basis of political action and direction. No substantive policy options are advanced or advocated; the appropriateness of policies vary with a country's level of develop-

TABLE 5-1
Trends in Policy and Institutional Reform among African Countries

10	countries have decontrolled producer prices
20	countries have frozen hiring or reduced public sector employment
13	countries have eliminated public agricultural marketing agencies or permitted private sector competition
7	countries have turned over import of agricultural inputs to the private sector
14	countries have privatized some state enterprises
21	countries have substantially increased producer prices
14	countries have reduced or eliminated agricultural input subsidies
8	countries have reduced or eliminated food subsidies
16	countries have realigned exchange rates to more closely reflect the real cost of foreign exchange
7	of the above have adopted floating market rates

Source: *West Africa*, 30 March 1987, 627.

ment, size, national endowment, specific conjuncture of external relations and political preferences, among other factors. The focus of this chapter is on the reform of organizational and managerial aspects of policy development and administration which respectively constitute its second and third parts. The first part examines the broader context in which these reforms are being made and the basis of the new mood of realism that underlay African declarations at the United Nations Special Session.

A NEW MOOD OF REALISM

The new mood of reform in official African circles has to be perceived against the broader background of dashed expectations of a new international economic order and little progress on the North-South dialogue.[5]

TABLE 5-2
African Countries[a] with Major Structural Reform Programs Planned or Underway as of March 1987

Burundi	Mali
Central African Republic	Mauritania
Chad	Niger
Equatorial Guinea	Rwanda
The Gambia	Senegal
Ghana	Sierra Leone
Guinea	Somalia
Guinea-Bissau	Tanzania
Kenya	Togo
Madagascar	Zaire
Malawi	Zambia

[a] IDA-eligible sub-Saharan African countries.

Source: Overseas Development Council (of the U.S.), "Should the IMF Withdraw from Africa?" *Policy Focus*, no. 1 (1987), 6.

The aspirations announced at the UN Special Session are the embodiment of a growing realization among African elites and technocrats that some desperately needed management and policy adjustments to a changing world are required in the region. It is a realization that stems from a recognition of some important changes in the world economy that have occurred since the 1960s, and a corresponding revisionism (the new emphasis on market forces) in development theory and practice that had emerged before the recession of 1974-76 came under the (revisionist) impetus, and became even more sharply defined after the 1980-82 recession.

In the twenty years between 1960 and 1980, there were significant changes in the locus of world manufacturing output and in the relative shares of gross world product of various countries and geographical groups of countries. As a result, the industrial market economies of Western Europe and North America have lost some ground to a number of "newcomers," among them, Japan, the most prominent, and two dozen or so "middle-income" countries—Newly Industrializing Countries (NICs) and/or oil exporters. These changes in the relative shares of gross world product were accompanied by new trends showing an increasing share of manufactures as distinct from resource-based commodities in the composition of the exports of the "newcomers." During the same period, the share of world product of the "low-income countries" (most of which can be found in Africa) declined, but only marginally; on the other hand, their share of manufacturing output also increased if only fractionally.[6] Aside from these outcomes, the changes also illustrate that the pursuit of industrialization has truly become a worldwide phenomenon. Economic nationalism in terms of prestige, technological capacity, and the wealth that industrialization brings underlies the commitment of the new "modernizing elites" to achieve facility in manufacturing as does economic justification in terms of diversification, value added, and growth.

On top of this, the success of the "newcomers," especially Japan and the Asian "gang of four" (Hong Kong, Singapore, South Korea, and Taiwan), was associated with a similar set of management practices and policies including the creation of appropriate public agencies for policy development and innovation; the follow-through of policy decisions and close monitoring of implementation but with enough flexibility for learning and relearning; a reliance on export markets to generate growth rather than the expansion of domestic or regional markets; the use of foreign capital and borrowing to finance local investment; the provision of a host of market incentives and disincentives to guide economic behavior along desired paths; a shift to floating exchange rates; and the exposure of export industries to market forces and international competitiveness. In contrast, the adherence to inflexible planning schedules, import-substitution and/or distribution policies which a number of "poor performers"—low-income and state socialist countries as well as some Latin American

NICs—pursued during the same period resulted in high-cost and low-quality industrial output, neglect of agriculture (and in some cases, growing food deficits), worsening income distribution, allocative inefficiencies, intractable inflation, combined with unemployment and/or underemployment, and thriving underground economies. These effects were especially pronounced in Africa where incomes fell throughout the 1970s (but partly also a result of the downward spiral of international commodity prices). It is generally believed that incomes per head at the end of the 1980s in Africa might be lower in real terms than in 1960.

In terms of an ideology of development, the success of the "newcomers" signalled the emergence of apparently viable alternatives to the theories and practices associated with postwar state intervention. As Harris suggests, "by the seventies, there was no such confidence in the capacity of governments to control their domestic affairs; the market, the invisible hand of a benevolent deity, was everywhere to be seen as the only means of allocating resources efficiently; economic growth and high employment were seen as the gift of the world market, not of domestic management."[7] The subsequent rise in influence of neoclassical theory in policy-making and public administration received impetus from the desperate search of many governments for a formula of adjustment to economic change and the postrecession climate of the late 1970s and early 1980s. This coincided with—but was not limited to—a shift in emphasis and strategy within the IMF and the World Bank toward a market-oriented philosophy and the coming to power in the United Kingdom and United States of the Thatcher and Reagan administrations with this ideological thrust. The result has been a retreat from Keynesianism (or supposedly Keynesian ideas) on the theoretical plane and, in the content of policy and process of management, a greater degree of latitude for the assertion of market forces.

But it has to be understood that neoclassical revisionism did not imply a decline in the role of the state in development or in economic management. On the contrary, the "visible hand" of government was very much in evidence orchestrating the policies that had brought about the success of the "newcomers" and directing adjustment policies in developing and developed, market and centrally planned economies alike. Some analysts of European and North American adjustment trends even identified corporatist tendencies in the neo-activism of the state amid premature paranoia over the alleged de-industrialization of these countries.[8]

The *mea culpa* tenor of African statements at the UN Special Session and their espousal of neoclassical policy, management, and institutional reforms, has to be seen as measures directed at adjusting to new international economic realities. It is a parallel of protectionist and corporatist adjustment trends in the industrial market economies of Western Europe and North America and of *glasnost* and other liberalizing tendencies in centrally planned economies.[9] At the heart of the emerging orthodoxy is the belief that there are strict limits on what governments *can* do effectively; and governments that ignore such limits, and instead restrict the allocative role of markets, are often rewarded with inefficiencies and intractable difficulties.

In Africa, the accumulating evidence suggests that organizational, management, and policy reforms revolve around a redefinition of the role of the state; institutional reforms within government to create an enhanced capacity for problem solving, policy development, and analysis; and, as a cornerstone of the former, a more enlightened approach to the various components of public personnel management; the restructuring of the public enterprise sector; more realistic planning and responsiveness to changing environments; a related emphasis on policy implementation; increasing attention to the needs of rural populations; encouragement of private business activity, foreign investment, and technology; the removal of price distortions; the realignment of exchange rates; and the provision of incentives to stimulate the productive sector (see Table 5–1). The next two parts of this chapter examine more closely the organizational and managerial aspects of reforms at the level of African central agencies.

ORGANIZATION REFORM IN CENTRAL AGENCIES

Central agencies are broadly defined to include secretariats of chief executives and individual ministers; the cabinet; central bank; budget, monetary, statistical, policy and planning agencies; aid and technical assistance coordination bureaus; and other units which provide political executives with staff services. Matters which require action by political leaders are processed by these agencies to facilitate decision-making and to coordinate action. While central agencies operate at the highest level of government, subcentral agencies, which include line or sectoral ministries, parastatal agencies, and the executive departments of regional and local authorities, carry out the work of government at other levels: they generate information for decision- and policy-making at these and higher levels; they implement policies and administer programs; and depending on the nature of the policy—they make possible some degree of decentralization which gives them discretionary (albeit limited) powers. Implementation is the distinguishing characteristic of subcentral agencies as control and direction are of central agencies.

Most African countries have various kinds of central agencies that constitute the nerve center of state economic management. Their origins can be traced back to the colonial period. This is particularly true of agencies such as secretariats of executive councils, treasuries, and establishment offices that performed staff services for colonial governors and other top administrators. Their roles were generally passive and routinized or hardly inspired by the kind of dynamism that is associated with the management of development in today's world. Indeed, the colonial state has been described as the administrative state *par excellence:* "colonies were administered . . . resources were managed with the goals of the metropolitan power in mind."[10] In the postcolonial state, the degree to which central agencies have responded to developmental challenges has not inspired much confidence in the past. Key central agencies in some countries have simply lacked analytical capacity (in terms of well-motivated, competent personnel capable of, and comfortable in, taking on nonroutinized roles) and/or have slavishly worked within the parameters of multiyear development plans in spite of rapidly changing environments. Where this has not been the problem, the tendency of rulers to make arbitrary decisions, irrespective of the consequences for development objectives, has undermined the institutionalization of analytical capacity in central agencies. The weaknesses of African central agencies is something of a paradox when the extreme centralization of resources—especially personnel—is taken into account. These weaknesses prompted the World Bank to urge in its third report on sub-Saharan Africa:

> Policy reform is a continuous process. The need for flexibility . . . is the single most important lesson of experience. . . . prescriptions and policy signals need to be assessed, analysed and internalised in the country's decision-making. . . . Governments need such policy-planning institutions and the strengthening of their management information systems to provide up-to-date policy analysis.[11]

An Economic Commission for Africa study echoes this view in noting that "at the national level . . . planning machinery still concentrates on merely collecting projects for submission to potential funding sources."[12] The institutionalization of analytical capacity in central agencies is crucial for economic progress. The best known study of this is perhaps Chalmers Johnson's work on the role of the Japanese Ministry of International Trade and Industry in providing the institutional context for policy analysis and planning to enhance that country's industrial and technological development.[13] In the case of South Korea, Wade and Kim have thrown some light on the operation of central agencies. The guiding principle of the regime of President Park, which emerged after the 1961 military *coup d'état* and put into effect the policies that transformed the Korean economy, was simply that "the effective performance of government as coordinator of basic decisions is indispensable to development."[14] Accordingly, a number of institutional mechanisms for policy development and coordination on matters ranging from the exchange rate and export promotion to manpower and health services were put in place. The key agencies in the central network included the Office of the President (which, in addition to having experts and personal staff responsible for advising the president on all aspects of government policy has an inspectorate division responsible for reporting back to the president on the implementation of policy at any level of the bureaucracy); the cabinet, its subcommittees and associated secretariats; the economic planning board; the vice-ministers' conference (a committee of top officials); the trade promotion corporation; and a number of think tanks including the Economic Science Council and the Korean Development Institute (which has a professional staff of over 230 personnel including a significant number of foreign-educated Ph.D.'s).[15]

As part of African state economic management reform initiatives, there is evidence of an effort to institutionalize analytical capacity at the central level. A growing trend is the establishment of interministerial committees or special units of key ministries, officials, and other experts to develop and recommend measures on structural adjustment, debt management, and coordination—a reflection of priorities in the less auspicious context of economic crisis and the struggle for survival. These bodies undertake a lot of the preparatory work for official negotiations with external creditors such as the London and Paris Clubs, the World Bank and IMF, and roundtable or consultative group meetings with donors. The proliferation of these committees and units and the *ad hoc* character which they sometimes take also reflects the more limited pool of talent that can be drawn upon at this level of government.

Recent reforms in Zambia provide a good example of efforts to establish the capacity for analysis and coordination at the central level. A Special Economic Unit, chaired by the Minister of Finance and composed of senior officials of the National Planning Commission, the line ministries, the central bank, major public enterprises, the cabinet office and State House (the Office of the President), was created in 1983 to prepare, coordinate, and monitor the government's attempts to stabilize and restructure the economy following persistent difficulties arising out of the collapse of international copper prices, the country's leading export. According to a 1984 assessment, in the year since the unit was created it proved invaluable in instituting important policy reforms and clearly satisfied the long-felt need for a high-level body capable of undertaking policy analysis and generating information for quick decision-making.[16]

A few African countries have consistently displayed an analytical capacity within central agencies. Botswana, frequently cited as an example of effective public sector management in Africa south of the Sahara, is a case in point. The leading agency in policy analysis and coordination is the Ministry of Finance and Development Planning (headed by the vice president since independence to emphasize its importance). As the government's nerve center of policy development, the ministry acts as a channel of information to the Economic Committee of the cabinet which is the key decision-making body on development issues.[17]

North of the Sahara, the *Conseil supérieur de la promotion nationale et du plan* in Morocco brings together senior staff and officials of key agencies and ministries not only to facilitate the national planning process, but in cooperation with the royal cabinet (the King's advisers and executive office), the Office of the Prime Minister and the Secretariat of the Council of Ministers, to process information for decision-making by the King and his ministers.[18]

These examples are part of a trend to reform and improve the capacity to plan, analyze, develop, coordinate, and monitor policy in central agencies. The limited supply of experts on a wide range of subjects continues to be a formidable constraint. And it must be acknowledged that in the cut and thrust of central agency operations, conflicts with line ministries and, indeed, even between central agencies arise out of differences in perspectives and interests of officials. For example, treasuries and central banks tend to be pro-IMF conditionalities, planning agencies against. These tensions are not necessarily disruptive provided the information reaching political executives is relevant and intelligible.

REFORM OF MANAGEMENT SYSTEMS AND PRACTICES

Very little research has been done on the actual managerial processes within African central agencies that facilitate the problem-solving approach to state economic management. Reference has already been made to selective organization reforms that have been carried out in Zambia, as well as the consistency of governments in Botswana and Morocco in nurturing this kind of capacity. But the paucity of knowledge of the managerial process is in sharp contrast to what is known about how central agencies operate in industrialized countries.[19] As the discussion above on central agency organization would suggest, flexible and organic structures as distinct from formal and mechanical ones are more supportive. The Special Economic Unit in Zambia, which brings together key officials of central agencies and line ministries, fits the bill of organic organization.

The paucity of knowledge on actual processes in developing countries' central agencies aside, it has to be recognized that there is no magic formula that could be applied to guarantee effective state economic management. This is not to suggest that certain minimum conditions that should be met cannot be identified: for example, smoothly functioning information systems on economic trends, the analytical capacity to make the information that is generated intelligible, and the commitment of political executives to make appropriate policy decisions. It is rather to emphasize that a number of subjective variables such as the leadership styles of political executives or the exigencies of national power politics intrude.

Lamb has put what we know about state economic management in a well-defined perspective:

> We do not yet have adequate knowledge or fully appropriate operational techniques to improve the management of economic policies—that is, to build up government structures and processes to support effective economic policymaking and implementation, and in particular to make sure that sustained rather than episodic policy improvements occur. Developing the institutional capacity for timely and flexible policy response is clearly central to successful policy reform and structural adjustment, but the sophistication of policy analysis has not yet been matched with corresponding knowledge about how to assist governments to strengthen and institutionalise their own processes of policy decision-making and implementation.[20]

It is clear that nonroutinized managerial processes and flexible organizational structures have not been extensively used in African public services in the recent past. The dominant managerial approach has been centered around planning—a managerial process noted for its high degree of formalism.[21] There is, indeed, no developing country in which serious attempts are not being made through multiyear plans to establish priorities and give the economy a direction. Many African governments are now in their fifth or sixth planning cycles since attaining independence; for example, Kenya's current (1984–88) plan is its fifth. Planning in African state economic management has colonial origins and reflected the triumph of Keynesianism over *laissez-faire* in the years following World War II.[22] The use and spread of planning after independence was inspired by conventional thinking in development theory and practice during the 1960s on the capital requirements for economic "takeoff."

The inherent limitations of planning as the dominant process underlying state economic management has been revealed by the turbulent environment of the 1970s and 1980s. Available analytical techniques used in forecasting are just not able to cope with the complexity of economic change and the necessity of concurrent adjustment to the change. Even as early as the beginning of the 1970s, analysts had identified a "crisis in planning"[23] around the elements of excessive rigidity; too much emphasis on the medium-term and the relative neglect of the short-term; more concentration on the formulation of the plan document than on its implementation; and differences in perspective and/or inadequate communication between politicians, planners, and officials in implementing or line departments.[24] Indeed, one study that appeared in the mid-1970s described planning as a "mode of problem avoidance; not problem-solving."[25]

To cope with these difficulties, it has long been advocated that planning should be integrated with budgeting.[26] The underlying rationale stems from the recognition that budgetary processes in government encompass one of two main instruments of managing and controlling the entire public sector (the other is public personnel management). To the extent that a government cannot effect public policy without spending money, the integration of planning and budgeting injects more realism into the former. Where the budgeting system functions properly, it provides a critical web of communications and becomes itself the hub linking all units and levels of government. Moreover, modern budgeting has become not only a process of resource management but also a mechanism for activating the policy levers and instruments of state economic management. It is a truism that budgeting literally gives coherence to the activities of government.[27]

As a managerial function in government, budgetary practices in most African countries have been stagnant. They have lagged behind reforms in other regions where efforts have been made since the 1950s[28] to introduce and refine variants of performance budgeting, control public spending, and grapple with the complexities of state economic management. A United Nations survey of financial management trends in developing countries during the 1960s and 1970s concluded that "while programme and performance budgeting has had widespread acceptance in Asian and Latin American countries where elements . . . have been in use . . . in Africa . . . many countries have expressed interest in the system, very few have actually made attempts to introduce it."[29] Far from being a substantive process of resource management and policy adjustment, budgeting in most African governments has been characterized by formalism and red tape. Consequently, planning remained unrealistic and inflexible at higher and strategic levels of African public services. Moreover, budgetary practices have remained stagnant at these and other levels. The inability of planning and budgeting processes to cope with changing demands and new challenges are familiar and well-known. The budgeting process also suffers from other defects, e.g., inadequate consideration of the recurrent cost implications of past and new investments; inadequate allocations for the operation and maintenance of existing capital stock; the low priority given to departments and agencies with important development functions; hidden (or unintended) subsidies to public enterprises; poor strategies of debt management; and weaknesses in accounting systems and in the application of analytical techniques of performance management.[30]

As part of the current reform agenda, several African governments have taken steps to overcome some of these difficulties. The case of Zambia, where a Special Economic Unit was created in 1983 to enhance analytical capacity and to become the "clearinghouse" of information for decision-making and the allocation of resources at the highest level of government, has already been cited. A Planning and Budgeting Committee, which is responsible for integrating future investment programs in the annual budgeting exercise, complements the work of the unit. The Ministry of Finance, whose officials are key participants on the committee and the unit, also introduces important changes in budgeting including realistic forecasts of resources (against a sharp decline of revenues from copper); a sharper focus on the consistency between recurrent and capital expenditures; increased allocations to priority sectors; and more effective accounting and performance evaluation procedures.[31] In Kenya, a budget rationalization program was adopted in 1985. Its objective is to introduce procedures for analyzing the composition of government expenditure more effectively and to redress imbalances such as inadequate allocations to projects and programs of high priority. The program also covered the operation and maintenance of existing government capital stock. The concept of a Forward Budget was also introduced as a rolling three-year plan for central government expenditure to link the priorities in the development plan with the annual budget.[32] In Algeria, attempts have been made to identify hidden subsidies from the treasury to public enterprises. The banking sector, which has grown appreciably in recent years, has been given a larger role in the financing of public enterprise investment on commercial terms.[33] With external debts of over U.S. $20 billion, important changes in structure and process have also been made in Nigeria to tighten policy coordination on debt management and service schedules. Investment and budgetary decisions are also streamlined through an interministerial committee that brings together key central agency officials including the central bank and the ministries of finance and planning.[34]

In essence, therefore, the salient features of the ongoing organizational and management reforms are flexibility, cost-consciousness, and performance monitoring. In addition, there is an increasing tendency on the part of policymakers to encourage extensive consultation within government, and with the private sector as well as the academic community. It is also recognized that an effective information system—especially as regards the key performance indicators—is crucial to sound economic management.

At this point it should be emphasized that the greater capacity for coordination, problem-solving, and policy analysis that is being built into the organizational and management reforms does not imply that planning has become redundant in Africa. Governments must perforce rely on medium- and long-term forecasting to clarify the priorities of public expenditure and investment and to give guidance to the private sector. Variables such as GDP, savings, investment, revenue and expenditure, export, import, foreign capital inflows, and domestic resource mobilization, need to be projected to provide an informed basis for decision-making. And as regards the main sectors, forecasts in such areas as power, energy, and transport are vital. Hence, the new approaches in organization and process have a continuing need for planning, the programming of investment and forecasting; they do not, however, leave the policy instruments and options of governments "frozen" in an environment that is characterized by change.

CONCLUSION

The priority being accorded by an increasing number of governments to development management reform is evidence of the new mood of realism prevailing in Africa. It is increasingly accepted that the continent is now part of a new and rapidly changing world, one which values flexibility in policy, and dynamism in management. It has become clear that policy measures of adjustment to global trends require sharp analytical skills in central agencies. These agencies in turn require appropriate organization and process. This is, of course, a recognition of one of the basic requirements of state economic management in a complex and changing environment; but just as important, it is a recognition of the structural constraints on economic development in the region and that for most countries, growth in the short- and medium-terms will owe as much to diversification as to innovative management. This latter point requires elaboration.

It is now clear that the disappointing economic performance in sub-Saharan Africa is of a far more serious nature than was originally assumed. There are, in fact, severe limitations to the gains that can be made from external trade, which incidentally constitutes the single most important stimulus to Africa's internal socioeconomic progress. Two recent studies project only a marginal increase over the next ten years in world demand for commodities in which the region has a comparative production advantage—coffee, cocoa, tea, cotton, rubber, and tobacco.[35] Palm oil production has declined dramatically in response to the loss of a buoyant export market, but inappropriate policies have also contributed to the loss of market share for other commodities. Similarly, precious metals and stones aside, projections for nonfuel minerals are not hopeful.

These difficulties are compounded by a tendency for world prices of commodities and nonfuel minerals to fall relative to world prices of manufactured goods. Between 1980 and 1982, for instance, even as the world was coming out of a recession, prices of nonfuel primary commodities declined by 27 percent in 1984 U.S. dollar terms. The loss of income as a result was 1.2 percent of GDP for the African region as a whole.[36] These indicators, not to mention other limiting prospects such as the increasing size of African populations (projected to grow by an annual rate of 3 percent until the end of the century), suggest that African governments are severely strapped. Private commercial lending to Africa has virtually ceased and debt servicing has become an added burden. According to one estimate, net resource flows to Africa declined sharply from U.S. $10 billion in 1980 to U.S. $4.9 billion in 1985 prices. A partial recovery in 1987 to U.S. $7.3 billion was expected in net flows largely as a result of official aid to finance adjustment programs. About 40 percent of current debt service payments—estimated at U.S. $11 billion in 1986–87—consists of payments to the IMF and the World Bank and of interest due to other creditors on debts which are not eligible for rescheduling.[37] In the meantime, the African countries face other serious problems, among them, sharp fluctuations in the exchange rate of major international currencies, instability of oil prices (although African oil importers have had some relief from higher prices), tariff and nontariff barriers including protectionism in agricultural commodities in North America and through the Common Agricultural Policy in Europe which hurt some existing and potential African exports. All these constraints underscore the view that future growth in Africa will have to come out of innovative state economic management as much as out of diversification. If the development history of the NICs has any lessons for holders of public offices in Africa, it is that the ingenuity of central agencies in fashioning and implementing appropriate policy instruments of intervention can make a difference to the level of prosperity that is attained. As the decade of the 1980s draws to a close, this is the challenge to African politicians and public administrators. African pronouncements and declarations on reform have been necessary. Effective leadership from central agencies is now required.

NOTES

1. See also OAU, *Lagos Plan of Action for the Economic Development of Africa 1980–2000*, 2d ed. (Geneva: International Institute for Labour Studies, for the OAU, 1982).

2. See also OAU, *Africa's Priority Programme for Economic Recovery 1986–1990* (Rome: Food and Agricultural Organisation, for the OAU, 1985).

3. See also OAU/ECA, *Africa's Submission to the Special Session of the United Nations General Assembly on Africa's Economic and Social Crisis* (OAU/ECM/2XV/Rev. 2, E/ECA/ECM. 1/Rev. 2, 1986).

4. See also *The Oxford English Dictionary*, vol. 8 (Oxford: Clarendon Press, 1983).

5. See also, e.g., Frances Stewart, "Brandt II—The Mirage of Collective Action in a Self-Serving World," *Third World Quarterly* 5 (1983): 640–49.

6. The best analysis of these changes is probably Nigel Harris, *The End of the Third World: Newly Industrialising Countries and the Decline of an Ideology* (Harmondsworth, U.K.: Penguin, 1986). But see also Chad Leechor et al., *Structural Changes in World Industry: A Quantitative Analysis of Recent Developments* (Washington, D.C.: World Bank Technical Paper, Industry and Finance Series, 1983).

7. Harris, *The End of the Third World*, 155.

8. See also, e.g., G. Lehmbruch and P. C. Schmitter, eds., *Patterns of Corporatist Policy-Making* (Los Angeles: University of California Press, 1982); John Goldthorpe, ed., *Order and Conflict in Contemporary Capitalism: Studies in the Political Economy of Western European Nations* (Oxford: Clarendon Press, 1984); P. J. Katzenstein, *Small States in World Markets: Industrial Policy in Europe* (Ithaca, N.Y.: Cornell University Press, 1985); and John Walley, ed., *Domestic Policies and the International Economic Environment* (Toronto: University of Toronto Press, 1985).

9. See also, e.g., Peter Knight, *Economic Reform in Socialist Countries: The Experiences of China, Hungary, Romania and Yugoslavia* (Washington, D.C.: World Bank Staff Working Paper no. 579, Management and Development Series, 1983).

10. See also Coralie Bryant and Louise G. White, *Managing Development in the Third World* (Boulder, Colo.: Westview, 1982), 25.

11. See also The World Bank, *Toward Sustained Development in Sub-Saharan Africa: A Joint Programme for Action* (Washington, D.C.: The World Bank, 1984), 39.

12. See also Economic Commission for Africa, *ECA and Africa's Development 1983–2008: A Preliminary Perspective Study* (Addis Ababa: ECA, 1983), 14.

13. See also Chalmers Johnson, *MITI and the Japanese Miracle: The Growth of Industrial Policy 1925–1975* (Stanford: Stanford University Press, 1982).

14. See also L. L. Wade and B. S. Kim, *Economic Development in South Korea: The Political Economy of Success* (New York: Praeger, 1977), 166.

15. *Ibid.*, 219–27.

16. See also The World Bank, *Zambia: Country Economic Memorandum: Issues and Options for Economic Diversification* (Washington, D.C.: The World Bank, 1984), 23–24; see also Government of Zambia, *Zambia's Implementation of APPER and UNPAAERD* (A document submitted to the International Conference on Africa: The Challenge of Economic Recovery and Accelerated Development, Abuja, Nigeria, 15–19 June 1987).

17. See also Nimrod Raphaeli et al., *Public Sector Management in Botswana: Lessons in Pragmatism* (Washington, D.C.: World Bank Staff Working Paper no. 709), 18–20.

18. See also The World Bank, *Morocco: Economic and Social Development Report* (Washington, D.C.: The World Bank, 1981), 6.

19. See also Colin Campbell, *Governments Under Stress: Political Executives and Key Bureaucrats in Washington, London, and Ottawa* (Toronto: University of Toronto Press, 1983). See also B. L. R. Smith, ed., *The Higher Civil Service in Europe and Canada: Lessons for the United States* (Washington, D.C.: The Brookings Institution, 1984); and Jean Blondel, *The Organization of Governments: A Comparative Analysis of Governmental Structures* (Beverly Hills, Calif.: Sage, 1982, especially ch. 5).

20. See also Geoffrey Lamb, *Managing Economic Policy Change: Institutional Dimensions* (Washington, D.C.: World Bank Discussion Paper no. 14, 1987), vii.

21. See also Aaron Wildavsky, "If Planning is Everything, Maybe It Is Nothing," *Policy Sciences* 4 (1973): 127–53.

22. See also B. Niculescu, *Colonial Planning: A Comparative Study* (London: Allen & Unwin, 1958); and Albert Waterston, *Development Planning: Lessons of Experience* (Baltimore: Johns Hopkins University Press, 1965).

23. See also Michael Faber and Dudley Seers, eds., *The Crisis in Planning*, 2 vols. (London: Chatto & Windus, 1972).

24. For a good review of these problems, cf. Diana Conyers and Peter Hill, *An Introduction to Development Planning in the Third World* (Chichester, U.K.: Wiley, 1984). See also Ramgopal Agarwala, *Planning in Developing Countries: Lessons of Experience* (Washington, D.C.: World Bank Staff Working Paper no. 576, 1983).

25. See also Naomi Caiden and Aaron Wildavsky, *Planning and Budgeting in Poor Countries* (New York: Wiley, 1974), ix.

26. See especially Waterston, *Development Planning*, ch. 7.

27. On the role of budgeting in government, cf. Aaron Wildavsky, *Budgeting: A Comparative Theory of Budgetary Practice* (Boston: Little, Brown, 1975); and A. Premchand, *Government Budgeting and Expenditure Controls: Theory and Practice* (Washington, D.C.: IMF, 1983).

28. See also United States Congress, *Report to the Congress on Budgeting and Accounting* (Hoover Commission Report) (Washington, D.C.: U.S. Congress, 1949). See also B. Guy Peters, *The Politics of Bureaucracy*, 2d ed. (New York: Longman, 1984), 211–36.

29. See also The United Nations, *Changes and Trends in Public Administration and Finance for Development: Second Survey* (New York: UN Department of Technical Cooperation for Development, 1982), 63.

30. Ibid., 63–65.

31. See also The World Bank, *Zambia: Country Economic Memorandum*, 23–24.

32. See also The World Bank, *Kenya: Policies and Prospects for Restoring Sustained Growth of Per Capita Income* (Washington, D.C.: The World Bank, 1986), viii.

33. See also The World Bank, *Algeria: The Five-Year Development Plan and the Medium-term Prospects for 1980–90, Volume I: General Report* (Washington, D.C.: The World Bank, 1982), 21–22.

34. See also *West Africa*, 24 November 1986, 2442–44. See also Government of Nigeria, *The Implementation of the United Nations Programme of Action for African Economic Recovery and Development (UN-PAAERD) 1986–1990 by African Governments and Institutions: A Case Study of Nigeria*. (A document submitted to the International Conference on Africa: The Challenge of Economic Recovery and Accelerated Development, Abuja, Nigeria, 15–19 June 1987.)

35. See also Shamser Singh, *Sub-Saharan Agriculture: Synthesis and Trade Prospects* (Washington, D.C.: World Bank Staff Working Paper no. 608); and The World Bank, *Commodity Trade and Price Trends* (Baltimore: Johns Hopkins University Press, 1985).

36. See also The World Bank, *Toward Sustained Development*, 11–12.

37. See also Overseas Development Council (of the U.S.), "Should the IMF Withdraw from Africa?" *Policy Focus*, no. 1 (1987): 6.

PART III

Impact of Restructuring Measures on the Public Service

CHAPTER SIX

The Impact of Structural Adjustment Programs on the Performance of Africa's Public Services

William N. Wamalwa

ABSTRACT

The deepening socioeconomic crisis in Africa has brought to the fore the issue of how to deal with the persistent recession and place the continent firmly on the course of self-sustained growth and development. Whereas some observers argue that the answer lies in "structural adjustment" (which in effect, means a drastic reduction in the scope of government and an enhanced role for private enterprise), others are of the view that a more effective strategy consists in promoting the institutional transformation capacity of both the public and the private sectors as a step toward increasing their productivity.

Structural adjustment and structural transformation—does it really make much difference which label we adopt so long as Africa overcomes the multiple obstacles to economic growth? To its advocates, structural adjustment is more than a label. It is an article of faith. According to the new evangelists of an old (classical) school of economics, the public sector is incapable of reforming itself or responding positively to external stimuli for reform. They (the supply-side economists) are convinced that the only way to promote the cause of development is to relieve the public sector of its development burden. Their favorite example of an overburdened public sector is Africa's. As their analysis goes, Africa's public sector has, over the past quarter of a century, grown by leaps and bounds—but unfortunately, without due consideration for rational economic principles. Having been shielded for too long from the realities of the marketplace, the argument continues, it is too late in the day to expect the public sector to understand, let alone live by, the law of supply and demand. Yet understand this law Africa must—if it is to survive in today's turbulent world. From the continent's standpoint, it is a world characterized by worsening terms of trade, mounting import bills, growing external debt burdens, rising interest rates, and crippling debt-servicing obligations. It is, in a nutshell, a less friendly world than it used to be.

But is structural adjustment the only prescription for survival in the increasingly hostile international economic environment? Proponents of the concept of "structural transformation" firmly believe that the "costs" of structural adjustment far outweigh its payoff. While it might have given the public service a "lean" look, and by so doing, made it more nimble on its feet and more adaptable to changing circumstances, structural adjustment might also have contributed in no small measure to the demoralization of public services. In other words, structural adjustment, while placing its patient (the public sector) on a calorie-controlled diet, might have overlooked the side effects, notably, administrative restlessness, loss of memory, and anemia, as it were. In any case, Africa cannot afford a drained and wobbly public sector, especially, since the private sector in Africa is itself far from being an epitome of managerial vitality and efficiency. The question is also frequently raised as to the ownership of enterprises in Africa's private sector. If equity participation is restricted to the multinational corporations, and to non-Africans, to what extent can the private sector be relied upon by African governments to contribute meaningfully to the recovery and development effort?

In discussing the impact of structural adjustment programs on the effectiveness of Africa's public services, this chapter starts by examining the main components of structural adjustment policies, and the type of problems that the policies were meant to solve. The second section of the chapter looks at the positive side of structural adjustment, while the third focuses on its adverse consequences on public administration and management. The fourth section discusses the structural transformation alternative and its possible impact on the public service.

STRUCTURAL ADJUSTMENT AND AFRICA'S DEVELOPMENT

Africa's development crisis did not emerge overnight. As was already pointed out, AAPAM perceived the danger and flashed the warning signals early enough. The ECA too, in a series of studies, sounded its own alarm. The declining growth rates over a twenty-year period should be enough indication that something was fundamentally wrong with the economies of African states. Table 6–1 shows that when compared with other Third World regions, Africa recorded the lowest rates of growth between 1960 and 1983. More disturbing is the generally downward trend in the rate of growth.

Almost every area of economic activity recorded negative rates of growth over the past two and a half decades. For example, in contrast to an annual rate of growth of 3 percent attained between 1971 and 1980 by the developing countries, generally in the area of agriculture, Africa reported a mere average of 1.6 percent per annum within the same period. And even though Africa's population was growing at an average annual rate of 2.8 percent in the 1970s, the rate of growth in food production was

TABLE 6-1
GDP Growth Rates in Asia, the Middle East, and NorthAfrica, 1960–83

Region Subregion	GDP Growth Rates (average annual percent change)					
	1960–73	1973–79	1980	1981	1982	1983
Asia	5.9	5.2	6.3	5.2	5.6	5.1
Middle East	5.2	3.0	4.2	−2.4	5.5	2.0
North Africa	3.5	2.1	1.3	1.2	0.2	−0.1

Source: *World Development Report*, (Washington, D.C.: OUP/World Bank, 1984), 11.

1.5 percent. It is therefore not surprising that between 1970 and 1980, food imports increased at an average annual rate of 8.4 percent.[1]

The problems facing Africa would still not have called for "structural adjustment," with its inherent element of urgency, but for the rapid depletion of financial resources. It would be recalled that the First and the Second Development Decades (1960s and 1970s) witnessed the launching of ambitious development plans and the corresponding growth in the size of the public bureaucracy. The expansion in public services was justified on the grounds of political and economic necessity. However, such expansion would not have been possible but for the liberal inflow of development funds. Official development assistance together with publicly and privately guaranteed loans provided the wherewithal for capital (and in some cases, recurrent) projects. At the same time, the export products provided a dependable source of revenue. However, as if diverse economic circumstances had joined forces to play a trick on Africa, all calculations upon which previous development policy and management were based suddenly turned out to be wrong. The international economic recession of the early 1980s tightened the credit situation and led to a critical appraisal by the creditor nations of their lending policies. Simultaneously, interest rates, which in the early 1970s scarcely went beyond 4.2 percent, climbed to 10.1 percent in the 1980s. Moreover, export revenue tumbled, largely as a result of the deteriorating terms of trade and the decline in the volume of exports (itself an outcome of the protectionist policies in some of the developed societies). The earlier assumption that African export products were doing well on the world market and would continue to fetch high prices needed to be revisited. But the countries of Africa faced a dilemma. Their governments were already committed to a policy of socioeconomic modernization, and this required massive government intervention in various aspects of life. Even if the leaders wished to retract the promise of government induced prosperity, it would not make much of a difference. The rate of economic growth might be declining, but not the tempo of social change and mobilization. The dramatic increase in population has particularly stepped up the pressure on governmental agencies. Additional resources are required to meet the increasing demands for food, school enrollment at all levels, improved health services, housing, infrastructural facilities, and jobs for the urban unemployed. Resources might not be adequate even for normal circumstances, but that does not insure national treasuries against demands for emergency and/ or disaster relief expenditures.

The new set of circumstances dictates a novel approach to public policy and administration. In specific terms, the hard economic realities call for a reordering of expenditure priorities, and the propagation of cost-saving (or penny-pinching) culture among the ranks of career officials. After all, what each African country was up against was a crisis of the worst kind. It was a serious malady which required careful diagnosis before the necessary surgical operation was carried out. The tragedy lies in the failure to recognize the symptoms early enough as the onset of a crisis. By and large, the negative economic indicators (food crisis, worsening terms of trade, declining resource inflows, and balance of payments difficulties) were perceived as "problems" which were amendable by short-term policy measures.

One immediate effect of these measures was a further expansion in the scope of the public bureaucracy. Thus, to cope with commodity shortages, a number of African countries introduced or strengthened the system of price control and set up agencies staffed by cadres of price control inspectors. Where the price control measure proved inadequate, some governments resorted to price subsidies. The services and commodities covered by subsidies include food items, fuel and energy products, and services rendered by public utilities. If price subsidies did not work, especially if the commodities in demand had to be produced by hard currency, governments were apt to enforce "belt-tightening" measures such as import licensing, prohibitive tariffs, and outright banishment of imports. It goes without saying that some of the actions distorted the realities in the marketplace quite apart from serving as a disincentive to productive activity. The clearest illustration of the ineffectiveness of the short-term measures could be seen in the agricultural sector. Up to the early 1960s, this sector occupied a strategic place in the economy of most African countries. It was the largest employer of labor, and one of the most dependable sources of export revenue. Soon after independence, many countries shifted attention to mining, manufacturing, and industry, and in the process, neglected agriculture. Farmers producing crops for export were frequently paid less than the market price of their products, the balance going to subsidize the expensive tastes of urban dwellers. Since they are utterly dependent on regular rainfall, any sudden change in climatic conditions exposed the farmers to grave dangers with little possibility of assistance from the government. Added to the inadequate investment in agriculture and the poor incentives to farmers are the inefficient price mechanisms; inadequate application of the results of research; defective and inadequate storage, marketing, and distribution systems; and poor rural infrastructural facilities.

Unfortunately, the neglect of agriculture was not compensated for by achievements in the newly favored sectors. If anything, export revenue declined substantially, thanks to the worsening terms of trade. In 1986 alone the value of Africa's exports fell by 28.7 percent.

To plug the resultant trade deficits, many African countries resorted to massive borrowing from external sources. The total external debt in 1985 was estimated at $175 billion, and the estimate for 1986 is $200 billion. The difficulty of repaying the burgeoning debt and meeting the heavy debt-servicing obligations led many African countries to negotiate the rescheduling of their debts, while at the same time pleading for new lines of credit. African countries have had more than thirty-two reschedulings in a period of less than three years. In addition at least twenty of them have reported payment arrears as at the end of 1984.[2]

Main Features of Structural Adjustment Programs

The ostensible aim of the structural adjustment programs formulated in collaboration with the IMF is to release productive forces from the strong grip of the public bureaucracy. The first target, therefore, had to be the sprawling bureaucratic realm. Since public officials had failed to allocate resources optimally and were likely to frustrate the efforts of the private sector in this direction, chunks of the empire had to be annexed and transferred to private hands. Structural adjustment meant not only reducing the size of government, but also narrowing down the range of decisions hitherto taken by executive decree or administrative fiat. Table 6–2 itemizes the structural adjustment measures adopted by the various African countries at the end of March 1987.

As at the end of March 1987, not less than twenty-three African countries were implementing one or a combination of the structural adjustment programs mentioned in Table 6–2. The question is how effective they have been in restructuring the economies and stemming Africa's development crisis. The next section focuses on the positive impact of the reforms.

POSITIVE IMPACT OF STRUCTURAL ADJUSTMENT-REFORMS

Regardless of what one may feel about structural adjustment measures currently being adopted by a number of African countries, there is no doubt that the reforms have achieved what a few years ago would have been considered impossible. To start with, structural adjustment has

TABLE 6–2
Number of Countries Implementing
Structural Adjustment Programs by March 1987
(classified by type of reform)

Type of Program	Number of Countries Implementing Program
Decontrolling producer prices	10
Freezing of public service vacancies	20
Elimination of public agricultural marketing agencies or permission of private competition	13
Handing over the importation of agricultural inputs to the private sector	7
Privatization of public enterprises	14
Substantial increase in producer prices	21
Reduction/elimination of agricultural input subsidies	14
Reduction or elimination of food subsidies	8
Realignment of exchange rates	16
Adoption of floating market rates	7

Source: Based on a table in David Fasholé-Luke, "African Development Management Reform: Political and Socio-cultural Constraints vs. the Neo-classical Imperative." (Paper presented at the International Conference on the Challenge of Economic Recovery and Accelerated Development, Abuja, Nigeria, 15–19 June 1987).

taken the practitioners of public administration from their bureaucratic fortresses to the marketplace, particularly the international marketplace. The immediate effect is to promote cost-consciousness at all levels. Before a decision is made (especially, if the decision has a foreign exchange implication), government officials now ask themselves critical questions, including questions as to whether there are local alternatives to what is being proposed. Structural adjustment has also brought in its wake a number of "austerity" measures. Jobs are not likely to be created for political or bureaucratic empire building purposes. If anything, jobs without visible contributions to the economic recovery efforts stand the risk of being phased out in the current series of "reorganizations." There are now stringent regulations, supplemented with control measures, governing the allocation of resources, such as official transport, fuel and lubricants, lighting, stationery, and office appliances. In many cases, salary increases for officials have been frozen, promotions suspended, and fringe benefits withdrawn.

The deregulation in some countries of certain economic activities, particularly, the abolition of the systems of price controls and import licensing, eliminated bottlenecks in commercial transactions and effectively dealt with a source of official corruption.

Of particular significance is the new wave of interest in administrative and institutional reform. Before the introduction of structural adjustment programs, the multifarious appeals for administrative reform fell on deaf ears. The First and the Second Development Decades, for instance, witnessed some valiant efforts to revitalize the institutions for policy-making and implementation, but with minimal results. With the advent of structural adjustment programs, policymakers and members of the higher civil service began to pay greater attention to measures designed to enhance the efficiency of operations. This is structural adjustment from the bright side. The next section looks at the not-so-bright side.

THE ADVERSE CONSEQUENCES OF STRUCTURAL ADJUSTMENT

The advocates of structural adjustment had an advantage over their opponents—they saw a big theoretical vacuum and moved rapidly to fill it. As the first section indicates, the individual countries' responses to Africa's development crisis consisted of no more than short-term, hit-or-miss, and uncoordinated attacks on specific "problems." Except in a few cases, little attempt was made to take a long-term, strategic view of Africa's development as a step toward the formulation of a comprehensive recovery and development policy. Sensing this omission in public policy, the advocates of structural adjustment simply dipped into the armory of classical and neoclassical economics and mounted a sustained attack on the hastily packaged recovery programs. The various African countries could not be accused of not putting up any resistance. As a matter of fact, many of them initially stuck to ongoing policies and programs. However, faced with an already bad situation and gloomy economic forecasts, the countries had to succumb to pressures to "restructure" their economies along certain prescribed lines. The impression which then started to gain ground, i.e., that structural adjustment programs were externally imposed, hardly endeared the policymakers and their civil service advisers to the local populace. In any case, by taking the initiative for policy formulation away from government leaders and passing it to non-African technocrats, or so it seemed, structural adjustment programs ran the risk of ignoring the real and basic needs of self-reliance. And the "belt-tightening" that formed part of the reform measures sparked off civil disturbances and threatened the stability of a few states. At the very least, such an explosive situation is likely to make policymakers and career officials very nervous.

Apart from feeling the impact of structural adjustment indirectly (i.e., through political pressures) the public service comes in direct contact with the consequences of the reforms in many other ways. First, the sharp drop in revenue substantially diminished the effectiveness (or program delivery capability) of government agencies. The situation is particularly acute in the rural areas. With the drastic cuts in recurrent allocations, the extension services operations of departments of agriculture have been paralyzed by lack of transport. Hospitals complain of shortage of medical supplies (vaccines, drugs, and dressings), and educational institutions have to do without badly needed textbooks, stationery, and instructional materials. Moreover, roads are left in a state of disrepair because of lack of construction equipment and material (such as graders, asphalt, fuel, and lubricants). Consequently, the transportation and marketing of agricultural products have been greatly handicapped.

The parastatal sector has been badly hit by the economic crunch. With a long tradition of relying on overseas sources for the supply of equipment, raw materials, and technical know-how, public enterprises in many countries now operate at such a low level of their capacity that their very existence is in question.

The embargo on the expansion of the public service coupled with the mass retrenchment of personnel are a corollary of budget reductions. However, they have adversely affected the motivation, morale, and productivity of officials. The situation has not been helped by the ceilings imposed on salary increases and by the freezing of vacancies. The incentive to "put in a fair day's job" has been undermined as a result of the feeling that the employee is not getting a fair day's pay. In such circumstances, palms have to be greased to "expedite" action on urgent matters. This is certainly not good for the institutionalization of the noble ethics of public service.

The open hostility toward government agencies displayed by the proponents of structural adjustment has also fostered a "siege mentality" among the ranks of public officials. The feeling of insecurity among the officials tends to be reinforced by the manner in which their peers are summarily removed and by the aspersion that is generally cast on their capability as a group. Unless urgent steps are taken to restore their collective self-confidence, the society would be the ultimate loser. After all, there was a time not far in the past when the public service in Africa exhibited the much needed development attributes of innovativeness, entrepreneurship, and creativity. Perhaps these are the attributes that the public service requires to face up to the challenges before it and to steer the society through the stormy phase of recession to an era of prosperity.

Yet another negative impact of structural adjustment programs is the escalating costs of production and the consequent increase in the prices of foods and services. For the ordinary citizens, the pains of structural adjustment can be translated into anger and frustration, and in extreme cases, to negative political actions (such as riots and civil disturbances). For the public official who suddenly finds that a month's salary does not buy a week's groceries, the harsh conditions of structural adjustment may be turned into personal advantage. It is then he demands "tea money" or "Kolanuts" in return for supplying a simple form. Even a messenger might be tempted to ask for a "dash" as an incentive to expedite the movement of files from one desk to another. Directly and indirectly, therefore, structural adjustment threatens the ethical fabric of public administration.

If the "inconvenience" is temporary, it would be difficult to fault the reasoning of belt-tightening underlying structural adjustment. However, while the structural adjustment program is frequently advertised as a cluster of short-term measures, it merely prepares its victim for another round (and endless rounds) of shocks. As one observer says, once a patient gets onto a structural adjustment operation table, the chances of his getting back on his own feet are remote. In that case, do we need an alternative to structural adjustment? The next section examines the merits of structural transformation.

STRUCTURAL TRANSFORMATION AND THE PUBLIC SERVICE

The realization in Africa and in the international community that Africa's socioeconomic crisis had persisted long enough prompted a new concerted effort toward recovery and development. A clear indication of this effort is the *United Nations Programme of Action for African Economic Recovery and Development* (UNPAAERD) which was adopted by the 13th Special Session of the UN General Assembly in 1986.[3] UNPAAERD is itself based on a program of action drawn up by the 21st Assembly of Heads of State and Government of the OAU in July 1985.[4] Starting with the affirmation of the African leaders' total commitment to the primary responsibility for the development of our continent[5] the new program of action attributes Africa's persistent economic backwardness to "the lack of structural transformation and pervasive low level of productivity, aggravated by exogenous and endogenous factors."[6]

With a renewed emphasis on agriculture, the program of action outlines policy and managerial measures designed to promote recovery in the short-run and development in the long-run. These include:

1. The strengthening of incentive schemes

2. Review of investment policies

3. Improved management of the economy (through efficient allocation of resources, improvement of the performance of public enterprises)

4. Encouragement of domestic resource mobilization

5. Formulation of effective human resource development and utilization policies (with particular emphasis on the development of entrepreneurial capabilities in *both* the public and private sectors)

6. Encouragement of grass-roots participation in the development process.

The recovery program sees structural rigidity as a barrier to growth, but it is as much a problem in the private sector as it is in the public. The cause of development would therefore be served not when we dismantle the governmental apparatus and assign additional responsibilities to the private sector, but when we recognize the complementarity of both. As one observer points out: "The secret of human happiness might be unlocked, and the equilibrium of the earth maintained, if governments and private individuals do what they are best placed by nature to do."[7]

What is required, therefore, is a sustained effort in the direction of institutional flexibility and reform in both the public and private sectors. It was in realization of this that the ECA prepared a proposal for revitalization of administrative and managerial institutions in Africa. The main elements of this revitalization and reequipment program are:

1. The restructuring, restaffing and reorganization of policy-making units, and the establishment of "open" (homeostatic) policy planning systems

2. The reinvigoration of subsystems in both the public and private sectors (the civil service, public enterprises, "field" administrative and local government units, the "organized" and the "informal" private sector)

3. The development of entrepreneurial capacity in the public and private sectors

4. Improvement of economic and finance management (including measures designed to instil budget discipline, promote accountability, and eliminate fraud)

5. Human resource development, management, and utilization

6. The dissemination of information about the goals, strategies, and tactics of collective self-reliance.[8]

THE PUBLIC SERVICE AND AFRICA'S DEVELOPMENT: A REVIEW

There is no doubt that the public service in Africa has expanded at a feverish pace. In the process, it might have acquired responsibilities which by rational economic criteria, could be argued to belong elsewhere. But then, the challenge of building a nation in postindependence Africa goes beyond economics. It includes the leaders' conception of the obligations of the state toward its people—particularly, the poorest and weakest segments of the society. The advocates of the structural adjustment formula might have correctly diagnosed Africa's development problems, but their prescriptions need to be carefully weighed in terms of the long-term consequences. If there has been a shortfall in the performance of the public service, there is no reason to conclude that this would be a permanent feature or that conscious efforts could not be made to revitalize it. Productivity enhancement is indeed what Africa needs considering that, in the present circumstances, even the private sector is yet to operate at an internationally competitive level. As Adebayo Adedeji has rightly argued:

> The future of Africa will be decided by the prevailing style of management in the public and private sectors. Unless the two sectors are committed to the goals of economic recovery and development, the prospects up to the end of this century are very bleak.[9]

NOTES

1. OAU/ECA, *Africa's Submission to the Special Session of the United Nations General Assembly on Africa's Economic and Social Crisis* (OAU/ECM/2XV/Rev. 2, E/ECA/ECM. 1/1 Rev. 2, 1986).

2. *Ibid.*, para. 30.

3. *United Nations Programme of Action for African Economic Recovery and Development, 1986–1990* (A/RES/S-13/2, 13 June 1986).

4. OAU/ECA, *op. cit.*

5. *Ibid.*

6. *Ibid.*

7. M. J. Balogun, "The Role of Management Training Institutions in Developing the Capacity for Economic Recovery and Long-term Growth in West Africa." (Paper presented at the Workshop for Heads of Training Institutions in West Africa, ASCON, Badagry, 2–6 November 1987.)

8. UNECA, "Re-dynamizing Africa's Administrative/Managerial Systems and Institutions for Economic Recovery and Development," ECA/EDI Senior Policy Seminar on Development Management (Addis Ababa, 6–10 July 1987) (ECA/PAMM/PAM/87/1).

9. Adebayo Adedeji, "The Evolution of the Public Service in Africa," *ACP-EEC Courier Magazine*, Brussels (forthcoming). See also his "Administrative Adjustments and Responses to Changes in the Economic Environment," in *The Ecology of Public Administration and Management in Africa* (New Delhi: AAPAM, 1986).

CHAPTER SEVEN

The Impact of the Economic Crisis on the Effectiveness of Public Service Personnel

James Nti

AFRICA'S ECONOMIC CRISIS

For almost a decade, the economies of most African countries have not been performing well—growth rates have been slow, in some cases even negative; inflation has been rising; there have been large balance of payments deficits, food shortages, and even famine in some countries. Persistently there has been a fall in outputs and services in all the productive sectors (viz., agriculture, mining, and manufacturing sectors) as can be seen from Table 7–1.

It will be noted that agriculture (including food) and manufacturing have been showing a consistently declining trend and that the growth rates in the mining sector have been negative since 1980. On the other hand, the growth rate of population in Africa is as high as about 3 percent per annum.

The crisis has been the result of a combination of factors. The oil price increases in the seventies caught both developed and developing countries off guard, and as the Brandt Commission put it, "Industrial economies transmit their troubles to developing countries by a number of routes. Uncoordinated policies in the North to eliminate payments deficits due to oil price increases or to reduce inflation have increased the adjustment burden of oil-importing developing countries."[1] The effect of this was the collapse of commodity prices, thereby reducing quite drastically the African countries' export earnings. And it should be noted that this happened during a period when there has been a slowing down in the flow of aid and private investment capital and when the prices for imported food and manufactures have risen steeply. "The developing countries," as the World Bank president put it, "are being battered by global economic forces outside their control."[2]

To overcome the balance of payments deficits, African countries have had to resort to external borrowing, in most cases, on extremely unfavorable terms. In fact, a number of these countries spend up to fifty percent of their export earnings on debt servicing alone.

The external debt-service burdens together with the low commodity

TABLE 7-1
Growth Rates of Manufacturing, Agriculture, Food,
and Mining Sectors in Africa
(in Percentages)

Period	Manufacturing	Agriculture	Food	Mining
1960–65	8.5	1.4	1.6	18.5
1965–70	7.3	3.7	3.8	16.2
1970–75	5.5	1.3	1.7	−1.8
1975–80	6.3	1.2	2.1	4.2
1980–81	3.6	1.1	1.0	−13.2
1981–82	3.7	3.4	3.7	−7.7
1982–83	0.4	0.4	0.2	−24.6[a]

[a]Provisional estimate

Sources: FAO, The State of Food and Agriculture, 1966 and 1981; United Nations Industrial Development Organization, Industry in a Changing World (UN, 1983), table V.2, 102; and Economic Commission for Africa.

prices have had the effect of undermining the economic performance of most African countries as "without adequate finance, imports cannot be paid for; without essential imports, production exports decline."[3]

As if these problems were not enough, African countries have also been suffering from deteriorating climatic conditions in the form of persistent drought, late rains, and desertification.

Attempts to Contain the Crisis

To deal with the crisis, a number of African countries have developed economic recovery programs delineating some restraints that they intend to impose on themselves. These usually include austerity budgets and import restrictions, the aim being to reverse the economic decline, achieve stabilization and adjustment in the short-term, and major restructuring in the long-term. In some cases, these restraints have been extended substantially by the IMF conditionalities to form part of structural adjustment programs. A SAP generally entails elimination or severe reduction in subsidies, substantial reductions in government spending, drastic reductions in the size of the public service, and steep devaluation of local currencies. According to the Abuja Statement, twenty-eight African countries were implementing such measures as at June 1987, and this was because of the dire need for external resources to relieve the balance of payments problems.[4]

A number of international conferences and special sessions of the Organization of African Unity and the United Nations have been held to find ways and means of containing the crisis. Among these may be mentioned the following:

1. The Monrovia Strategy for the Economic Development of Africa and the Monrovia Declaration of Commitment on Guidelines and Measures for National and Collective Self–Reliance in Social and Economic Development for the Establishment of a New International Economic Order (July 1979)

2. Special OAU session on economic problems which produced the Lagos Plan of Action and the Final Act of Lagos (April 1980)

3. Africa's Priority Programme for Economic Recovery (1986–90) (APPER) adopted by the Ordinary Session of the Assembly of Heads of State and Government of the OAU in July 1985

4. Special Session on the Critical Economic Situation in Africa (25/5/86–1/6/86) resulting in Resolution 5 - 13/2 of 1st June 1986 on UN Programme of Action for African Economic Recovery and Development 1986–90 (UN-PAAERD)

5. At the subregional level, the Authority of Heads of State and Government of the Economic Community of West African States (ECOWAS) have pledged individual and collective support to initiate a West Africa subregional recovery process through a joint plan of action (July 1986).

Despite all these efforts on the part of African governments, "there is hardly any country that has been able to mobilize adequate resources to support its adjustment programmes."[5]

CONSEQUENCES OF THE ECONOMIC CRISIS ON PUBLIC SERVICE PERSONNEL

The economic crisis has, for the ordinary person in Africa, meant shortages of basic needs, or what in some countries have been termed "essential commodities." The effect of these shortages has been a daily struggle by many people to seek and obtain these items for their families and themselves. Cases have been reported in a number of countries of citizens having to queue for two or three days before obtaining a fifty-kilo bag of rice, or six tins of milk, or a packet of sugar, or a few liters of petrol.

Public service personnel have not been exempted from this preoccupation to keep body and soul together. As a result, more time and energy have been spent on the efforts to get "essential commodities"/basic needs than on the public service jobs that they were recruited to perform. As Douglas McGreggor put it, "Man tends to live by bread alone when there is no bread."[6]

Even for those who do not care much about imported food items, shortages of cutlasses and other imported farming implements have meant that farmers have been restricted in their production of local food items which could have provided some relief. There is empirical evidence in some countries that the economic crisis has brought about a deterioration in the diet and overall welfare of the people.[7] Shortages of basic medicines, such as antimalarial tablets, paracetamol, and vitamin tablets have meant that many people do not enjoy good health, and cannot, therefore, be as productive as they were before the changes in their diet resulted in malnutrition, anemia, diarrhea, and other food-related maladies.

Where these items of basic need can be found, prices are so high that they tend to be beyond the means of many people. In some countries, people have had to part with their personal belongings to find money to purchase some of these items. Public servants with low and heavily taxed salaries tend to feel the biting effect of inflation very deeply.

This has resulted in a number of public servants, particularly the professionals, spending official working hours moonlighting as a means of supplementing their meager salaries. Others have set up private businesses. Yet others use vehicles bought with governmental advances, ostensibly for the efficient performance of their duties, as taxis, which they drive themselves during and after official working hours.

Even the limited period during which public servants genuinely carry out their official duties is also beset with many frustrations. The economic crisis has meant that in attempts to balance budgets, the "other charges" votes are normally cut close to the bone. This results in employees receiving their salaries without having the necessary tools, materials, and supplies with which to work. Shortages of stencils, duplicating papers, functioning typewriters, and photocopiers are rampant in many ministries and departments in a number of African countries. Hospitals without drugs and dressings but with full complements of specialists, general practitioners, pharmacists, and nurses; schools without books, or in some cases, without desks, are well-known illustrations of the problems confronting the African public service today. The monitoring and supervision of subordinates in the field, visits to projects, and the performance of extension work have also been frustrated by the immobility of public servants, an immobility resulting either from the lack of serviceable vehicles or the shortage of fuel. In some cases, vehicles are declared unserviceable because of the lack of minor parts such as brake pads or tires!

As a means of containing the economic crisis, and on the insistence of the IMF, which always prescribes reduction in the size of the public service as one of its conditionalities, many African governments have resorted to mass retrenchment of staff. The IMF stand is based on its belief that the public services in Africa are "too big," despite a view to the contrary published in a World Bank document: "The empirical evidence supports the view that the public service in developing countries, on the average is not 'too big' at least not bigger than what would be expected on the basis of their population and level of income."[8] Despite the view of the World Bank, the IMF insists on the reduction of the public service by a certain percentage as a condition for releasing funds. How the percentages are arrived at remains a mystery, as no proper studies or staff audits are undertaken before the percentage reductions are announced. In one case, the consultants who were to conduct a study in pursuance of "Administrative Reform" announced upon their arrival in an African country that they were going to reduce the civil service of that country by a certain percentage even before they conducted any studies. When asked how they came by that figure, the answer was that the budget was skewed in favor of staff emoluments, i.e., that the percentage of the budget that went into paying staff emoluments was too high, and that the ratio between staff emoluments and "other charges" should be set right. In other words, there is an ideal theoretical ratio between the two components of a budget that should be maintained, no matter what the circumstances. As it turned out, none of the experts carrying out that "Administrative Reform" study had ever worked in any civil service before. Consequently, as was to be expected, the consultants concentrated on reducing the budget component for staff remuneration with scant attention paid to efficiency, which indeed should have been the main thrust of the ("Administrative Reform") exercise. To use their own words, "The main thrust of the unit review has been to identify cost savings and opportunities for better utilisation of staff."[9] They proceeded to state: "Despite the fact that we have deliberately made limited use of O & M techniques, we consider that the Civil Service would benefit from a series of such studies."[10] Why then did they not use those techniques? Without a proper examination of the departments and ministries, the consultants recommended that the number of established posts be reduced from 9,075 to 7,517 (−17 percent) and unestablished staff from 993 to 653 (−34 percent) and, in addition, 340 nonestablished positions should be abolished. "This gives a total annual saving of D 5.4 Million,"[11] they stated.

In another country where about 45,000 civil servants have been retrenched over a three-year period as part of the measures to reduce the budget deficit as a proportion of gross domestic product,[12] a circular was issued in April 1987 indicating that the civil service should be further reduced by October 1987 by as many as 15,000 positions, without an attempt to conduct any studies, such as a staff audit, or an examination of the organization structure.

While it is possible that public services in Africa are "too large," the question is can we not approach the issue in a more scientific manner?

Reduction in the size of the public service has admittedly a number of advantages. It could result in better utilization of human resources and make money available for the procurement of equipment, materials, and supplies required for the proper functioning of the service. It offers an opportunity to get rid of deadwoods and lazy workers who tend to frustrate the conscientious officers. Retrenchment also carries the implicit warning that no one can count his job secure unless he performs well. An argument that can validly be advanced, however, is that deadwood and non-performing workers can be separated from the system through the normal application of proper personnel policies and regulations, without the need to resort to mass retrenchment. Furthermore, the adverse effects of reduction in the civil service through retrenchment are serious and many. Certain individuals join the public service and are prepared to receive lower remuneration because it provides security of service. Retrenchment shatters this belief, and creates a sense of insecurity, especially, because of the stop-and-go manner in which many African countries carry out the retrenchment exercise. A feeling created among those not retrenched is that lightning does strike twice in the same place. This sense of insecurity creates diversion of energies and of time, with public servants using official time to seek alternative jobs as a contingency measure. This implies that they have divided attention and do not perform their duties full-time or properly. In effect, morale and the relationship between management and staff could be very adversely affected. It could result in a significant drop in productivity.

In considering retrenchment, one should not lose sight of the social and political effects. In the African context, with our extended family system, the effect of retrenchment goes far beyond the person who is retrenched; it is felt by members of his extended family for whom he may be the only breadwinner. Added to the other measures, such as removal of subsidies leading to increases in prices of commodities, retrenchment could result in a greater number of people suffering from hunger and starvation. It could even affect the next employer, who may find a resentful, ex-redundant employee not the easiest individual to integrate into his organization. It needs to be remembered that there is a direct relationship between poverty and unemployment, the poorest being the jobless. Without social security systems that provide unemployment benefits, the unemployed in Africa cannot in most cases fulfill their basic human needs.[13]

The view that after retrenchment a lesser number of officers can provide the same services efficiently because of proper utilization of personnel and the fact that one has got rid of deadwood and lazy workers could be valid. Its validity, however, depends upon the fulfilment of other conditions such as provision of adequate incentives in the form of good salaries and allowances, regular supply of tools, and intensive in-service training. In many African countries engaged in economic recovery programs, this is not the case. The tendency generally is to freeze salaries or, at best, award increases in no way related to the level of inflation and high cost of living resulting from "devaluation," "floating," or "adjustment" of the currency. And yet such measures usually erode the purchasing power of the salaries received by public service personnel.[14]

The economic crisis in African countries has had other effects. In some cases, as in Ghana, it has had the effect of intensifying the brain drain, encouraging the exodus of public service personnel with good qualifications and experience to seek greener pastures elsewhere—in other countries, in international organizations, in the private sector as big-time farmers, businessmen, and consultants, or working for private companies. One sad aspect of this is that in a number of cases, some of these highly trained persons have not had the opportunity to practice their profession. They, therefore, settle for something lower, for instance, trained administrators and engineers become teachers in high schools.

In other cases, it has had the effect of increasing the incidence of corruption among public service personnel who find their remuneration insufficient to maintain the living standards they are used to. One hears of cases where citizens have to offer bribes (some call them "tips") before they can obtain services to which they are entitled. Many instances of embezzlement of public funds by public service personnel can be cited in most African countries, and even such severe penalties like public executions have not deterred some people.

There are the happy cases where the economic crisis has helped to build up the character of some public service personnel, making them more careful in their use of funds (dispensing with habits such as heavy drinking and heavy smoking), making them more attuned to accepting challenges and hardships.

SUGGESTIONS FOR CONTAINING THE ADVERSE IMPACT OF THE ECONOMIC CRISIS

What can African governments do to lessen, if not eliminate, the adverse impact of the economic crisis on the effectiveness of public service personnel? It would seem that the most effective way to achieve such an objective is to find ways and means of eliminating the root cause of the malaise—the economic crisis. This implies finding a way of achieving a quick turnaround of the economies of the African countries. As indicated earlier, African countries have not in the past been able to mobilize enough resources to support their adjustment programs relying, as they are, on donor governments and agencies.

In any case, structural adjustment programs (SAP) as being implemented under IMF directions are mainly an exercise aimed at reducing budget deficits as a percentage of the gross domestic product (GDP). It does not cover other aspects of the economy that could help to achieve lasting structural economic recovery. The current structural adjustment programs do not lead to the restructuring of the economy. The structure remains the same except for the readjustment of the budget figures. And this is the crux of the matter. Macro level decisions regarding the reduction of budget deficits should be accompanied, and their feasibility established, by micro level studies. Every available means of reducing budget deficits should be explored before such major decisions are made. Weighty and momentous decisions such as the reduction of the size of the public sector and retrenchment of staff should not be based on rule-of-thumb techniques.

Given that the current SAP does not lead to restructuring it is possible that after implementation of the program, the economic crisis would persist. Indeed the latest World Bank annual report published on 17 September 1987 reinforces this gloomy forecast by stating that fifteen of the poorest African countries were on the brink of collapse: "In spite of attempts by governments to implement SAPs negotiated with the Bank, growth has proved elusive."[15] As Tinbergen and others put it, "economic stagnation (and stagflation) can only be overcome by a parallel increase in production, productivity and purchasing power. A lasting structural economic recovery and a general increase in welfare can only be implemented through a maximization of employment."[16]

NOTES

1. The Brandt Commission, *Common Crisis: North-South Cooperation for World Recovery* (London: Pan Books), 17.

2. Speech to the Annual Meeting of the IMF and The World Bank, Toronto, September 1982.

3. The Brandt Commission, *op. cit.*, 19.

4. *The Abuja Statement*, The International Conference on Africa: The Challenge of Economic Recovery and Accelerated Development (Abuja, Nigeria, 15–19 June 1987), 10.

5. *Ibid.*

6. Douglas McGreggor, *The Human Side of Enterprise* (1984), 41.

7. Dorothy Mutemba (of the National Commission for Development Planning, Lusaka), Paper presented at a recent London conference on "The Impact of the IMF and World Bank Policies on the People of Africa," reported in *West Africa*, 21 September 1987, 1833.

8. Salcuk Ozgediz, *Managing the Public Service in Developing Countries* (Washington, D.C.: World Bank Staff Working Paper no. 583), 3.

9. Peat Marwick, *Government of The Gambia, Review of the Organization, Staffing and Efficiency of the Civil Service,* Interim Report, 3.

10. *Ibid.,* 49 para. 5.5.

11. *Ibid.,* 55, 56, paras. 5.20 & 5.23.

12. A paper presented by Kwesi Jonah of the University of Ghana at a recent London conference on "The Impact of the IMF and World Bank Policies on the People of Africa," quoted in *West Africa,* 21 September 1987, 1832.

13. J. T. Tinbergen, J. N. den Uyl, J. R. Pronke, and W. Kok, "A New World Employment Plan," *IFDA Dossier* 21 (January/February 1981): 7.

14. At the forty-ninth weekly foreign exchange auction in Accra on September 25, the cedi dropped in value for the seventh consecutive week from ¢171 to a record low of ¢176 to U.S. $1 (*West Africa,* 19 October 1987, 2046). Until December 1985, five dalasis could be exchanged for £1 sterling. Now one requires D12 to obtain a pound. In 1985, salaries in Zaire's public sector were less than 10 percent of their 1975 value. In the Central African Republic, apart from the Army and the Police, no public worker had had a wage increase in the last five years. The minimum guaranteed wage of 1980 remains unchanged.

15. Quoted in *West Africa,* 28 September 1987, 1926.

16. J. T. Tinbergen et al., *op. cit.,* 5.

CHAPTER EIGHT

Economic Crisis, Budgetary Constraints, and Effectiveness of Government: A Critical Review

Michael A. Bentil

THE SCOPE OF THE SOCIOECONOMIC CRISIS

In one of its publications, the World Bank has attempted to summarize the prevailing economic conditions in contemporary Africa:

> Africa's economic and social conditions began to deteriorate in the 1970's, and continue to do so. Gross domestic product (GDP) grew at an average of 3.6% a year between 1970 and 1980, but has fallen every year since then. With population rising at over 3% a year, income per capita in 1983 is estimated to be about 4% below its 1970 level. Agricultural output per capita has continued to decline, so food imports have increased. Much industrial capacity stands idle, the victim of falling domestic income, poor investment choices, a failure to develop export opportunities, and inadequate foreign exchange for materials and spare parts.[1]

The data that have been assembled to illustrate the gravity of the crisis in sub-Saharan Africa is presented as Table 8–1. It indicates the annual average rate of changes over the period 1960 to 1986.[2]

A major factor that has precipitated the African economic crisis is the drought that began in Southern Africa in 1983 and went on to affect more than twenty countries by 1985. The ensuing famine took a devastating toll in human and animal life. Many farmers and nomadic cattle rearers joined the already swollen ranks of urban poor; families broke up; systems of community support were weakened; and the strain on government services increased further. Fortunately, most parts of Africa were blessed with good rainfall in 1985, and the situation started to improve. This improvement is reflected in Table 8–1, which shows a remarkable increase in the annual rate of GDP by more than 3 percent between 1985 and 1986. By the same token, the per capita GDP annual rate also rose significantly from −2.9 percent to 0.4 percent, an increase of 3.3 percent.

Notwithstanding the improvement recorded between 1985 and 1986, the World Bank indicated that the welcome developments would still not enable low-income Africa to recover the ground it had lost in the past years. Per capita income was expected to fall by 12 percent compared with

TABLE 8-1
Changes in GDP, Population, and GDP Per Capita in Sub-Saharan Africa, 1960–86

Factors	1960–70	1970–75	1975–80	1981	1982	1983	1984 (preliminary)	1985 (estimated)	1986
GDP	3.6	2.4	2.3	1.7	−0.8	−0.1	0.8	0.0	3.6
Population	2.5	2.7	2.8	3.0	3.0	3.1	3.1	3.1	3.2
Per Capita GDP	1.0	−0.3	−0.5	−1.2	−2.2	−3.0	−2.2	−2.9	0.4

the level at the start of the 1980s. The decline in Africa's per capita output during the 1980s together with the decline in the 1970s according to the World Bank study, would wipe out all the gains in per capita output since 1960.[3] It is explained that many institutions have been and are still deteriorating, both in physical capacity and in their ability to perform efficiently. Even though the situation differs from country to country, it is further reported that even those countries with good records in the 1970s are also facing serious difficulties.[4]

The scope and intensity of the African crisis are demonstrated in several other ways. It is reported that in many African countries, people are having to do without public infrastructural services, as governments are compelled to concentrate their limited resources and energies on sheer political survival. Several others have been compelled to allocate a substantial share of their annual budgets, both recurrent and development, to defense spending because of the inevitable need to provide for and ensure maximum internal security.

The dismal picture also reflects a continuing deterioration in facilities and a denial of features of modern society to which many Africans had been previously exposed. The plain fact is that the entire continent is poorer today than it was in the 1960s. The efficiency of health, education, and physical infrastructural services has been increasingly undermined. For example, (a) transport services and facilities have almost broken down, and in some cases become nonexistent, because trucks, ferries, and other vehicles no longer operate because of lack of spare parts and the deteriorating conditions of roads and railway networks; (b) aircraft no longer land at night in some places because of the breakdown of power supply systems to keep the airports operational at all times; (c) a clean water supply is hard to come by in many places, even in the national and provincial capitals, which are supposed to be developed; (d) many children continue to be denied opportunities to attend schools; and (e) ready access to health care facilities is becoming a privilege available to a few and denied to the majority of the population.

A review of the African economic crisis and its budgetary impact and constraints cannot be complete without making reference to other crucial factors and their impact, as well as analyzing some of the factors that have been mentioned previously.

Deteriorating External Environment

The principal factor under this heading is the unfavorable impact of the terms of world trade and the associated loss of income in sub-Saharan Africa. The World Bank study reports that while world trade has stagnated and commodity prices have declined, many developed countries have increased protectionist barriers for goods from developing countries. For sub-Saharan Africa, restrictions on sugar and livestock have particularly aggravated economic deterioration.[5] The decline of Africa's share in the world trade according to the report has occurred generally with respect to commodities in which the continent has a comparative advantage and which are likely to remain its main potential source of foreign exchange earnings.

In addition to the trade barriers imposed by the developed countries, the terms of trade in respect of African export commodities worsened in recent years. Between 1980 and 1982, prices of non-primary commodities declined by 27 percent in current dollar terms. The middle income oil-importing countries suffered the most; their income dropped by about 3 percent of GDP. The percentage changes in terms of trade and the associated loss of income as a percentage of GDP in sub-Saharan Africa during 1980–82 are reported to be −4.7 and 1.2 respectively.[6]

Deepening Debt Problems

Since 1980, debt servicing has emerged as a major problem in sub-Saharan Africa. During the four-year period from 1980, it was reported that of the thirty-one reschedulings agreed to with the Paris Club, thirteen were initiated by sub-Saharan countries. In addition, eleven countries have rescheduled their commercial debt.[7] During that period, the region's debt service payments (including payments to the IMF) increased from 18 percent of export earnings to 26 percent, according to World Bank sources.[8] In some countries such as Malawi, Niger, and Zambia, the ratio is reported to have risen to more than 30 percent. But for the reschedulings that had been allowed, a buildup of arrears would have attracted higher debt service payments in 1984, much higher than 38 percent of the export earnings for low-income African countries as a whole. In real terms, it is estimated that the total of Africa's disbursed public and publicly guaranteed medium- and long-term debt at the end of 1982 was over $48 billion.[9] The majority of the debt was on nonconcessional terms. Public debt servicing has been expected to increase dramatically. For example, the rate was estimated to rise to an average of $11.6 billion a year between 1985 and 1987.

It is to be noted that repeated reschedulings and arrears of debt hinder development. They do not only use up the scarce management time of Africa's policymakers, but they also create a climate of uncertainty that makes sustained development very difficult. Payment arrears can further halt new loan commitments and disbursements from existing loans. In particular, payments due to multilateral organizations can hinder the process of formulation of an adjustment program, which in turn can block debt relief from private and bilateral creditors.

The World Bank study gives a number of reasons for the rise in debt service obligations. The reschedulings in the last few years, mostly on concessional terms, gave short-term relief, but at the expense of increasing the debt service burden from 1984 onward. In many sub-Saharan African countries, significant increases in assistance were needed to repay IMF loans falling due. Taking into consideration IMF loans outstanding at the end of 1983, repurchases and charges were expected to total some $0.9 billion in 1984 and $3.5 billion during 1985-87.[10]

In conclusion, when Africa's arrears of debt are taken into account, its debt service outlook looks even more dismal. Servicing obligations in 1984 were expected to jump about 30 percent if all arrears had been repaid in that year. Unless corrective measures are taken, the external resource position of sub-Saharan Africa is likely to become disastrous in the next few years.

Declining Investment and Capital Inflows

According to the World Bank's 1984 report, Africa's record of investment in the 1970s was good compared with the investment situation of the 1960s. Part of the reason was that the increase in foreign capital inflows more than compensated for the lower terms of trade and the fall in domestic savings at that time. The level of investment remained at around 18 percent of GDP in the 1970s, but in the 1980s, the rate of investment dropped. In fact, it was estimated to have fallen to 14 percent in 1984. The investment rate in Africa is reported to be the lowest of any other developing region and is indeed less than what the region needs for its sustained development. It is too little to provide for additional productive capacity or even to maintain and rehabilitate existing capacity.

The fall in the investment rate during the 1980s has reflected some decline both in external capital inflows and internal savings. The latter averaged about 15 percent of GDP until the mid-1970s. Since then, the savings rate has dropped steadily. Two significant factors explain this trend. One stems from falling per capita incomes. The other factor, more important perhaps, is the increasing public sector deficits or negative public savings due to unchecked government budget deficits and losses incurred by state-owned enterprises. Also, the net inflows of foreign savings have fallen from 11 percent of GDP in 1980–82 to 8 percent of GDP in 1983–84. This has happened primarily because of the increase in debt service payments and lower inflows of commercial capital, because of reduced debt servicing ability.[11]

African Response to Crisis

The African economic problems became a subject of grave concern in 1984, within Africa as a whole, following two years of severe drought. In this regard a United Nations conference on the emergency situation in Africa was held in Geneva to mobilize international support for the countries most seriously affected by the drought. In addition, the United Nations Secretary General established the Office of Emergency Operations in Africa to facilitate and coordinate the mobilization and disbursement of emergency assistance.

In response to the crisis, the OAU convened in July 1985, a major summit meeting to prepare short- and long-term programs for dealing with the emergency. The summit adopted the African Priority Programme for Economic Recovery 1986–1990, which embraces short-, medium-, and long-term measures to cope with both the symptoms and fundamental causes of the crisis. It was believed that the food crisis which had sparked much international concern and sympathy was, in fact, a symptom of a deeper malaise which needed to be seriously addressed, if such a crisis were to be prevented from becoming endemic in Africa.

Following the special summit of the OAU held in July 1985 to address and critically analyze the crisis, a special session of the United Nations General Assembly was convened in May 1986 to address the same subject. In its submissions to the Special Session, the African bloc acknowledged that both internal and external factors contributed to the development crisis. Attention was drawn in particular to: (a) the shortcomings in domestic economic policies, (b) the collapse of primary commodity prices, (c) the decline in concessional assistance, and (d) the effect of high interest rates on the burden of external debt. It was also recognized that pervasive low productivity, particularly in the agricultural sector, was central to the issue of Africa's structural crisis. At the end of the Session, a United Nations Programme of Action for African Economic Recovery and Development was adopted unanimously.

Highlights of the Economic Crisis and Its Impact on Budgetary and Public Service Effectiveness

The nature of the ongoing socioeconomic crisis can be understood in terms of its impact on the effectiveness of government. The depletion of resources, as well as the inability to generate them adequately to satisfy budgetary requirements prevents the machinery of government from running smoothly and undermines the efficiency and responsiveness of the public services.

The steep decline in standards of living consequent upon the depletion of resources has contributed, in no small measure, to social upheavals. Political instability due to continuing changes of governments and administrations follow largely from coups d'état. The effects of such changes include costly delays and sometimes wasteful abandonment of public programs and projects into which huge and irrecoverable sums are sunk and the establishment of time-consuming and often unproductive commissions of enquiry into the alleged abuses and excesses of previous regimes. About forty coups d'état have taken place in some twenty different countries between 1960, when African countries started to gain their political independence, and September 1987. Another incidence of political instability is armed conflicts between governments and rebellious factions such as guerrilla groups. This has necessitated the investment of large sums of public funds (in some cases, more than 30 percent of a government budget) to build and maintain armed forces and their equipment and logistical support.

REVIEW OF PURPOSES AND SCOPE OF GOVERNMENT BUDGETING PROCESS

Before the negative effects of the African economic crisis on the budgetary and public service effectiveness are analyzed and assessed, a general understanding of some important aspects of the budgetary process in government is considered essential.

Budgeting is an integrated part of the financial management system of which accounting and auditing are the remaining parts. In addition, budgeting complements planning and provides the key to the government's financial policies. Despite the complementary relationship between planning and budgeting, the degree of harmonization between the two functions has often been weak and inadequate in practice. There are several reasons for the divergence between planning and budgeting. First, the role of planning agencies in many countries is limited to advisory services, whereas budget agencies are essentially operational; also, budgeting being historically older, wields more influence in the mobilization and allocation of resources. Second, there are differences between the two in time perspective: planning is essentially a forward-looking exercise and takes a long-term view, while budgeting is an annual exercise and often has to conform to short-term situations and political realities. Third, planning and budgeting differ in their scope; the latter is limited to the operations of the government sector, while the former covers the entire economy.

In view of the foregoing, there is a need to provide measures that will ensure the success of planning and budgeting as complementary activities, as well as their effective coordination. The fundamental requirement for achieving this is a clear enunciation of socioeconomic goals and objectives by political leaders, as well as a clear and comprehensive understanding of such goals by both planning and budget officials.

Budgeting as an element of financial management plays two significant roles in contrast with accounting and auditing. First, budgeting provides the policy guidelines as well as the legal framework along which public accounting processes should be carried out, especially with regard to the limits of public spending. In contrast, accounting is concerned with: (a) proper recording, generally, of all financial transactions, in the form of receipts and expenditures of departments and other organizational units within the government; (b) maintenance of records that reflect the propriety of transactions and give evidence of accountability for assets and other resources in public use; and (c) classification of data in a way that provides useful information for control and for the efficient management of programs.

The linkage between budgeting and auditing consists of the provision by the former of yardsticks against which the monitoring and evaluation of financial and management performance (otherwise called auditing) is carried out. Equally, budgeting provides the standard against which financial accountability is measured and auditing is that measurement. A United Nations publication on *Government Auditing in Developing Countries* defines government auditing as:

> the objective, systematic, professional, and independent examination of financial, administrative and other operations of a public entity made subsequently to their execution, for the purpose of evaluating and verifying them, presenting a report containing explanatory comments on audit findings, together with conclusions and recommendations for future action by the responsible officials and, in the case of the examination of financial statements, expressing the appropriate professional opinion regarding the fairness of their presentation.[12]

Along the lines of the foregoing definition, the purpose of auditing may be summarized as follows:

A. Ascertaining whether, in the auditor's professional opinion, the financial statements of the organization examined present fairly and accurately its financial position, results of operations and changes in financial position, in conformity with generally accepted accounting principles

B. Determination of compliance with legislative provisions relating to the operations examined

C. Evaluation of the degree of economy and efficiency in the management and use of resources

D. Evaluation of the effectiveness with which the operations of the organization concerned attain the objectives established by the government and by the organization's own management.

Functions of Budgeting

As an independent management function, budgeting is a process by which a government formulates its goals and objectives for the fiscal year, establishes priorities for the use of scarce resources, mobilizes and allocates resources among specific programs and activities, identifies policies and operational modalities to implement programs and projects efficiently, and provides for an evaluation of results in relation to the objectives, targets, and utilization of resources. It is a continuing and flexible process that should respond to changing conditions. In this context, budgeting is an important instrument in the implementation of national development strategies and in the management of the national economy.

Budgeting involves different tasks on both the expenditure and revenue sides. On the expenditure side, it involves the determination of the total size of the budget in terms of what needs to be done, as well as the size and magnitude of the outlays on different programs and functions. On the revenue side, the size of overall receipts from all possible sources to match the total outlays, needs to be determined. A decision is also needed on the size of the deficit, as well as the component and sources of its financing, including the assessment and ownership of public debt that may be necessary. These tasks are common to all countries, irrespective of their political ideology, economic and social system, and cultural orientation. All of them need to recognize and take appropriate measures to respond efficiently to the requirements of the three functions of the modern budget: *allocation, stabilization,* and *distribution.*

The three functions of budgeting mentioned above are very crucial in the sense that they provide the foundation upon which a sound and objective budget formulation can be based. It should be noted in this regard that budget preparation involves the interplay of several forces and therefore deals with different institutional factors, different demands, and different patterns of accountability and responsibility. *Allocative* responsibilities revolve around, and are concerned with, the balanced sharing of resources between the public and private sectors among competing demands within the government, and the assessment of trade-offs between allocational and other objectives. *Stabilization* concerns the impact of government operations on the economy and the need to adjust the budget in light of macroeconomic changes. This is achieved through a variety of devices and mechanisms such as adjusting the national income accounts, as well as adjustments to provide for increases or reductions in taxes and expenditures to meet unforeseen changes in the economy, or to apply a specified degree of restraint or a stimulus to the economy.

Distribution, as the third function of the budget process, concerns the incidence of public expenditures, and the extent to which different groups are expected to gain or lose from a particular budget strategy. Alternatives such as cash payments in lieu of government services may have to be envisaged, or programs may have to be redesigned to meet the needs of specified income groups. In endeavoring to meet these objectives, conflicts arise. For example, how to establish an equilibrium in the distribution of resources between the public and private sectors is sometimes a problematic issue. Equally, it is not always easy to determine the level of the right trade-offs between the allocation and stabilization functions, on the one hand, and between the stabilization and distribution functions, on the other.

Roles and Responsibilities in Budget Functions

The roles and responsibilities stemming from the functions of allocation, stabilization, and distribution in budget formulation and implementation constitute the hard core of public policy, and as such, are largely a matter of political choice. However, in terms of administrative responsibilities, *distribution* would tend to be the concern of executing and spending agencies, while *allocation* and *stabilization* would fall within the jurisdiction of central coordinating agencies. In light of the foregoing division of responsibilities, there may be times when the spending agencies lack sufficient appreciation of the issues of *allocation* and *stabilization* functions. Therefore, as a precondition to sound budgeting, there should be adequate communication and understanding on these matters during the process of determining annual budgets and medium-term financial plans.

With the close linkages between budgeting on the one hand, and on the other hand, planning, accounting and auditing as already pointed out, responsibilities for sound formulation as well as effective and efficient implementation of the budget should devolve not only on budget specialists in the Ministry of Finance or the Treasury, but also equally substantially on the staff of planning, accounting, and auditing units.

In summary, the foregoing analysis reflects that the budget process generates a network of relationships transcending different levels of responsibility which may be classified as follows:

A. Policy responsibilities exercised by the central resource mobilization, coordinating, allocating, and stabilization institutions and agencies, such as the Parliament/National Assembly/National Congress; Office of the President/Prime Minister/Chief Executive; the Cabinet/Council of Ministers; and Ministries of Finance, Planning, Public Service/Establishments/Personnel Administration and Supplies. The central role of the last two named agencies is especially emphasized, because their significance in the budget process is often not sufficiently recognized, compared with the role of financial and planning agencies. The Ministry of Civil Service or Establishments is centrally responsible for mobilizing, allocating, and stabilizing manpower resources, which constitute between 60–65 percent of national budgets in financial terms. Supplies ministries, on the other hand, exercise central responsibility for the procurement, and balanced allocation of material resources, which are estimated to constitute between 20 and 25 percent. Those directly involved at this level include politicians and top administrators.

B. Staff responsibilities involving specialist functions of data collection, analysis, synthesis, utilization, and control in planning, budgeting, accounting, and auditing. The specialist staff at this level include economists and analysts, statisticians, budget officers, accountants and accounting staff, and auditors and auditing staff.

C. Operational responsibilities exercised overall at the level of all implementing agencies where in particular, program managers and the teams of personnel they lead or supervise are required to take the following broad actions:

   1. Advise top executives and policymakers on their budget requirements and priorities

   2. Feed information to the planning, budget, accounting, and auditing specialists to facilitate the preparation of periodic budgets, and also cooperate with them in complying with the necessary rules and regulations relating to the mobilization and utilization of public resources, i.e., money, manpower, and materials.

CAUSES OF BUDGET DEFICIENCIES

Budgetary weakness and deficiencies have been sufficiently documented and are too widely known in most African countries to merit repetition in this chapter. Accordingly, we shall now focus on a brief review of the persistent but *avoidable* or controllable problems that are common to African countries.

The problems in question exclude those that have arisen out of natural disasters, such as the widespread drought of 1982–84, the global recession and accompanying rising inflation commencing in the 1970s, unfavorable international trade conditions and terms, and other situations that might be presumed to be beyond the control of the countries and the governments concerned. The concern here relates more to those problems that stem mainly from internal factors such as general incompetence at different levels of responsibility in managing government business; blatant dishonesty and corruption in the public services; indiscipline and lack of control; ineffective systems of accountability; and political opportunism, selfishness, and disharmony often leading to unnecessary coups d'état; and internal armed conflicts and civil wars coupled with insecurity.

Core of the Problems

Despite the severity of the economic problems caused by unforeseen and uncontrollable factors mentioned above, their effects on budgets and public service performance would not have been catastrophic if the internal problems (to which reference has been made) had been identified and effectively controlled. Those internal problems have become perennial, leaving the resource base of governments so weak and fragile that the least external shock leads to economic and financial disaster.

The most painful and disturbing of all the internal sources of problems is the widespread *corruption*, much of which is regrettably linked with, or can be traced to bankrupt and dishonest leadership steeped in selfishness and insatiable avarice. Unless this problem is effectively uprooted, the different efforts to deal with all other resource draining deficiencies will not yield positive results.

It is well known that genuine but unsuccessful efforts have been made since the 1970s if not earlier, and are still being made both at the national and international levels, to seriously address budget related, or resource-draining problems. Administrative and financial reforms have been launched and carried out in almost all developing African countries with the aim of promoting efficiency, maximization in the use of public resources, and cost-effectiveness in the overall administration of the government. The current requirement of the International Monetary Fund (IMF) and the World Bank for structural reforms, as a precondition for financial assistance, is a further evidence of the concerted effort being made globally to stamp out some of the problems under review.

Another concrete example of the concerted efforts to bring about improvements and rationalization in resource management and utilization is the increasing number of training programs, publications, and special studies undertaken by national governments, as well as international and technical cooperation agencies. At the national level, one recent and classic example is a six-day residential workshop for *all* Permanent Secretaries in the government of Uganda which was held from 29 November to 4 December 1984. The workshop was exclusively devoted to studying and searching for the means of *Improving Budget Management and Financial Control in the Uganda Civil Service*.

At the African regional level an illustration can be drawn from a program initiated and executed between May 1983 and September 1984 by AAPAM in cooperation with public enterprises in four African countries. The exercise was to study and advise on problems of financial management in electricity and power corporations. The collaborating countries were Ethiopia, Liberia, Tanzania, and Zambia. The program ended with an Experts Workshop held in September 1984 in Zambia on financial management problems in public enterprises.

The various studies, publications, training programs, technical assistance services, and other forms of reform efforts have identified more or less the same set of problems. These include:

A. *Unsound Policy Formulation* sometimes because of lack of clarity in the definition of roles between policymakers (ministers, board members of public corporations) and policy advisers and administrators (permanent secretaries, managing directors, general managers). Other factors accounting for policy deficiencies are shortage of data, partisan political influence, and other affective considerations impinging on decision-making.

B. *Deficiencies in Accounting and Auditing Systems Because of:*

1. outdated financial rules and regulations

2. failure to comply with, or direct flouting of, prevailing financial rules and regulations, particularly by policymakers and top officials

3. failure to effectively enforce compliance with financial rules and regulations

4. delays in the bookkeeping and processing of accounts. In some countries, the government treasury final accounts are known to have fallen behind deadlines for as long as five to eight years

5. poor record-keeping

6. slowness in modernizing and streamlining accounting procedures

C. *Weak Systems of Control and Accountability Reflected in:*
1. mounting unheaded audit queries and failure to enforce compliance
2. unauthorized and uncontrolled overspending of public funds because of unauthorized overstaffing, excessive procurement of materials and equipment; fraudulent practices in public purchasing and tendering procedures and practices
3. absence of effective cost standards or yardsticks to provide the necessary guide for measuring budget performance
4. laxity in the system of recording losses
5. ineffective reporting and inspection systems

D. *Shortage of Skilled and Qualified Staff Because of:*
1. poor recruitment and staff employment practices
2. absence of meaningful training and staff development schemes
3. lack of proper schemes for staff performance appraisal and training needs assessment
4. unattractive low wages and other poor conditions and terms of employment, leading to loss of staff morale
5. lack of interest and support in promoting and developing professionalism in financial and accounting work in the public service, particularly among civil servants and local government employees

E. Poor maintenance and control of public assets and facilities, including building, equipment, furniture, machinery, and plants.

Positive and constructive actions based upon sound recommendations are known to have been made continually, both nationally and internationally since African countries started to attain political independence more than two decades ago, to rectify the problems summarized above. The outcome of these efforts has been disturbingly discouraging. The problems persist, reflecting either the failure to identify and eradicate the roots of the problems, or the lack of interest and boldness to take appropriate corrective measures.

NOTES

1. The World Bank, *Toward Sustained Development in Sub-Saharan Africa: A Joint Programme of Action* (Washington, D.C.: The World Bank, 1984), 11.

2. The World Bank, *Financing Adjustment with Growth in Sub-Saharan Africa, 1986–90* (Washington, D.C.: The World Bank, 1986), 9.

3. *Ibid.*

4. The World Bank, *Toward Sustained Development*, 9.

5. *Ibid.*, 11.

6. *Ibid.*, 12.

7. *Ibid.*

8. The World Bank, *Financing Adjustment with Growth*, 11.

9. The World Bank, *Toward Sustained Development*, 12.

10. *Ibid.*, 13.

11. The World Bank, *Financing Adjustment with Growth*, 10.

12. *Handbook on Government Auditing in Developing Countries* (New York: United Nations, 1977), 1.

BIBLIOGRAPHY

Other World Bank Publications

The World Bank Atlas 1987.

Developing Country Debt: Implementing the Consensus, 1987.

Other United Nations Publications

A Manual for Economic and Functional Classification of Government Transactions (1958).

Budgeting and Planning for Development in Developing Countries (1976).

Handbook on Government Auditing in Developing Countries (1977).

Government Auditing in Economic Development Management (1977).

Report on Budget Management Techniques in Selected Development Countries (1978).

A Manual for Programme and Performance Budgeting (1965).

Priority Areas for Action in Public Administration and Finance in 1980's (1981).

Accrual Accounting in Developing Countries (1984).

Part IV

Country and Subregional Case Studies

CHAPTER NINE

Government Response to Economic Crisis: The Experience of Ethiopia

Asmelash Beyene

INTRODUCTION

While the current socioeconomic crisis is of continental magnitude, countries on the lower rung of the development ladder have been hit much harder by the impact of the economic crisis. Like all other least developed African economies, Ethiopia has been a victim of the global and regional economic crisis. The country's predicament seems to have been further complicated by the drastic societal restructuring embarked upon in the 1970s, the political upheavals that accompanied the restructuring, and by the repeated natural calamities to which the country was exposed.

In the subsequent paragraphs, we shall briefly examine recent economic developments in Ethiopia against the background of the revolution that took place thirteen years ago, the challenges confronting the revolution from internal and external forces, and their effects on the economy, the impact of drought and famine that devastated the economy and the subsequent government responses. The chapter will start by providing a glimpse of the state of the economy and then proceed to examine how the government attempted to revitalize the economy through the launching of the development campaigns, and how resettlement and villagization policies were used to combat drought. Attempts by the World Bank and donor agencies to force the government to undertake structural adjustment reforms and the government's reaction to such pressures will also be briefly discussed.

THE STATE OF THE ECONOMY OF ETHIOPIA

Situated in the Horn of Africa, Ethiopia covers an area of 1,221,900 square kilometers and has a population of 45,958,700 (1987), making it the third most populous country in Africa.

Endowed with fertile soil and a good climate, it has been suggested that Ethiopia could be a bread basket of Africa. However, recurring natural calamities have made it impossible for the country to feed itself, let alone generate surplus for use by others. In 1984, the world witnessed an unprecedented human tragedy in the form of drought and famine in

Ethiopia. Millions of people were on the verge of extinction until massive international assistance, coupled with internal initiatives, contained the disaster.

Ethiopia, whose history dates back to the fourth century A.D., had for long suffered under a backward and exploitative feudal economic system. This situation arrested the development of productive forces, and as a result the country remained one of the poorest countries in the world. In 1974, the Ethiopian revolution erupted resulting in the overthrow of the old imperial regime and the establishment of the Provisional Military Council (PMAC). Socialism was proclaimed as a state policy and the antiquated land tenure system abolished with the enactment of the rural land proclamation, which brought the feudal system to an end. Subsequent measures taken in nationalizing industries, financial institutions, insurance, urban land, and housing were further evidence of the country's determination to lay a foundation for socialist construction.

When a change of the magnitude introduced in Ethiopia is experienced and results in the radical restructuring of society, it is bound to provoke a hostile reaction by groups affected by the change. The aftermath of the revolution was, therefore, hardly peaceful. The military government was confronted with threats from secessionist forces in the north, the Somalia invasion in the east and south, and the destabilizing acts of the various groups contending for power. This was to force the government to concentrate its energy and resources of fire fighting, thus diverting its attention from developmental activities. Worse still, the drought and famine of 1974 returned in 1984 with a more devastating blow to the economy.

Ethiopia's GNP per capita was estimated to be U.S. $110 in 1984, and about 60 percent of the people live below the poverty line. The GDP at market price for 1985 was $4,835.9 million.[1] Agriculture, the mainstay of the economy, contributes about 50 percent of the GDP and accounts for 85 percent of employment. Ninety percent of the export earnings come from agriculture. Industry's share of GDP is estimated at 16 percent, and services constitute 39.7 percent.[2] A recent World Bank report summarizes Ethiopia's overall economic trends in the following manner:

> The Ethiopian economy has experienced low growth stagnation in commodity production for more than a decade. The recent drought exacerbated but did not cause these adverse trends which were evident before the drought. In the decade ended 1983/84, GDP growth (2.5 per cent per year) failed to keep pace with population growth (2.7 per cent per year), and there was a sharp decline in per capita agricultural production. Production growth was impeded by the low level of investment reflecting relatively low level of both domestic savings and external resource flows. Public savings have diminished as government current expenditure, especially for defence and public adminis-

tration, rose faster than revenues. Meanwhile, private saving and investment did not respond adequately to various government initiatives. Agricultural producer prices have remained virtually unadjusted for the past six years, leading to an erosion of incentives.[3]

The report further asserts that the current account deficit has continued to widen over the past decade. Between 1974–75 and 1983–84, the volume of exports grew at an average rate of only about 1.4 percent per year while import volume grew by nearly 7 percent per year.[4] As a result, the value of merchandise imports has more than doubled the value of merchandise exports.

It is common knowledge that there cannot be growth without investment, and that investment is financed by domestic savings or external resources. Ethiopia's performance in this regard has been discouraging. Domestic savings as a proportion of GDP have steadily declined from 5.7 percent in the aftermath of the revolution (1975–78 to 1977–78) to 4.3 percent, 3.2 percent and 0.3 percent in 1978–79 to 1979–80, 1980–81 to 1982–83, and 1983–84 to 1984–85 respectively. With the decline in savings, the dependence on external resources to finance investment increased progressively. According to the World Bank:

> The share of investment financed from external resources increased progressively from 39 per cent during 1975/76–1977/78 to about 72 per cent during 1980/81–1982/83. During the period 1983/84–1984/85 namely the drought years, domestic savings turned negative, with consumption exceeding total output. In other words a part of net capital inflows went into consumption during this period.[5]

Even though the growth rate prior to the revolution was not remarkable, it was nevertheless much better than trends observed following the revolution. During the seven years ending 1973–74, the GDP growth averaged 3.3 percent per year. The first three years following the revolution recorded a serious slowdown in economic growth. Between 1975–76 to 1977–78 the GDP growth averaged 0.4 percent per annum.[6]

The slowdown experienced in economic growth was understandable. Following the revolution, the country's unity appeared very fragile. The secessionist movements in Eritrea, the emergence of the Tigrean Liberation Front, confrontations with groups loyal to Ali Mira, former Sultan of the Afars who fled to Saudi Arabia, armed uprising by feudal elements disaffected by the rural land proclamation, and the scramble for power among various elements, resulted in a serious political turmoil marked by bloodshed. It was also this moment that the Somali government considered opportune to strike and realize its long-cherished dreams of territorial aggrandizement. As a result, it invaded Ethiopia in the east and south and penetrated seven hundred kilometers into Ethiopian territory. All the events narrated above disrupted production and transport activities. As a consequence, existing production capacities could not be fully utilized. The level of investment during the period was too low to make any significant impact on production. Not only did the production level decline, the value of exports also fell sharply. In contrast, the war effort required imported goods resulting in increased import bills.

With a tremendous sacrifice in human and material resources, the government finally succeeded in repulsing the Somali invaders and containing the internal threats posed by the secessionist forces in the north. The government then embarked upon a recovery strategy through special development campaigns known as *Zemetchas*. The campaigns lasted from 1978–79 to 1980–81 and aimed at revitalizing the war-torn economy. They met initial success by recording a GDP growth of 5.2 percent and 5.5 percent in real terms during the years 1978–79 and 1979–80 respectively.[7] However, the encouraging surge of the economy was soon to experience a major setback. Between 1980–81 to 1981–82, the GDP growth rate dropped from 3.0 percent to 1.5 percent.[8] According to a report by the World Bank:

> The economy . . . witnessed a setback in the third period, i.e. 1980/81 to 1982/83. The growth of real GDP slowed down to an average rate of 2.9 per cent per annum during this three-year period, despite a moderate recovery in 1982/83. This slowdown was due mainly to conditions of persistent drought, capacity constraints in industry, and the low level of total investment, the last as a consequence of increasingly severe constraints on domestic as well as external resources. The deceleration in economic growth was coupled with a sharp deterioration in the external economic environment. Ethiopia's terms of trade declined by about 27 per cent over this three-year period, reflecting a further decline in coffee prices and sharp increases in import prices. Efforts to raise non-coffee export earnings were not successful owing to internal factors as well as poor marketing prospects. Consequently, Ethiopia's current account deficit widened significantly, reaching around 7 per cent of GDP in both 1981/82 and 1982/83.[9]

A moderate recovery was registered in 1982–83 when the GDP recorded a 4.2 percent growth. But this trend was short-lived when in 1984–85 a severe drought hit the country. This resulted in a 25 percent drop in domestic food production amounting to a grain deficit of 1.8 million tons.[10] The drought was followed by a severe famine affecting about eight million people. The severity of the famine was such that massive international relief support had to be sought to cope with it. According to the report by the World Bank:

> The 1983/84 drought plunged the economy to a period of negative growth. GDP declined by 3.7 per cent in 1983/84 primarily due to the 9.9 per cent decline in agricultural output (value added). GDP further

declined by about 6.5 per cent in 1984/85 owing mainly to a drop of 16 per cent in agriculture.[11]

GOVERNMENT RESPONSE TO ECONOMIC PROBLEMS

It has already been mentioned how the country passed through a political turmoil following the revolution, resulting in an armed uprising by forces opposed to the revolution, secessionist movements, and external invaders. These events had dire consequences for the economy. The PMAC subsequently embarked upon a strategy intended to revitalize the economy through the introduction of annual development campaigns (*Zemetchas*) beginning in 1978–79.

As may be recalled, the first three years following the revolution recorded a serious slowdown in economic growth, the GDP growth averaging 0.4 percent per annum between 1975–76 to 1977–78.[12] To reverse the economy's declining trend, the development campaign was officially launched. The National Revolutionary Development Campaign and Central Planning Supreme Council was established, with the Head of State as its chairman, to oversee the campaigns.

The campaigns were conducted through a series of (six) annual development plans. The objectives of these development campaigns were:

> To restore war-damaged physical assets and infrastructures; to alleviate urgent economic problems prevailing at the time; to lay down social and economic infrastructure necessary for accelerated development; to find ways and means of solving the prevailing social problems and to create the necessary institutional framework and gain the requisite expertise and experience for the preparation and implementation of long term plans.[13]

The National Revolutionary Development Campaign Central Planning Supreme Council (NRDCCPSC) was established by a proclamation in November 1977 to implement the development campaigns. The Supreme Council was composed of a congress, executive committee, a secretariat, provincial development campaign and planning offices, and *awraja* and *woreda* development campaign and planning congress and executive committees.

The Congress of the Supreme Council was composed among others of high officials in the PMAC, members of the Council of Ministers, Commissioners, chief and deputy provincial administrators, high-ranking military officers, and the chairmen of national mass organizations, viz., the Urban Dwellers' Association, the All Ethiopian Trade Union, the All Ethiopian Peasants Association, Revolutionary Ethiopia Youth Association, and the Revolutionary Ethiopia Women's Association.

On the basis of studies submitted to it by the Executive Committee, the Congress of NRDCCPSC was to have the following powers and duties:

A. To give general guidelines concerning the development campaign

B. To establish the country's development strategy on the basis of which short-, medium- and long-term plans will be prepared

C. To give general policy guidelines concerning the strategy for the mobilization of the country's resources, determine the preparation of investment and consumption in the total resources, determine sectoral allocation of resources and the size of the domestic or foreign loans and technical assistance required during the development campaign and plan period

D. To give general policy guidelines concerning the production, trade, finance, and credit policies of the country

E. To mobilize and coordinate the financial, material, and human resources of the country for the purpose of implementing the development campaign and the plan.[14]

As a strategy for increasing productivity in the agricultural sector, the campaign focused on "cooperativization," conservation, and development of natural resources and settlement. Fertilizers, improved seeds, pesticides, improved farming implements, and technical assistance were made available to agricultural cooperatives and private farmers. During the campaign period, 3,815 agricultural service cooperatives were organized with a membership of 16,845 peasant associations. At the same time 1,275 agricultural producers' cooperatives were established.[15] Measures for combatting deforestation and soil erosion were undertaken with encouraging results. Government afforestation programs were expanded, the participation of the people in forestry development was enhanced, and efforts in the area of land terracing and diversion of rivers were intensified. The government set up two peasant training centers (Agarfa Multipurpose Agricultural School and the Yekatit 25 Cooperative Institute) to ensure a constant supply of trained manpower to be deployed in the effort to increase agricultural productivity.

Another area in agriculture that was given special attention by the campaign was the development of state farms. The total acreage of state farms under cultivation rose from 68,000 in 1977–78 to 221,000 hectares by the end of the campaign year. The total output jumped from 1.5 million quintals to 2.8 million quintals.[16]

As mentioned earlier, the campaign lasted for six years and the success scored in the first two years was remarkable. The 0.9 percent growth rate in GDP recorded on the eve of the campaign took an upward turn in 1978–79 and 1980 with growth rates of 5.2 percent and 5.5 percent, respectively. These increases in output were a result of the measures taken to boost production in the agricultural and industrial sectors and to improve distribution facilities and trade flows. However, the growth trends observed earlier were not sustained for long, as the growth of GDP declined to 3.0 percent, 1.1 percent, −5.3 percent, and −3.7 percent in 1980–81, 1981–82, 1982–83, and 1983–84 respectively.[17] Despite the decline in GDP, the campaigns indeed contributed to the revitalization of the war-torn economy.

In the first place, the campaign programs provided useful experience in the preparation and implementation of economic plans at the national and regional levels. Even though the campaigns proved useful in tackling the problems that they were set up to handle, it eventually became clear that they had to give way to more regular planning. As a result they had to be discontinued. In providing the rationale of the shift from the campaign to regular planning, it is remarked:

> It was in due course realized that valuable as the annual campaign programmes have been their objectives fell short of fully satisfying the long-term development needs of the country which must be addressed if the root causes of economic backwardness are to be tackled. The annual campaign programmes proved effective in mitigating urgent economic and social problems, but it was beyond their scope to effect a structural transformation of the national economy which, of necessity, is a long-term process entailing, among other things, the mobilization of domestic and external resources on a large scale for the implementation of an integrated long-term development programme.[18]

The annual development campaigns were replaced by a ten-year perspective plan (1984–85 to 1993–94), which was approved by the central committee of the newly established Workers Party of Ethiopia (WPE). The perspective plan is divided into three subplans with a time frame of two, three, and five years respectively.

The objectives of the ten-year perspective plan are to:

A. Enhance the productive capacity of the economy by developing and improving the productive forces

B. Based on domestic resources, build a strong national economy with adequate intersectoral linkages

C. To conserve, explore, develop, and rationally utilize the country's national resources

D. To expand and strengthen socialist production relations

E. To gradually raise the material and cultural well-being of the people

F. To ensure balanced development of all the regions in the country.[19]

The strategy devised to realize the objectives of the ten-year perspective plan include self-sufficiency in food production; raising labor productivity; developing a rural infrastructure; enlarging and diversifying export and import substitutes where found economically feasible; developing domestic capability in research, science, and technology; strengthening the country's trade relations and cooperation in economic, scientific and technological areas; developing and strengthening the state institutions, producers' cooperatives, and service cooperatives sectors to guarantee a socialist economy; carrying out settlement programs; improving economic management and organizational capabilities of the state; strengthening the principle of democratic centralism in plan implementation; and increasing the level of saving and investment substantially.[20]

The plan envisages a 6.5 percent growth rate of GDP per annum but because of unforeseen developments (particularly, the drought that set in immediately after the launching of the plan) the performance of the economy has been more modest than what was expected.

Dealing with Drought

Drought and famine have a long history in Ethiopia, dating back to the beginning of the country's history. Written evidence regarding the occurrence of famine in the country goes back to the ninth century. Since then, a number of famines have been recorded.

The famine of 1974 claimed over two hundred thousand lives in Wollo province, and this was one of the immediate causes of the demise of the imperial regime.

One of the immediate measures taken by the government following the revolution was to set up the Relief and Rehabilitation Commission and provide it emergency powers to deal with a wide range of problems associated with the natural calamity. The Commission, which is the only one of its kind in Africa, has proved useful and effective in dealing with relief operations. It has built over time the necessary capacity for predicting and managing the problems of famine. In cases where the problem was beyond its means, it has succeeded in effectively mobilizing resources for relief operations.

In 1983–84, drought struck the country again. Unlike the 1972–74 drought, which affected only a few administrative regions, the 1983–84 drought encompassed twelve out of fourteen regions in the country. This resulted in human sufferings on an unprecedented scale, and could only be contained with massive assistance from the international community.

In order to cope with the natural calamity, the party (WPE) set up a National Committee for Relief and Rehabilitation, which drew up an action plan for combatting the drought and the consequent famine. This action plan had the following objectives:

A. To save millions of human lives through relief work

B. To lay the groundwork for the long-term solutions to the problems of drought and the attendant suffering by means of the various resettlement and rehabilitation schemes

C. To restore the fertility of the soil and correct the imbalance of the ecological system in the drought-affected areas.[21]

The government also took measures intended to save domestic resources. The measures included rationing fuel by allowing private motor vehicle owners to buy eighteen liters of fuel per week, banning driving on Sundays, requiring government employees to wear khaki uniforms and to pay a surtax amounting to one month's salary.

Resettlement as a Strategy to Combat Drought

The recurrence of drought led to a serious examination of long-term solutions to the problem. It was obvious that certain areas of the country having been overutilized for a long period were exposed to environmental depletion. It was further realized that in some parts of the country, there was a wide expanse of virgin land that could easily accommodate many of the people in the overcropped parts of the country.

As a result, the ten-year perspective plan, and other party directives issued from time to time, recognized resettlement and villagization as the cornerstone of the nation's agricultural policy. The government accordingly started to devise strategies for the implementation of the resettlement policy.

Resettlement is not a new phenomenon in the country. There were some resettlement attempts by the government and voluntary agencies prior to the 1974 revolution. By 1974, some twenty thousand families, mostly retired soldiers and unemployed persons, were settled in the southern and western parts of the country.[22]

Following the revolution and the subsequent enactment of the rural land proclamation, a settlement authority was established under the ministry of agriculture. In the first few years of its existence, the authority is reported to have settled some twelve thousand families, 43 percent of whom were from the urban unemployed and 41 percent peasants and nomads.[23] Other government authorities like the Relief and Rehabilitation Commission and the Awash Valley Authority were involved in settlement schemes. In 1979 the settlement authority was dissolved and its responsibilities were transferred to the Relief and Rehabilitation Commission (RRC).

Following the defeat of the invading Somali forces, there were attempts by the government to settle the displaced dwellers, and this provided a major impetus for the expansion of RRC resettlement activities. By 1980, RRC had over four hundred centers in the Bale region. By 1983, RRC was running over eighty settlement sites containing about two hundred thousand people.[24] Despite the gradual increase in resettlement activities, the number of people resettled from the famine-prone areas was not that significant, amounting to less than 1 percent.[25]

However, the ten-year perspective plan that considers resettlement as a strategy for agricultural development, envisages the resettlement by 1994 of some eight hundred thousand families, involving some four million people.[26] Even though the government had planned to implement the resettlement schemes in a gradual manner, the 1984 famine disaster necessitated an emergency settlement of some three hundred thousand people in a year.[27]

According to the Head of State, Comrade Mengistu, the objective of the program is to resettle the section of the population who:

A. Have been repeatedly hit by recurrent drought, particularly in the north

B. Live on land whose fertility has been totally destroyed as a result of extremely backward agricultural practices

C. Because of the high density of population, do not have enough land to work on and need to move to fertile parts of the country where they can have enough land to cultivate and build decent lives for themselves.[28]

The logistics of the resettlement as well as the resource requirements were indeed massive. According to Clarke:

> The resources for the settlement programme were to come from the redirection of existing funds, personnel and equipment from various government departments and organizations, from voluntary contributions and labour by people right across Ethiopia, from additional funds raised through the special revenue measures that had been introduced to meet the famine emergency and finally from material, transport and other assistance given by foreign countries. Over 3,400 civil servants were reassigned from their normal duties to work on the

immense organizational task that the emergency resettlement programme entailed, along with hundreds of WPE workers and officials.[29]

In addition to the government's efforts, mass organizations were mobilized for the relief and rehabilitation activities. The mass organizations collected money and materials for the resettlement effort, provided volunteers to assist in program implementation, and entertained the settlers at their rest stops. The Revolutionary Ethiopian Youth Association (REYA), for example, mobilized twenty thousand volunteers up to August 1985 to support the efforts of local volunteers and government workers.[30]

The outcome of all these measures was the construction of:

> 200,000 rudimentary buildings, all from locally available materials (these are huts and *tukulus* of various types and sizes both for residential and common service purposes such as stores, clinics, meeting halls and offices); 1,500 kilometers of road had been laid; 285 wells had been dug and 273 springs cleared; and more than 84,000 hectares of land had been cleared for cultivation.[31]

The achievement, given the haste with which it was undertaken, was indeed remarkable. But it was by no means a completed task. Nor was it easy to accomplish. As John Clarke puts it:

> Much of the terrain surrounding the village sites is still virgin bush and forest; the land that had been cleared for cultivation still needed to be planted and worked in order to produce a crop; and the villages themselves consisted of only extremely rudimentary buildings. The establishment of viable independent settlements with decent living conditions and sufficient agricultural production would still take a great deal more work both on the land around the site and within the villages themselves.[32]

The movement of large numbers of people (most of them victims of malnutrition and persons exhausted by journeys over long distances) is likely to be fraught with all kinds of problems, particularly, health problems. The government, however, had mobilized health personnel to the different sites. By November 1985 there were eighty-five health stations, ten health centers, and five hospitals in the resettlement areas with a total staff of over six hundred full-time personnel, both Ethiopian and foreign.[33]

The health centers undertook antimalarial campaigns involving the screening of settlers as they arrived and the provision of antimalarial drugs (both curative and preventive). According to Clarke,

> In the region of Wellega, Illubabour, Gojjam, and Keffa, at the peak breeding time of the mosquito in September and October 1985, the incidence of malaria across these areas was only 0.7 per cent, which was

much higher than the normal level of 0.1 per cent, but still a very low figure and, given the circumstances, a great achievement for the Ethiopian Ministry of Health.[34]

In addition to the measures taken against malaria, the Ministry of Health also took steps to immunize the settlers against a range of communicable diseases, particularly measles, meningitis, and yellow fever. Hand in hand with these measures, community health units engaged in teaching health education, particularly, basic sanitation and hygiene, the traditional skills of birth attendance, and the promotion of child vaccination.

Since the whole objective of the resettlement was to make the settlers self-sufficient by enabling them to work on productive land, the government had to supply the necessary agricultural inputs that would support these efforts. According to one report, between November 1984 and August 1985,

> 23 tonnes of seed, 19,000 plough oxen and 1.2 million hand tools were supplied to resettlers and this was in addition to the several hundred tractors from the state farms operating in the resettlement areas.[35]

The Ministry of Agriculture dispatched over five-hundred agricultural workers to the resettlement areas to aid the development of production, to give advice on soil type, fertilizer, ploughing, irrigation, and new types of crops suited to the environment.

By the end of the first year of the emergency resettlement program, seventy-five thousand hectares were cultivated out of the eighty-one thousand hectares cleared.[36]

> It is true that, even in overall terms, it was not without its problems, and it failed, perhaps inevitably, to fulfill all the plans and ideal models that the Government had initially set out to achieve. Although the target for resettlement in the first 12 months had been 300,000 families in fact only 203,000 were actually moved, consisting of 587,785 people—well short of the figure of well over a million people which the Government had been hoping for. It was also true that many health problems among the resettlers had not been solved and agricultural production was not yet at the level of self-sufficiency in most new settlements. Nevertheless, over half a million people had been moved out of the famine areas, easing both the burden on the relief agencies there and the pressure on the environment. Also, they had been settled in areas where they were already beginning to produce for themselves and where they had the potential in the near future not only to become self-sufficient but to actually produce surpluses that would help others in the country as well as themselves.[37]

The settlement program has provoked much criticism from abroad. The Western governments and the media, which perceive the measures taken by the government as moves in the direction of accelerating the socialization of agriculture, were harsh in their criticisms. In addition, there was the campaign by the liberation fronts in Tigray and Eritrea, who branded the resettlement schemes as a deliberate policy of depopulating the area in which they had been operating, depriving them of a base for recruitment. Such criticisms were echoed by groups supporting the cause of the liberation fronts. As a result, the program has been branded by some as "a policy of genocide, involving oppression and enslavement of millions of people and, indeed, the deaths of a great many."[37a] The organization, Medicine sans frontières, has gone so far as to say, "The main problem in Ethiopia is that people are dying not from famine but from resettlement."[38] The critics of the resettlement have not only accused the government of forcing the people to move and of doing little to abate the appalling conditions on their journey, but also of imprisoning them in armed camps within the resettlement areas, which are themselves in regions totally unsuitable for agricultural development.[39]

The irony of this accusation lies in the fact that the United States government, which is one of the harshest critics of the resettlement program in the north had, before the revolution, drawn up plans through the USAID for the resettlement of three million people from northern Ethiopia to fertile, unpopulated areas of the south and west. As Michael Simons puts it "that was in the days of Haile Selassie. Now that Ethiopia has an avowedly socialist government, the USAID has changed its tune."[40] The American assault on the settlement schemes was soon followed by similar opposition from its allies, Britain and West Germany.

Villagization as a Policy Response

Villagization, like resettlement, is a strategy devised by the WPE and the revolutionary government to enable the peasants to benefit from modern methods of agriculture and improved social services. More than 85 percent of the Ethiopian people live in rural areas where settlements are scattered. The peasants live in isolated and inaccessible homesteads and are consequently deprived of basic social services. The traditional settlement pattern is partly blamed for the ecological imbalances repeatedly experienced in the country. In an effort to combat the ecological imbalance and protect the peasants from continuous harassment by natural calamities, the government adopted villagization as one of its strategies.

> Villagization (is) a multipurpose scheme the central aim of which is to introduce a coherent land use or land recovery programme through concentrated and collective efforts. The aims of the villagization programme are fairly simple—to move people into villages where it will be possible to provide them with basic essential services ranging from

medical care and educational facilities to access roads and clean water.[41]

The overall aims and objectives of the villagization programs are:

1. To ensure that basic infrastructural facilities and services are provided for the enhancement of the livelihood and socioeconomic upliftment of the rural masses

2. To enable the rural population to develop the tradition of "familihood," in other words, sense of community self-help and coordinated efforts toward the solution of rural problems

3. To ensure that the rural population, in close cooperation and collaboration with local organs entrusted with the tasks of education and agitation, raises the level of its consciousness and discharges, to the full, its role in the nation's socioeconomic life

4. To provide the means for enabling the rural masses, more particularly the peasantry, to safeguard local peace and security as well as to protect their own property

5. To help arrest the galloping tendency in the unwise use of the nation's valuable natural resources and make judicious utilization of the same

6. To create conditions whereby expert advice and the benefits of latest technology to promote agricultural productivity are brought within easy access of the peasantry with a view to improving its livelihood

7. To create the means whereby the rural population has maximum access to basic infrastructural services like roads, irrigation facilities, and dams, which are vital for transforming the quality of rural life, but which, in the present stage of economic underdevelopment, cannot possibly be created through individual means and resources

8. To create the conditions whereby the peasantry has an opportunity to channel its exploitation free produce to service cooperatives and obtain industrial products and commodities needed to uplift its livelihood and thereby narrow the current imbalance in urban-rural exchange of goods and services.[42]

To oversee the realization of the objectives, the government set up the national villagization coordinating committee (NVCC) to plan at the national level. Among its other tasks are the overseeing of the preparation of standard designs for villagization procedures in respect of cooperatives and infrastructure facilities. They are also entrusted with the responsibility for overseeing the work of the provincial villagization coordinating committee.

The NVCC comprises the Deputy Chairman of the Council of Ministers as Chairman (now the Prime Minister); Deputy Chairman of the National Committee for Central Planning, second Deputy Chairman; the Ministers of Construction, Agriculture, Interior, Education, Health, Mining and Energy Resource, Domestic Trade, Housing and Urban Development; the Commissioner of the National Water Resources Development Commission; and the Chairmen of the Ethiopian Peasants Association, Ethiopian Trade Union, Revolutionary Ethiopia Youth Association, and Revolutionary Ethiopia Women Association.

The NVCC stretches right down to the *kebele* peasant association (PAS).

> At both the provincial and district levels, the coordinating committee takes appropriate steps to ensure that the villagization programme is conducted voluntarily and that it enjoys the full confidence of the local community. They also prepare plans for local initiatives and follow up their execution, oversee local party, government and management involvement and participation in the villagization drive.[43]

By September 1986, 53 out of the 102 provinces had been reached through the villagization program. This covers 4,299 *kebeles* making up a total of 5,164 villages. These villages have 3,899,634 dwellers.[44] A work program devised by the NVCC for 1986–89 envisages the construction of the following facilities under the auspices of the Ministry of Agriculture:

- 2,420 kilograms of feeder roads
- 1,728 self-help grain silos
- 124 fruit and vegetable warehouses
- 939 medium-sized grain stores
- 939 medium-sized potato storage facilities
- Clean water distribution in 855 villages
- Workshops in 380 villages
- Grain mills in 370 villages
- Solar pumps in 155 villages and air pumps in 47 villages
- Biogas in 255 villages
- Electrification of 74 villages.

Likewise, the plan provides for the supply of potable water to 190 villages during the fiscal year, 325 during the second, and 500 during the third year.[45]

Like resettlement, the villagization program drew much criticism and uproar from abroad. Western critics have branded the program as a violation of human rights and forced collectivization. Some have also tried to associate the villagization program with socialism as a whole. In replying to questions directed at him by a group of editors from the American magazine, *Time*, Comrade Mengistu, the Head of State, is reported to have categorically denied the allegation made about forced collectivization by stressing that "the choice and right of peasants who move to villages for individual or cooperative farming is absolutely free and guaranteed."[46] On the attempt to link villagization to socialism, the Head of State also pointed out that "villages exist in all societies the world over but that it does not follow that where there are villages there is also socialism, or that those who build socialism necessarily build villages."

He underscored that the building of socialism takes more than villagization to be effective. He pointed out that it takes more than villages to bring together the whole complex of factors, above all, the level of consciousness of the people that go into the movement which makes the building of socialism possible.[47]

INCREASING AGRICULTURAL PRODUCTION THROUGH *WOREDAS*

Ethiopia is divided into 570 *woredas* (districts). These fall in the different agricultural zones and have different fertility potentials. However, the country's limited resources have not enabled the government to provide farmers with all the inputs they need to increase production. The attempt to distribute evenly among the *Awrajas* whatever limited inputs it has at its disposal has resulted in spreading its inputs thin. Following the recent famine, the Ministry of Agriculture, on the basis of the directives given to it by Central Committee of WPE has devised a new strategy for increasing agricultural production by concentrating its efforts and resources in 148 surplus-producing *woredas*. The selected *woredas* will benefit from enhanced extension services and supply of inputs. The number of *woredas* covered is supposed to eventually reach three-hundred. Unlike the four to five extension workers assigned to each *woreda* prior to the implementation of this new strategy, the surplus *woredas* now have 18 to 25 extension workers. It is hoped that through the allocation of extension workers and other required inputs, the surplus *woredas* will ultimately increase their agricultural production. In view of the fact that this strategy has only been put into effect recently, it is too early to assess its impact. But informed sources believe that it has a fair chance of succeeding in areas with normal rainfall.

REINVIGORATING THE ECONOMY: THE CONTENDING VIEWS

From the foregoing discussion, it is clear that the performance of the Ethiopian economy was not up to the desired level. The economy does not seem to show any signs of coming out of the stagnation it has been in for the last few years. What strategy to follow to increase production in the agricultural sector, the mainstay of the economy, has been a subject of debate. Western governments and donors, who are the major sources of the external funding required by this sector, believe that the only way to increase productivity in the agricultural sector is to concentrate on private smallholder agriculture. On the other hand, Ethiopia has not found the smallholder strategy appealing in light of its commitment to a socialist society. The disagreements over policies as to how best to invigorate the agricultural sector in particular, and the economy in general, have reduced external resource to a trickle. Pressure is being exerted on the Ethiopian government, by the World Bank and other western donor countries, for the introduction of structural adjustment.

The advocates of the private smallholder agriculture argue that with the right price incentives, and the support of a progressive rural structure based on research, extension and market linkages, smallholders can dramatically increase their output. It is argued that:

> The increase in rural incomes will stimulate employment in small towns and urban centers that sell goods and services to rural producers. The small holder model is based on a well functioning reliable private sector and good price incentives.[48]

Those who consider the smallholder strategy as a way out of stagnation for the agricultural sector in Ethiopia base their argument on the fact that Ethiopia's agricultural sector is dominated by smallholders. The smallholders are estimated to constitute 80 percent of the rural population and they work 94 percent of the land and produce 50 percent of the national agricultural output.[49]

Advocates of the small farmer approach further argue that the policy currently pursued by the government is lowering the farmer's incentives to produce. Cohen and Issaksson summarize the criticisms directed at the government's policies:

> Foremost among these policies are unfavourable input output price ratios, low producer prices, burdensome AMC quotas, and restrictions on private grain traders operating more efficiently than the AMC and offering higher price to farmers. Further, they argue that the government has promoted PCs and state farms to the detriment of the

largest peasant sectors largely by focussing extension agents time on PC formation and support, giving PC and state farms priority over improved seeds, fertilizers and credit, and channeling limited supportive government investments in agriculture outside the peasant sector.[50]

Western donors like the World Bank and SIDA, unhappy with the government's reluctance to heed their advice (to concentrate on the smallholder development model), have refrained from assisting with the present Agriculture Development Extension Programme (ADEP). The program was designed to support the continuation of the minimum package program and proposed "to extend to the peasant sector a scaled down ARDU programme based on intensified agricultural research and the training and visit system developed in the World Bank."[51] Four zonal projects covering eight regions were to be established to promote increased smallholder farm production and resource conservation. In order to avail the resources required for the sector, the World Bank set forth conditions that ought to be met by the government. It called for:

1. Increasing the price paid to farmers to a level offsetting the rise in input costs and promoting the profitability of agriculture

2. Narrowing the role of the AMC to procurement only to ensure urban supply and provide food security

3. Ending government restrictions that hamper private traders while maintaining regulations that promote fair consumer prices

4. Rationalizing the distribution of inputs and credit so that they reach smallholders on a timely basis in the quantities needed and locating it in organizations like service cooperatives that are accountable to peasants

5. Rebuilding the faltering agricultural research system and improving its capacity to breed and upgrade high-yielding seed varieties tailored to specific areas

6. Upgrading training of extension agents and improving their salaries and terms of service

7. Ending the practice of using extension agents for mobilizing PCs and collecting funds for government campaigns.[52]

The World Bank has also called for a number of policy measures which presumably would stimulate the economy in general. The policy recommendations made by the World Bank include:

- A substantial adjustment in the exchange rate to bring it in line with the scarcity value of foreign exchange
- Restoring an open market for grain within and between all regions by removing interregional barriers to, and taxes on, the movement of grain by private traders
- Restricting AMC's operations to its demonstrated capacity in terms of its transport, storage, staff, and management resources
- Increasing AMC's procurement prices to a level which would provide incentives for the adoption of technical packages, based on the import parity prices of each comparable crop, at the shadow exchange rate
- Providing greater autonomy to industrial public enterprises managers, including in the pricing of commodities to reflect supply and demand conditions, and encouraging a wider use of project evaluation criteria used by the DPSA
- Encouraging the growth of small-scale private industry by improving the investment and overall business environment by reducing government regulations and increasing accessibility of entrepreneurs to production inputs, including foreign exchange and credit
- Improving domestic resource mobilization by strengthening the collection mechanism for agricultural taxes, converting specific taxes to ad valorem taxes, reducing nondevelopmental related 67 percent recurrent expenditure, taking measures to encourage farmer savings in the rural areas, and strengthening incentives to encourage private savings and investment in the modern sector
- Preparation of a public investment program
- Improving external resource mobilization through an improved policy framework to attract donor-financed projects, improving the government's aid-coordinating and planning mechanisms, and strengthening institutional mechanisms for promoting foreign investment.[53]

The other donor agency associated with PADEP is SIDA. For reasons that are similar to those of the World Bank, SIDA expressed reluctance to support PADEP as planned. According to Cohen and Issaksson:

> The Swedes declared it impossible to disregard the national policy context any longer, even in a project specific context. Specifically, the SIDA delegation told the government that its policies of villagization,

suppression of private grain trade, maintenance of artificially low agricultural prices and subsidization of producer cooperatives were difficult to justify given the clear ARDU evidence on the agricultural potential of the SEAD zone, the project generated data on the higher productivity achieved on small-holder land, the inappropriateness of mechanized production on group farms, and the severe food shortages facing the country.[54]

The Ethiopian government thus seems to be under pressure to abandon some of its socialist policies, but this has only increased its resolve to pursue its avowed goal. The government has confronted its critics with the argument that the ideological factor has been exaggerated and that its policies were based mainly on Ethiopia's national interest.

In responding to the accusation that the Ethiopian government is spending too much on the state farms, the government argues that the state farms constitute less than 2 percent of the cultivated land, but account for 3 percent of the total agricultural output. The acreage under state farms is expected to grow to 5 percent at the end of the ten-year plan period. While admitting that the level of investment on each farm is quite high compared to those on small farms, the government argues that "the level of investment in the few state farms that exist (there are not more than 25) would make only a marginal impact if distributed among several million peasant farmers."[55] The state farms are supposed to supply export products like coffee, raw material for industry like leather, and food crops for urban dwellers. John Clarke summarizes the Ethiopian point of view for preferring state farms as a long-term strategy for increasing agricultural production:

> The majority of peasant farms in Ethiopia are extremely small (almost all are below two hectares) and many without even the benefit of a pair of plough oxen. The potential to develop agricultural production on such peasant farms is, inevitably, limited with the peasants simply lacking the resources for any substantial investment in inputs and improvements to boost yields. The Ethiopian authorities commitment to state farms was not simply a matter of political ideology, it was also due to a pragmatic assessment of the economic value of such a farm to the development of the country's agriculture.[56]

Another area of policy disagreement with western donor agencies has been "cooperativization." This is an area that involves less than one hundred thousand out of more than seven million peasant farmers in the country. The donors have little quarrel with service cooperatives which are managed mainly by individual peasant producers. But the producer cooperatives, which represent socialist ownership, have been the target of criticism.

Clarke, in addressing some of the criticisms directed to producers' cooperatives, argues as follows:

> While it is undoubtedly true that the Ethiopian Government sees the development of state farms and producer co-operatives as important elements in their policy of socialisation of agricultural production, it would be quite wrong to attribute this to an ideological dogmatism blind to economic realities. The economic development of agricultural production is the main priority of the Ethiopian Government and they see both co-ops and state farms as important elements in this strategy. They believe that it is through large economic units able to use investment effectively that the future of agriculture must lie.[57]

The government has also been criticized for its pricing policy of agricultural products and the measures it took in some provinces in eliminating private trade. The lack of growth in the agricultural sector has been attributed to lack of incentives for the farmers. The Ethiopian government has disputed the argument that lack of incentives is discouraging food production. The government policy required the peasants to sell 30 percent of their produce to the Agricultural Marketing Corporation at a fixed price which sometimes could be much lower than what the farmer could have obtained in the market. While conceding that such policies could have some disincentive effects, the government argues that there are many other more fundamental problems limiting agricultural production and even with price incentives, it doubts whether a substantial increase in production could be achieved.[58]

In justifying some of the measures taken to restrict the activities of private merchants, the government argues:

> The fact is that in a system of private trade it is not the peasants who benefit but the merchants. The individual peasant has no ability to travel to seek out the best price. Indeed the peasant often has to pledge his harvest to merchants before it has even been reaped in order to meet debts.[59]

THE NET EFFECTS OF ECONOMIC PROBLEMS AND POLICY RESPONSES

From the foregoing discussion, it is clear that the performance of the Ethiopian economy leaves much to be desired. The last three years have been trying moments for the country as a whole. A revolution that did away with the old order and was accompanied by political upheaval, continuing secessionist movements that put a lot of pressure on the country's limited resources, a full-fledged war with Somalia that was prosecuted at a huge cost (human and material), two devastating droughts, all these must have contributed to the slow growth of the economy.

The government has tried to respond to the economic crisis with policy measures that it considered appropriate. No doubt, the measures opted for have ideological implications. The country, having committed itself to a socialist path of development has ensured that whatever measures were taken to invigorate the economy were also consistent with its long-term political goals. This point of view is well articulated by the Head of State when he remarked:

> When we planned our country's economic development, we had the strategic objective of our Revolution in mind. It was not planned for economic development (to be) solely an end in itself. . . . There are some who have forgotten that the sole basis of our revolutionary struggle was the ideology and politics which we follow . . . there are some who tend to neglect political and ideological issues, taking the priority we have given to economic reconstruction as a reason.[60]

The pressures for structuring the economy as reflected in the policy proposals by the World Bank have not been heeded. The locally initiated solutions to the problems faced by the country have provided some relief but what their long-term effects will be is difficult to speculate. The various policy measures taken to deal with the economic changes like the development campaigns, settlement, and villagization, have required immense human and financial resources. The country's ability to mobilize the peasants, youth, and women, has, however, lessened the burden on the government.

The supreme Planning Council established in 1979 to revitalize the economy was staffed with high-level manpower by transferring economists and other professionals of "significance" to this economic command center. How the deployment of the scarce high-level manpower in such an organization affected the operation of other agencies has not been properly investigated, but no doubt, the impact must have been serious.

In spite of the recurring economic problems, a decline in the size of the bureaucracy has not been witnessed. The civil service jumped from 93,965 employees on the eve of the revolution to 200,269 in 1986—a 213.2 percent growth.[61] Employment in the public industrial sector likewise jumped from 47,000 in 1974, to 81,430 in 1986, an increase of 173.2 percent.[62]

With the government expanding its hold over the economy through the takeover of various enterprises formerly in the hands of private owners, the growth in the bureaucracy was inevitable. With the exception of the first three years after the revolution, when an austerity budget was in force and there was a freeze on employment, the civil service has continued to expand.

The establishment of the People's Democratic Republic of Ethiopia in September 1987 has also resulted in the setting up of more institutions. The administrative regions have been increased from fourteen to twenty-nine, including the five autonomous regions. This will require additional manpower to fill the various positions. Even though ministries have been merged and commissions have been reduced in number, the net savings had been one ministry and three commissions. At the same time, many new authorities have been created. This is an indication of the government's determination to organize itself in a manner that would make it possible to deal with its socialization objectives. The current economic problems do not seem to put any pressure toward the reduction of the size of the bureaucracy. How much longer the bureaucracy can expand in the face of the present economic problems is hard to tell.

Side by side with the expansion measures, the government has introduced a number of austerity measures. In line with its declared policy of narrowing the income gap between the highest and lowest public servants, it imposed a freeze on salary increases immediately after the revolution. Only employees who earn 347 birr per month were allowed to get salary increments, and these they are entitled to, by law, every two years. This figure was later raised to 600 birr. The highest salary in the public service is 1,500 birr, and that is the salary of a minister. Since the freeze came into force thirteen years ago, the middle- and high-level employees have not had any salary increases. The freeze has continued even though the cost of living index has been steadily rising. For example, the retail price index of Addis Ababa, taking 1963 as a base year, has risen from 170.1 in 1967–68 to 459.4 in 1978–79.[63] Such a prolonged freeze in the face of the rising cost of living can easily affect the morale and motivation of middle- and high-level civil servants with obvious implications for efficiency. As it stands now, the higher level incentives consist essentially of prospects for promotion.

The diminishing foreign exchange earning capacity is likely to affect the importation of input, machinery, and spare parts urgently required in the different developmental fields. Foreign exchange constraints could result in the lack of resources for replacement and rehabilitation of old, and worn-out equipment in the public enterprises. Such a situation could easily lead to a serious undercapitalization in some enterprises. Even though the management of its foreign exchange has won praise, that by itself will not get the country far, unless the foreign exchange earning capacity is adequately enhanced. The shortage of foreign exchange had become so serious that a high-powered political committee is now involved in its management and allocation. In addition, a study is underway to look into measures that could be taken to promote foreign trade and thereby increase the foreign exchange earning capacity.

Even though the fiscal and monetary management is generally regarded as conservative and prudent, there has nevertheless been a steady growth of expenditure with revenue lagging behind. The overall deficit reached a peak in 1982–83 with a figure of -1305.7 million birr. By 1984–85 the deficit had dropped to -802.1 million birr or -8.1 percent of GDP.[64]

It has been mentioned earlier that the scope for savings is narrowing increasingly and prospects for substantial improvement in this regard do not appear encouraging. With limited resources for investment, immediate economic recovery and growth do not look probable.

One need not forget that the country is still facing armed confrontation from secessionist forces, and that the struggle with drought is far from over. Under these circumstances, the government would be forced to divert a substantial percentage of its meager resources to the war effort and other nondevelopmental areas.

Various pressures for structural adjustments exerted by the World Bank and other donors have been resisted. However, with heavy dependence on external resources for investment, it is not clear how much longer the country can fend off the pressures for structural adjustment reform.

It is too early to judge the impact of the strategies pursued by the government to boost agricultural production. Resettlement and villagization have come under severe criticism by westerners, but that has not persuaded the government to abandon its policies.

Although the obstacles to immediate economic recovery appear formidable, the future may not be that bleak, as one report puts it:

> The country is faced with a challenging set of obstacles to development, and it has experienced over the past decade a number of severe "shocks," including the devastating drought of 1984–85. Yet more so than many countries, Ethiopia has some comparative advantages stemming from its size, natural resources, location, and its competent civil service. Its potentialities for economic development are therefore considerable. Moreover, its economic management has in certain respects been exemplary. For example, owing largely to its traditionally conservative and prudent monetary management, Ethiopia has generally avoided heavily bank-financed deficit spending and consequent inflation. The country's external debt burden has so far been kept within manageable bounds, and in (favorable) contrast to the experience of many African countries, its rates of capacity utilization in industry have been quite high. Its record of project implementation has been relatively good, and its technocrats and civil servants have a reputation for honesty, dedication and competence. These are indeed important strengths and successes of economic management to build upon.[65]

NOTES

1. Central Statistical Office, People's Democratic Republic of Ethiopia, *Facts and Figures*, 1987, 22.

2. The World Bank, *Ethiopian Recent Economic Developments and Prospects for Recovery and Growth*, Report no. 5929-ET, 25 February 1987, 13.

3. *Ibid.*, 15.

4. *Ibid.*, 23.

5. *Ibid.*, 15.

6. *Ibid.*, 17.

7. The World Bank, *Ethiopian Recent Economic Developments and Future Prospects*, Report no. 4683a-ET, 31 May 1984, 3.

8. *Ibid.*, 5.

9. *Ibid.*, 4.

10. The World Bank, Report no. 5929-ET, *op. cit.*, 19.

11. *Ibid.*

12. *Ibid.*, 17.

13. Workers' Party of Ethiopia, *Guideline on the Economic and Social Development of Ethiopia (1984/85–1993/94)*, Draft, Unofficial Translation, Addis Ababa, September 1984, 5.

14. Provisional Administrative Council, Proclamation no. 156 of 1976, National Revolutionary Development Campaign and Central Planning Supreme Council Establishment Proclamation, *Negarit Gazeta*, no. 4 (29 October 1987): 61–62.

15. Workers' Party of Ethiopia, *op. cit.*, 7.

16. *Ibid.*, 8.

17. The World Bank, Report no. 5929-ET, *op. cit.*

18. The Relief and Rehabilitation Commission, *The Challenges of Drought: Ethiopia's Decade of Struggle in Relief and Rehabilitation* (Addis Ababa: The Relief and Rehabilitation Commission, 1985), 51.

19. Workers' Party of Ethiopia, *op. cit.*, see 20–21.

20. See *ibid.*, 22–24.

21. The Relief and Rehabilitation Commission, *op. cit.*, 46.

22. John Clarke, *Resettlement and Rehabilitation, Ethiopia's Campaign Against Famine* (London: Harney & Jones, n.d.), 44.

23. *Ibid.*

24. See *ibid.*, 45.

25. See *ibid.*

26. *Ibid.*, 46.

27. *Ibid.*

28. National Villagization Co-ordinating Committee, Mender, Addis Ababa, May 1987, 27.

29. John Clarke, *op. cit.*, 51.

30. *Ibid.*, 61.

31. *Ibid.*

32. *Ibid.*, 61–62.

33. *Ibid.*, 62.

34. *Ibid.*, 67.

35. *Ibid.*, 68.

36. *Ibid.*, 69.

37. *Ibid.*, 70.

37a. *Ibid.*

38. *Ibid.*, 71.

39. *Ibid.*

40. *Ibid.*, 153.

41. National Villagization Co-ordinating Committee, *op. cit.*, 20.

42. *Ibid.*, 14.

43. *Ibid.*, 17.

44. *Ibid.*, 30.

45. *Ibid.*, 30–31.

46. *Ibid.*, 23.

47. *Ibid.*, 24.

48. John M. Cohen and Nils-Ivar Issaksson, *Villagization in the Arsi Region of Ethiopia*, Report Prepared by SIDA Consultants to the Ethiopio-Swedish Mission of Villagization in Arsi Region, 1–14 December 1986 (Uppsala: Swedish University of Agricultural Sciences, International Rural Development Centre, February 1987), see 117.

49. *Ibid.*

50. *Ibid.*, 117–18.

51. *Ibid.*, 120.

52. *Ibid.*, 121.

53. The World Bank, Report no. 5929-ET, *op. cit.*, 72–73.

54. Cohen and Issaksson, *op. cit.*, 122.

55. John Clarke, *op. cit.*, 132.

56. *Ibid.*, 133.
57. *Ibid.*, 135–36.
58. *Ibid.*, 136.
59. *Ibid.*, 137.
60. Cohen and Issaksson, *op. cit.*, 123.
61. See *Yemengist Seratengotch Mesriabetoch Astedadr* Commission (in Amharic) 1954–79 (Addis Ababa: Tahasas, 1979), 33.
62. Central Statistical Office, *op. cit.*, 52.
63. *Ibid.*, 104.
64. The World Bank, Report no. 5929-ET, *op. cit.*, 25.
65. *loc. cit.*

CHAPTER TEN

The Adaptation of Government to Economic Change: The Case of Senegal

Amadou Sadio

INTRODUCTION

Since the mid-seventies and the beginning of the eighties, the Senegalese government has become conscious of the necessity to undertake important measures to restructure its economy for a quick and significant recovery from the persistent crisis.

The government's General Policy Statement, presented to the Consultative Group Meeting in December 1984, made clear that the underlying causes of the country's economic crisis were structural and not temporary. These causes were:

A. An unstable international economic environment

B. A limited and increasingly fragile resource base to support agricultural development and the needs of a growing population

C. The inability of any sector of the economy to generate enough savings for investment.

In the diagnosis leading to the working out of the medium- and long-term adjustment program, it was noted that "the Senegalese economy remained fundamentally weak, vulnerable, with precarious government finances, an overextended public sector, substantial domestic arrears and an unsustainably large external current account deficit."

Following the first Stabilisation Programme (1979–81) and the economic and financial recovery plan of 1981, the adjustment process has taken a wider scale since 1984.

By the time the Consultative Group Meeting took place in December 1984, the government had concluded that the first adjustment efforts (1979–83) had been insufficient and needed to be intensified and sustained over a much longer period. The government therefore set a target of 1990 as the year when the following objectives ought to be accomplished:

A. Resolving the external debt problem and paying off the government's large domestic arrears

B. Eliminating the overall deficit on the government's budget

C. Building up a much more efficient public investment program, concentrated on rehabilitation and expansion of key public services and giving a freer rein to private sector activities by combined measures on administrative regulations, pricing, promoting competitive production, and export incentives for manufacturers.

The medium- and long-term adjustment is therefore an overall plan with sector strategies for 1985–93. Its first phase has been worked out during 1985 and has been supported by the World Bank's structural adjustment credit approved in early 1986.

THE MEDIUM- AND LONG-TERM ADJUSTMENT PROGRAM: A GENERAL REVIEW OF ITS OBJECTIVES AND SECTORAL POLICIES STRATEGIES

Taking account of the policy orientations and specific measures incorporated in Africa's Priority Programme for Economic Recovery (APPER) and the United Nations Programme of Action for African Economic Recovery (UN-PAAERD), Senegal's adjustment policy seeks to:

A. Lay the foundation of the economic recovery, through a coherent and well-planned process of a medium- and long-term policy, maximizing the country's production potential, while eliminating all obstacles to optimum resource allocation and higher performance from the factors of production

B. Create a new environment for growth in production depending on mechanisms of training and income distribution that encourage production, reward individual and private initiatives, and lessen regional disparities.

These objectives have led the Senegalese government to implement sectoral strategies to achieve overall recovery in production and employment.

Sector Strategies

Achieving recovery in economic activities and employment is a key objective of the adjustment policy. In that respect, new policy instruments to revitalize supply in the agricultural and industrial areas were put into effect in 1985 and 1986. In addition, in order to make such policies more effective, the government has introduced a set of supporting measures that focus on the reorganization of the commercial and banking sectors and a reformulation of employment policy.

Senegal possesses a large agricultural sector providing employment for nearly two-thirds of its population and representing 20 percent of the gross domestic product (GDP). The New Agricultural Policy (NAP), which the government is implementing within the framework of its adjustment efforts, aims at increasing production and income by emphasizing productivity based on farmer accountability, and by limiting the government's role to more effective supervision.

As such, the NAP calls for:

- A reorganization of the rural areas
- A redefinition of the role of the extension agencies, most of them being public enterprises
- An introduction of a "grains policy"
- Formulation of a policy on management and distribution of the factors of production
- An implementation of a policy of price incentive
- Measures for protection of the natural environment

As a matter of fact, the new agricultural policy aims to change radically the institutional environment, and to promote diversification of the Senegalese economy. As part of this new policy, Senegal is expected to achieve food self-sufficiency by the year 2000. Other objectives are:

- Stabilization of rice imports
- Organization of market for local grains
- Deregulation of the distribution and marketing of inputs and factors of production (seeds, fertilizers, plant health products, and farm equipment)
- Limitation of the role of the extension agents to providing services for rural groups, consulting on community development, and functional literacy training
- Creation of a fund to enable personnel, dismissed from their jobs as a result of the New Industrial Policy, to be retrained in different skill areas. At the same time, a Reintegration Fund is created to help personnel declared redundant in the other sectors to estab-

lish their own businesses. This Fund will gradually be made available to civil servants of a certain age and experience leaving their jobs in the public service.

Other Key Sectors

Besides emphasizing agriculture and industry, the adjustment program focuses on tourism and fisheries, two sectors that are very important for their potential. The fisheries sector growth rate projected for 1987–92 is 4 percent a year, confirming its importance to economic growth in the country. The main objectives in this subsector are supposed to bring forth, by combined measures, the development of a nonindustrial fishery, and high productivity of an industrial fishery through a modernization of the processing facilities. As for tourism, a promotion campaign is to be launched to make the sector contribute more significantly to increase economic activities and employment.

Trade has also been a concern of the adjustment program. Two major steps are expected to foster better distribution of industrial products and create a freer environment. These steps consist of a deregulation of distribution channels as well as a deregulation of prices.

Reform of the banking system is also part of the adjustment policy. The government is fully conscious of the fact that a recovery in production cannot be achieved without a restructured banking system able to infuse new vitality into the economy. The government therefore decided to recycle a major proportion of available resources through the banking system. The development of savings incentives, and implementation of a judicious credit policy geared to the financing of economic growth, are the main tasks assigned to the banking system.

Employment Promotion Policy

The ongoing crisis has had a devastating effect on employment: growing unemployment and underemployment have characterized the labor market. This situation has led the government to take direct action to increase employment by setting up integration and reintegration funds in the productive sector for individuals who have been declared redundant. The long-term solution to the problem of unemployment lies in a resurgence of activity among Senegalese enterprises. To this end, the government decided to simplify administrative procedures by allowing enterprises themselves to make whatever staffing adjustments are imposed by current economic circumstances, and by making the regulations governing temporary employment more flexible. Measures have also been introduced to increase the productivity of labor by upgrading skills appreciably and improving shop floor organization. This first series of actions in the productive sector has been complemented by a set of institutional and financial measures.

POLICIES IN SUPPORT OF THE RECOVERY STRATEGY

The policies in support of the recovery strategy are part of the adjustment program. They are both institutional and financial. The institutional component deals with the redefinition of the role of the government, while the financial relates to the search for financial equilibrium in public finance and in the balance of payments.

Role of Government

The considerable role played by the government in the main economic sectors has produced a particularly large parastatal sector operating at a cost that the national economy could not sustain any longer. In view of the current constraints, and of the necessity to concentrate the scarce resources on the key economic sectors, it was decided that the role of the government must be redefined and limited to its original mission. This entailed the withdrawal of government from commercial operations and substantial reform of the parastatal sector.

The underlying principle of the new policy, is that government should cease providing a service or good if this could be offered by the private sector at a lower social cost. The strategy is based on a famous *leitmotiv*, *"moins d'état, mieux d'état,"* regarded by many observers as contradictory to the socialist ideology of the Senegalese government.

Actually, the withdrawal aims at promoting private investment in order to revitalize the production sector. It is based on the following five principles:

A. Regrouping of enterprises

B. Partial or total disposal of government shares

C. Dissolution of enterprises found not to be viable

D. Winding up of organizations that have served their purposes

E. Reassigning to regular status of public agencies and services that have so far had special or individualized status.

By applying these principles, the government has identified a hard core of enterprises which will be kept in the public sector. In addition, a rigorous policy of planning and managing public investment is being implemented as part of the national planning system.

Reform of Parastatals

Within the context of government withdrawal, the enterprises remaining in the public sector have to be restructured in order to increase the volume of services provided and improve their quality. To this end, a series of measures have been introduced, designed to:

A. Upgrade the public sector information system

B. Put the relationships between the government and the public sector enterprises on a contractual basis through program contracts and recovery plans (it should be noted that the first management contract was released in 1979, thus predating the structural adjustment program)

C. Incorporate recognized standards of efficiency into the enterprises' charter (Decree on the public enterprises' management is called the Management charter)

D. Simplify the authorities' monitoring procedures and strengthen their supervision.

In conclusion, the redefinition of the role of government in the economic process has brought forth practices tending towards privatization. The new policy seeks to increase direct private investment from 62.48 billions CFA to 137.04 billions by the end of the adjustment program in 1983.

Establishing Financial Equilibrium

Financial disequilibrium is fundamentally a consequence of the comparative rigidity affecting both overall consumption and the domestic supply of goods and services. In order to solve these structural problems, which have been aggravated in recent years, the government has adopted a series of measures for reestablishing financial equilibrium at macroeconomic level. Encouragement of an austere approach in public spending and of mobilization of savings and resources are the main objectives of the policy. Increases in revenue are to be effected by extending the tax base and combating fraud. An improvement of the property tax system is also expected by means of a more accurate assessment of the real estate belonging to private developers. In respect to these objectives, new tax and custom codes have been elaborated and adopted by the National Assembly.

In its austerity policies calling for strict management of expenditure, the government has decided to peg the labor costs at an annual rate of increase of 5.6 percent. To this end, the number of government employees is to be limited. Staff reductions would take various forms, but the most typical include eliminating unnecessary positions, refusal to replace retired officials and encouraging voluntary departures of civil servants from their jobs, restricting recruitment to the graduates of training schools and limiting enrollment in these schools, and granting wage and salary increases only in cases of promotion. The policy of austerity also incorporated measures that severely limited the expenditure on materials, equipment, and supplies. Thus from 1981–86, the government remarkably reduced the vehicle fleet, transferred many administrative services to government premises (direct labor), and introduced policies for improving the management of civil service housing.

As part of the effort to bring about financial equilibrium, the government introduced measures considerably reducing the subsidies allocated to parastatal enterprises which now had to adopt pricing policies to underscore their autonomy.

Given the considerable requirements for financing adjustment and economic growth, the government has drawn up a debt policy in line with its macroeconomic option. As a result, guarantees to parastatal enterprises have to be reduced. At the same time, preference is given to grants and soft loans from multilateral organizations to finance public investment. Finally, the repayment of the government's accumulated debt to banks and the private sector is being speeded up to facilitate quick economic recovery.

Improving the Balance of Payments

The trade balance and current account deficits have, in recent years, reached alarming proportions: 83.2 billion CFA. This negative external position is expected to be reduced from 6.2 percent to 3.6 percent as efforts are made to increase exports by 8.2 percent and peg imports at 6.3 percent. Positive changes have been noted as a result of improvements in the non-factor goods and services account. Moreover, the adjustment program, in its concern for financial equilibrium, aims at establishing a dynamic financial process harmonizing financial adjustment with the funding of growth in economic activities and employment.

CONSTRAINTS AND CONDITIONS OF SUCCESS OF THE ADJUSTMENT PROGRAM

Senegal's structural adjustment program faces at least three types of constraint: financial, social/human, and political.

Financial Constraints

The demands of the adjustment program have been evaluated through the aggregate of the public investment program and the budgetary and balance of payments support. They have been estimated at $600 million (U.S.).

The Senegalese government cannot, under the present conditions, make such a huge sum available from internal sources. That is why it relies on its partners to help finance the medium- and long-term program. In this respect, the conditionality attached to the provision of the external assistance must not constitute an obstacle to the achievement of the objectives of the program. The donor countries generally prefer bilateral arrangements whereas it is much more beneficial for the recipient countries to accept multilateral assistance.

In any case, Senegal also has to rely on resources drawn from its own economy. Steps toward this end have been taken through the various reforms instituted to promote public savings.

Social/Human Constraints

The medium- and long-term adjustment program has been negatively perceived by the labor force because of its devastating impact on employment. The government has to persuade its social partners (the workers and their trade unions) to commit themselves to the implementation of these new measures. It is the price for survival. The Social Pact (Social Agreement) signed by the government, the trade unions, and the employers in August 1987 is an attempt to create a social environment conducive to the successful implementation of the adjustment program. Publicity campaigns are also mounted regularly to enlist support for the program. However, the private entrepreneurs must show enough evidence of their ability and dynamism to exploit the new environment created by the government through its decision to withdraw from commercial operations. Moreover, the New Agricultural Policy requires a new spirit of mind and new attitudes from the rural communities. The farmers have to know that they have responsibilities far more important than they had before NAP was launched.

Political Constraints

Although these constraints are less important than the two categories of constraints discussed earlier, the government is sensitive to the general feeling of disaffection against the structural adjustment program. For many Senegalese ideologues, the medium- and long-term adjustment program has opened a new era of liberalism that is not in accord with the socialist ideology of the leading political party. The trend toward privatization, according to the political opponents, is undoubtful evidence of the new liberalism. The point is that they do not offer alternative prescriptions for dealing with the crisis.

CONCLUSION

The adjustment program is still at an early stage and does not yet permit any general evaluation of its impact. Nevertheless, it gives indications of the way the Senegalese government has faced difficult choices. In view of the considerable interest that this program has generated among the Senegalese government's development partners, there are reasons to be confident. However, we must be conscious that the road to recovery is a long one, and that it calls for radical changes in the economic process as well as in the public administration's organization and procedures.

CHAPTER ELEVEN

The Adaptation of Government to Economic Change: A Case Study of Tanzania

B. Mulokozi, W. H. Shellukindo, and R. Baguma

INTRODUCTION

This chapter is concerned with the experience of the government of Tanzania in responding to the economic crisis that started in the 1970s and became more acute in the 1980s. Since we are concerned with reactions to the crisis, we should warn at the outset, that the framework within which this chapter was prepared is narrower than the heading, "The Adaptation of Government to Economic Change." We feel that economic change is rather broad and refers to both positive and negative changes, and could very easily stand for economic development, which is currently not the case. The current government reactions are geared toward economic adjustment rather than development. As Please has noted,

> Adjustment programmes can be differentiated from development programmes in terms of the time horizon. Development programmes embody measures—improved provision of infrastructure, technological change, education, health, population and so on—that are required to ease the basic constraints on growth and development and, therefore, have a long-term focus. Adjustment programmes on the other hand, embody measures which aim at achieving viability in the medium-term balance of payments while maintaining the level and rate of growth of economic activity at as high a rate as possible. Thus adjustment programmes take the basic constraint as given, and ask the question 'How, through changing the policies and institutional arrangements in a country, can existing productive capacity be more efficiently used?'

The general economic crisis can be explained by the structural features of the LDCs' economies. These economies are heavily dependent on the primary sector, mainly agriculture and/or mining, which produce most of the internationally tradable goods and services, and the manufacturing sector, which produces mostly local consumables. However, both sectors greatly depend on the revenue from tradable goods. An economic crisis normally sets in when the economic linkages between and among the internal sectors are asymmetrical, and when international trade results in consistent payment deficits, leading to a balance of payments crisis.

There are other factors that may lead to, or aggravate, the economic crisis without necessarily being structural. Examples of nonstructural factors are negligence, laxity and lack of accountability by the work force, and absence of monitoring mechanisms to spur corrective actions.

Given the nature of the problem facing Africa, structural adjustment is the response of an economy to an unviable balance of payments deficit and an attempt to reach some equilibrium. The Tanzanian case, as will be shown shortly, is a typical case of a country that has faced a structurally induced balance of payments crisis, and the government has been involved in devising appropriate measures to revamp the economy.

MAIN FEATURES OF THE TANZANIAN ECONOMY

Tanzania's economic structure is typical of most underdeveloped countries. The structure has a dual character. At one level, it consists of a large traditional sector and a small urban sector. The rural, traditional sector is involved in the production of most export items, food, and raw materials for the local industries. The urban sector is mostly involved in manufacturing and managing the services sector. It also produces goods for the local market.

Both the urban (especially the manufacturing subsector) and the rural economic sectors are highly dependent on foreign imports for their operations. Surprisingly, there is little linkage between the two domestic sectors of the national economy. As we will see, this lack of linkage (a basic structural problem) has been the main cause of the country's balance of payments problems and the major explanation for the current economic crisis.

Population of Tanzania

The population of Tanzania is currently estimated at about 22 million 45 percent of whom are estimated to be economically active. Out of the total, about 90 percent constitute the rural population and are involved in different sorts of agricultural activities, mainly crop and animal husbandry, and fisheries. While the population density is low (about twenty-two people per square kilometer), the distribution is not even. There is a relatively high concentration of the population in the peripheral regions. This has important implications for transport and communication.

The number of people in formal employment is low. Currently only about seven-hundred-thousand (or less than 8 percent of the economically active population) are in wage employment. Half of these are in the public service and are more or less equally distributed among the civil service, the armed forces, and the parastatal sector. Again, the majority of those in the public sector are employed in the services and related sectors, while a limited number is engaged in directly productive, industrial, or manufacturing operations.

Transport, Energy, and Mining

The transport system is relatively well established, but because of financial problems, it is inadequately maintained. There are altogether 3,600 kilometers of railroads, about 50,000 kilometers of roads that link all ports of the country to the national capital, Dar es Salaam. There are three major ports, two international airports, around fifty domestic airfields, and telecommunication links with Dar es Salaam.

Tanzania's energy resources comprise biomass fuel (92 percent), petroleum (7.4 percent), while hydroelectricity and coal provide the rest. Total per capita energy consumption was estimated at 470 kilograms of oil.

NATURE, CHARACTER, AND CAUSES OF THE ECONOMIC CRISIS

The economic crisis of Tanzania is discernible from several economic indicators, including low or negative growth rates, balance of payments deficits, budget deficits, decreasing capacity utilization, high rates of inflation, and high cost of living, among others. Below we present information related to the indicators as a basis of understanding the magnitude of the Tanzanian economic problem.

Our time frame will be ten years starting from 1975–76. While it is true that the economic problems started earlier, with the 1972–73 abrupt increase in the price of petroleum, we believe also that ten years is a long enough period to carry out an objective and generalized assessment of an economy's performance. In any case, the economic crisis in Tanzania became acute starting around 1980. In Table 11–1 we present the GDP and per capita income for the years 1982–86 with 1976 as base year.

TABLE 11–1
GDP and Per Capita Income (PCI), 1976–86
(at 1976 Prices)

Year	1976	1982	1983	1984	1985	1986
GDP in Millions of Shillings	21,652	24,104	23,472	23,930	24,561	25,486
PCI in Shillings	1,328	1,255	1,185	1,167	1,159	1,164

Source: *Annual Economic Review—1986* (Dar es Salaam: Government Printer, 1987).

As a measure of real income, the fall in the per capita income over the years indicates that production has not kept pace with population growth. However, the magnitude of the decline also indicates that it is not only the population growth that has outpaced economic growth, but that the growth of the productive sectors has been negative in absolute terms.

Table 11-2 indicates growth in different economic sectors, and two things are obvious here. One is that there has been consistent growth in the services sector. For example, public administration has grown by 54.5 percent over the period, representing an annual growth of 6 percent. The same is true of money and banking. In contrast, however, the productive sector recorded declining growth or stagnation. An illustration is agriculture, whose annual growth has been marginal; and industry, which has witnessed a fall of nearly 30 percent between 1978 and 1986, equal to an annual decline of 3.6 percent.

The information presented in Table 11-2 corroborates that presented in Table 11-1. However, growth alone is a partial indicator of the crisis, since it does not include, for example, the position of balance of payments. Table 11-3 shows the exports and imports position for the years 1975 to 1985.

Table 11-3 clearly shows that for quite a long period, Tanzania's exports could only meet part of its imports. The chronic balance of payments deficit highlights the grim economic situation in Tanzania. An economy that depends for its growth on imported items has to be sensitive to anything that erodes its import capacity. Tanzania's economy reached a critical stage when exports could no longer finance imports. This was when the symptoms of the crisis manifested themselves in the form of budget deficits, increasing rates of inflation, commodity shortages, and rising cost of living. The recurrent budget deficit reached an all-time high of 12 percent of the GDP between 1978-79 and 1981-82. Deficit financing does not necessarily mean that the national economy has a problem. If it is a deliberate short-term policy geared toward the financing of productivity-inducing projects, a deficit budget may be justified in terms of the long-term payoff. However, when deficit financing becomes a regular habit and persists over a long period (and especially when it is meant to finance recurrent services) it should be regarded as a danger signal, an indicator of decreasing productivity, and of an eroded revenue base. In plain language, chronic budget deficits are clear evidence of an economy living beyond its means.

Another danger signal that has been flashing for some time is the rate of inflation. Like budget deficits, inflation may be a short-term price to pay for long-term economic expansion. Besides, inflationary measures may be adopted to make a country's products more competitive in international markets, that is, when inflation is used as a strategy to stimulate production and external trade. However, when inflation persists over a

TABLE 11–2
Economic Growth in Different Sectors, 1978–86
(at 1976 Prices; Figures in millions of shillings)

Sector	1978	1979	1980	1981	1982	1983	1984	1985	1986
Agriculture, Forestry, etc.	8,998	9,066	9,418	9,511	9,639	9,597	9,463	9,788	10,045
Mining	189	200	189	193	193	174	176	163	160
Industry	2,730	2,821	2,683	2,382	2,304	2,103	2,159	2,075	1,935
Energy and Water	286	318	400	417	420	413	439	461	523
Construction	783	879	932	890	930	549	629	577	572
Commerce and Trade	2,797	2,839	2,839	2,925	2,668	2,612	2,640	2,662	2,669
Transport, Storage, and Communication	1,699	1,634	1,818	1,652	1,694	1,473	1,703	1,848	1,887
Money and Banking	2,208	2,338	2,483	2,529	2,702	2,817	2,920	2,993	3,073
Public Administration	2,937	3,349	3,657	3,916	4,221	4,450	4,555	4,761	5,394
Less Bank Charges	485	501	531	549	667	716	754	767	772
Total	22,142	22,943	23,888	23,666	24,104	23,472	23,930	24,511	25,486

Source: *Annual Economic Review—1986, op. cit.*

TABLE 11–3
Tanzania's External Trade, 1975–85
(in millions of shillings)

Period	1975	1976	1977	1978	1979	1980	1981	1982	1983	1984	1985
Exports	2,764.0	4,108.0	4,464.2	3,670.6	4,484.3	4,165.7	4,807.4	4,028.6	4,270.1	4,354.8	4,265.9
Imports	5,709.4	5,349.5	6,161.3	8,792.7	9,073.2	10,307.9	10,047.2	8,595.6	8,876.5	9,652.8	15,287.8
Balance	−2,945.4	−1,241.5	−1,697.1	−5,127.1	−4,588.9	−6,142.2	−5,239.8	−4,567	−4,605.4	−5,297.9	−11,021.9

Source: Bank of Tanzania, *Economic and Operations Report*, June 1986, Bank of Tanzania, Dar es Salaam, Table 21.

long period, this is an indication that the economy has ceased to enjoy good health, and that production is lagging terribly behind consumption. The inevitable outcome is a rising cost of living and a substantial erosion in the real value of money. Table 11–4 depicts the situation between 1977 and 1985.

The general features and character of the economic crisis in Tanzania are reflected in the decline in production, leading to limited exports and export earnings, which have resulted in acute balance of payments problems and a reduced import capacity.

These problems have had other negative spillovers. Those whose real incomes have been severely reduced (agricultural income has declined by 13.5 percent between 1979 and 1984 and nonagricultural by 65 percent) have reacted by engaging in "black" (or parallel) market operations, smuggling, tax evasion, and other illegal activities.

Causes of the Economic Crisis

Over a period of time, there have been concerted efforts by the government, scholars, and members of the public to search for the real causes of Tanzania's economic crisis. Local initiatives have been complemented by the efforts of the international community, particularly, the IMF, the World Bank, and countries which have interest in the development of the economy. So far the causes identified may be classified as structural, policy, and natural. They have also been classified as domestic and external.

The most glaring cause of the crisis is the country's dependence on a weak primary sector, which is sensitive to natural disasters and to external factors, such as fluctuations in international commodity prices. Internal policies, especially pricing and investment policies, have also constrained the performance of the primary sector. Thus, the primary cause was the decline in the performance of the agricultural sector, which was aided and abetted by the fall in international commodity prices. This contributed in no small measure to the lowering of national income and undermined the capacity to finance much-needed imports.

What are the remote and immediate causes of the decline in agricultural production? At least six different factors have been identified as in-

TABLE 11–4
Tanzanian National Consumer Index, 1977–85
(1977 = 100)

Year	1977	1978	1979	1980	1981	1982	1983	1984	1985
Index	100	106.6	120.3	156.7	196.9	253.9	322.6	439.2	585.4

Source: Bank of Tanzania, *Economic and Operations Report*, June 1986, Table 27(a).

fluencing the performance of the agricultural sector. These include the pricing policy, lack of incentives, low commodity prices in the world market, poor infrastructure, bad weather, and lack of production inputs. It is thus a combination of domestic, external, and natural factors.

Pricing and Price Policy

Up to and including the early 1970s there was a steady growth in the agricultural sector, while between 1974 and 1984, it grew at a low rate (2.2 percent per year, which was well below the population growth rate of 3.2 percent per year). During the same period, the principal export crops actually declined. One explanation is that over a period of time, agricultural prices remained either stagnant or declined in real terms, and the peasants reacted by cutting back on agricultural production in favor of alternative activities. Table 11–5 shows the price paid for the major export crops.

It has been recognized now that the peasants' production started to fall, because of the fall in real prices, among other reasons, at the time when the value of money was falling and prices for merchandise were going up.

Decline in Export Prices

Concurrently, as the domestic prices for agricultural commodities were falling, the export commodity prices were also experiencing a downward trend especially beginning with the 1972–73 oil price rise. At the same time, import prices of essential inputs, machinery, and spares went up. The resultant negative terms of trade contributed to the worsening of the balance of payments position.

TABLE 11–5
Producer Prices for Peasant Export Crops, 1973–79
(1966 prices in Tanzanian cents per Kilogram)

Year	Coffee	Cotton	Cashew Nuts	Tobacco	Tea	Pyrethrum
1973	243	86	72	445	57	244
1974	341	91	64	356	46	255
1975	308	108	54	300	41	216
1976	498	83	46	290	37	269
1977	448	74	36	237	48	208
1978	—	70	48	211	43	185
1979	244	81	49	238	41	175

Source: Bank of Tanzania, *Credit for the Development of Agriculture in Tanzania*, 1979, tables; and *Bulletin of Crop Statistics, 1980/81*, (Dar es Salaam: Ministry of Agriculture, 1981).

Unfavorable Weather

Although Tanzania is well endowed with surface water, the country does not yet have the capacity or the technology to harness the water for irrigation. Agricultural activities, therefore, continue to depend on rainwater. During the late 1970s and in 1981, Tanzania experienced an extended drought, and this adversely affected agricultural production.

Agricultural Management

Agricultural management, especially extension work and marketing, had traditionally been handled by the local government and the cooperatives, respectively. Beginning from 1972, local governments were abolished and a deconcentrated central government was set up instead. In 1972 cooperative unions were also abolished and crop authorities were created in their place. Unfortunately the new institutions, especially the latter, were insensitive to the peasants' needs in agricultural management. They turned out to be expensive in their operations and often failed to purchase, and/or pay peasants for, their crops promptly, further discouraging the peasants. These factors and others, like poor transport, did contribute to the decline in agricultural production. It is also true that the government investment policy favored industry at the expense of agriculture.

Industrial Decline

As noted earlier, one of the features of the economic crisis in Tanzania is low capacity utilization in industry. Initially, this was a consequence of the fall in agricultural production and the deterioration in the balance of payments position. As a result of an acute shortage of foreign exchange, it became increasingly difficult to import industrial raw materials and spare parts. Within a short period, production declined in most industries, in some cases, to as low as 20 percent of installed capacity.

Reduced capacity utilization led to an acute shortage of locally manufactured goods. This encouraged the incidence of smuggling and profiteering and the growth of black markets. In the urban areas many workers spent most of the time scrambling for the few goods available, and therefore, less time doing effective work. This further lowered the productivity in both the industrial and the services sectors. Thus what started as an effect (of the unhealthy balance of payments position) became a cause (of economic deterioration and declining productivity).

Monetary and Fiscal Policies

It is now realized that monetary and fiscal policies pursued earlier did contribute to the economic decline, even if not directly. Two aspects of the policy are important, namely, the exchange rate and deficit budgeting.

The exchange rate of the Tanzanian shilling which is pegged to the SDR had, for a long time, remained constant. At a time of escalating inflation and rises in the domestic cost of production, this policy resulted in the overvaluation of the shilling in relation to other tradable currencies. It also had a negative effect in that Tanzanian products could not compete effectively in the international markets.

GOVERNMENT RESPONSE TO THE CRISIS

Tanzania's economic crisis is particularly exacerbated by the lack or shortage of foreign exchange. The Tanzanian government's efforts to contain the situation have thus focused on ways and means of raising the needed funds and on judicious management of available resources. Actions taken so far can be categorized as structural, administrative, and diplomatic.

Structural Adjustment Measures

From 1981, Tanzania launched three consecutive broad-based structural adjustment programs. Although they carried different names they had similar features and objectives. They are the National Economic Survival Programme (NESP), launched in 1981, which was the forerunner of the Structural Adjustment Program (SAP) of Tanzania, 1983. This was succeeded in 1986 by the Economic Recovery Programme (ERP).

By 1981, the government had come to realize that what started earlier as a temporary decline in economic growth was exhibiting permanent and disturbing features. Concerted efforts had to be made to contain the situation. Attention then focused on four factors: the increases in the price of petroleum, increase in the prices of other essential inputs, stagnant or decreasing export prices, and unfavorable weather.

Having recognized the problems, the government set new objectives, notably, an increase in export earnings in 1982 by 31 percent over the 1981 estimates of TSh 6,185 million; strict control of recurrent expenditure, and a sustained attack on conspicuous consumption and extravagance; thrift and judicious use of foreign earnings; increase in food production coupled with the motivation of farmers.

The NESP never realized its objectives as production and other indicators continued to take a negative form. A critical review of the NESP revealed that the program suffered from at least three constraints. First, it was overambitious and unrealistic, especially in its projections of growth. Second, it lacked a well-defined implementation program. Other than mentioning that planning activities should be related to the stated objectives, everything else was left to chance. Third, it was wrong, even then, to ignore the internal factors' impact on the decline of the economy.

In 1982, after further analysis of the causes of economic decline, the government recognized that internal factors were as potent as the external ones in the development process. In particular, the following internal factors were identified:

1. Insufficient resources for agricultural development compared with the high priority given to industry

2. Inadequate producer incentives and marketing/distribution systems

3. Expansionary, fiscal, and monetary policies which added inflationary pressures to the exchange rates' overvaluation

4. Rapid growth in the size of government sector and related management problems.

Among the external reasons was the huge cost of waging the war with Idi Amin's forces between 1978 and 1979.

The main objectives of the SAP are:

1. To restructure future economic activity through better incentive systems and revise priorities in government spending to achieve a more sustainable external balance and renewed growth

2. To rationalize production structures to achieve increased capacity utilization, improved manpower utilization, and to reduce unproductive activities.

3. To improve planning and control mechanisms through more effective budgeting, evaluation, and enforcement of agreed priorities.

A number of steps were subsequently taken to realize the broad objectives. In the agricultural sector, these include a review of producer prices. Starting with the SAP period, producer prices were raised by at least 5 percent per year, and deliberate steps were taken to cushion the producers against domestic inflation. Despite these efforts, however, real prices were still half what they had been in the early 1970s.

The marketing structure was also reviewed. Thereafter, the crop authorities were abolished and replaced by cooperatives and marketing boards. The advantage in using the cooperatives lies in the fact that their leadership originates from the peasants themselves; they are therefore likely to be responsive to the farmers' needs.

SAP also brought about substantial improvement in agricultural inputs supplies through the export rehabilitation credit from the World

Bank and through import support by donors. Besides, the government introduced the Export Retention Account, whereby exporters retained a percentage of their foreign earnings for the purchase of inputs and spares.

In the industrial sector, the major thrust was a shift from investment to rehabilitation. This was intended to step up production and increase the utilization of installed capacity. Measures taken to stimulate exports of industrial goods included export retention schemes, export credit guarantees, concessional interest rates, and liberalization of imports through the own-funds import scheme (ERP 1986). These measures were in addition to exchange rate adjustments and price decontrol.

Major changes have also taken place in the budgeting and public expenditure programming. The new thrust was toward reducing government expenditure, broadening the revenue base, and attaining thrift through efficient management.

Measures to curtail the rise in the government budget covered:

1. The removal of subsidies to crop parastatals and on food items
2. Stricter control of the use of fuel for government vehicles
3. Stricter control of the subventions given to nonrevenue-yielding institutions
4. Reduction in the size of Government through the retrenchment and closure of some public corporations
5. Transferring some financial responsibilities to local governments
6. Suspension of new projects.

The strategies for generating additional revenue and mobilizing resources included:

1. Introducing parents' contributions toward the cost of secondary school education
2. The introduction of development levy payable by every citizen aged eighteen years and above
3. Increasing discretionary indirect tax rates by using presumptive income to assess the income tax due from small business enterprises.

Despite the efforts undertaken, Tanzania was unable to rehabilitate its economy by the end of the SAP period. The major explanation is that the problem of foreign exchange liquidity still persisted. However, a number of positive achievements attributable to the measures were recorded. Among them are the following:

1. In the agricultural sector there were remarkable increases in the production of food crops, especially, maize, as well as some export crops. Official purchases by the National Milling Corporation increased from 71,000 tons in 1983–84 to 105,000 tons in 1985–86, and 262,000 tons in 1986–87. Cotton picked up from an all-time low of 130,150 bales in 1982, to an all-time high of 400,000 bales in 1986–87. With good weather there is every promise that production in most crops will continue to rise.

2. The budget and fiscal sector also started to show some improvement. For example, because of the adjustment of the exchange rate in 1984, and partial trade liberalization, revenue from custom duties almost doubled in 1984–85, and local currency value of external aid rose by over 40 percent. The recurrent budget deficit was 27 percent less in 1984–85 than in 1983–84. Government deficit financing (through bank borrowing) declined from 74 percent in 1983–84 to 47 percent in 1984–85. At the same time, government revenue increased by 26 percent in 1984–85 over the estimated figure.

In contrast, the balance of payments position did not improve. The decline in the volume of exports, which had averaged 5.6 percent between 1973–80 was reduced to 1.2 percent annually in 1981–84 and began to show an upward swing in 1986. At the same time, however, the value of imports was rising, with the result that the foreign trade deficit grew from TSh 5 billion in 1981 to TSh 11 billion in 1985. This position has been compounded by the volume of the external debt which in 1986 was about $3.5 billion, or nearly 70 percent of the GDP; while remittances amounted to about 60 percent of the export value.

The Economic Recovery Programme (ERP)

The SAP lasted for three years, 1982–83 to 1984–85. In 1986, the government launched the Economic Recovery Programme (ERP). The objectives of the ERP are stated as:

1. To increase the output of food and export crops through appropriate incentives for production, improving marketing structures, and increasing the resources available to agriculture

2. To rehabilitate the physical infrastructure of the country in support of directly productive activities

3. To increase capacity utilization in industries through the allocation of scarce foreign exchange to priority sectors and firms

4. To restore internal and external balances by pursuing prudent fiscal, monetary, and trade policies.

The spirit as well as the operational focus of the ERP are more or less the same as those of the SAP. The new measures include periodical review of agricultural incentives, export promotion, containing the level of government recurrent expenditure, improving measures of tax collection, streamlining public institutions and enhancing their efficiency, adjusting of the shilling's exchange rate, and as far as possible containing budget deficits.

An area which has received greater attention in the ERP than under the SAP is the rehabilitation of the infrastructure and industries. Thus under ERP "new projects will be undertaken only exceptionally and if (i) they directly increase export earnings, (ii) promise to remove serious bottlenecks impeding present production, and (iii) provide for the basic needs of the population in terms of essential goods and services. Consequently resources will be directed mainly towards the rehabilitation of existing social and physical infrastructure and the reactivation of existing capacities" (*ERP,* 1986).

However, the rehabilitation exercise requires huge sums in foreign exchange. Yet as already stated, Tanzania's foreign exchange position is highly precarious particularly because of the low level of exports, the negative terms of trade, and the external debt burden. It was in recognition of this situation that the government, through the ERP, appealed to the international community for assistance. It stated that

> debt service obligations currently take up about 60 per cent of current exports earnings and the debt burden will remain high during the recovery period. In view of the need to channel scarce foreign exchange resources to supporting the recovery efforts, the Government will try to get a consolidation of trade arrears and multi-year rescheduling and whenever possible conversion into grants of its external obligations which will enable Tanzania to re-open commercial lines of credit and resume orderly debt-servicing payments as soon as possible (*ERP,* 1986).

It added that

> the Government is committed to a programme of policy reform designed to provide a framework for economic recovery, but only with increased aid will the Government be able to make a major effort to rehabilitate the productive sectors, boost exports and enhance Tanzania's own capacity to generate foreign exchange earnings.

Table 11-6 shows the minimum import requirements for the ERP period (to be borne mostly out of external support).

Measures to Increase Efficiency: Managerial

As the economic crisis intensified, it became apparent to the government that among the factors that contributed to poor performance of both government and parastatal institutions was poor management. This was probably because of lack of exposure and training in modern management techniques. A consultancy team was commissioned by the government to study the problems and identify training areas. As a consequence of that study, the government launched what is known as Top Executives Programme lasting between four and eight weeks. The program is designed for all top executives in the public sector, including principal secretaries of government ministries and managing directors of parastatal organizations.

Another measure has been to enforce accountability of all public servants, especially the leadership. In 1971 the party had announced a policy known as *Mwongozo wa Tanu* (i.e., the Party, TANU or Tanganyika African National Union Guidelines), which cautioned leaders in the public sector against bureaucratic excesses, and high-handed treatment of subordinates. The spirit of the policy was grossly misinterpreted by the workers to mean that they were free to do what they wished. Management having been caught unawares, equally refrained from the enforcement of rules and regulations. Thus cases of absenteeism, truancy, and laxity became rampant and this naturally undermined productivity. Nobody, however, cared to take remedial action as that would be branded bureaucratic and tyrannical.

This state of affairs prevailed for a long time. However, as the economic crisis deepened, it became obvious that urgent steps ought to be taken to curb laxity and careless handling of public property. The remedial actions have now been instituted through the presidential announcement calling for enforcement of accountability, particularly by the leadership for

TABLE 11-6
Minimum Import Requirements
(in U.S. $ millions)

Year	1986–87	1987–88	1988–89
Investment/Rehabilitation	443.2	417.5	407.5
Recurrent	412.6	812.7	892.9
Total	1,205.8	1,230.2	1,300.4

Source: United Republic of Tanzania, *Economic Recovery Programme*. Dar es Salaam: Government Printer, 1986. Table 4.2, 23.

the performance of their organizations and for the activities of their subordinates.

As was pointed out earlier, one of the consequences of the economic crisis in Tanzania was a shortage of essential goods. This had given room to smuggling, unofficial price escalation, hoarding, and other vices. The situation provided fertile ground for corruption and abuse of office, which, in turn, aggravated the crisis and eroded public confidence in the government.

To counter those activities and contain the situation, the government in 1983 adopted the Economic and Organized Crime Act, whereby known and suspected people involved in what might be termed economic crimes were arrested and tried in special courts. Even now economic crimes can only be tried by the High Court and they carry special penalties when the culprit is proved guilty.

It should be noted that in addition to the measures described in the preceding sections, the government explored diplomatic means in the effort to overcome the obstacle posed by the chronic shortage of foreign reserves. Moreover, after a protracted negotiation with the IMF, an agreement was reached on the rescheduling of the debt payment due to the Paris Club. Tanzania has further derived immense benefits from its membership of subregional institutions such as the Southern Africa Development Coordination Conference (SADCC) and the Preferential Trade Area (PTA).

A few issues remain unresolved, however. First, the tough economic restructuring measures introduced by the government (particularly the substantial devaluation of the Tanzanian shilling) have hit individuals with fixed incomes hardest. How to reconcile the need for collective sacrifice, which underlies economic restructuring, with the requirements to keep body and soul together is going to be a major issue in public policy for some time to come. The second issue that needs to be addressed quickly is that relating to the external debt and debt-servicing obligations. Whether or not a debt is rescheduled, it is essential to give serious thought to the repayment modalities. Unless this is done, increasing debt-servicing obligations may constitute yet another major impediment to growth.

BIBLIOGRAPHY

Bank of Tanzania. *Economic and Operations Report*. Dar es Salaam, June 1986.

Bank of Tanzania. *Quarterly Economic Bulletins*. Dar es Salaam.

President Ali H. Mwinyi. *Government Five-Year Implementation Report on Resolutions of the Second (1982) General Conference of Chama cha Mapinduzi (CCM) to the Third (CCM) General Conference (October 1987)*. Dar es Salaam: Government Printer, 1987.

President Ali H. Mwinyi. *Speech to the Third CCM General Conference, 22nd October 1987*. Dar es Salaam: Government Printer, 1987.

Tanzania Government. *Programme for Economic Recovery*, Report by the Government of Tanzania for the Meeting of the Consultative Group for Tanzania. Dar es Salaam, 1986.

UNDP. *Development Cooperation Report, 1986, for United Republic of Tanzania*. Dar es Salaam, 1987.

UNDP. *Development Cooperation Report, 1985, for United Republic of Tanzania*. Dar es Salaam, 1986.

The United Republic of Tanzania. *Annual Economic Surveys, 1976–86*. Dar es Salaam: Government Printer.

The United Republic of Tanzania. *Economic Recovery Programme (ERP)*. Dar es Salaam: Government Printer, 1986.

United Republic of Tanzania. *Report of the Presidential Export Promotion Commission*. 1985 (unpublished).

CHAPTER TWELVE

The Adaptation of Government to Economic Change in Zimbabwe

S. Mahlahla

INTRODUCTION

Since independence (1980), Zimbabwe has been experiencing severe economic problems that result from internal and external imbalances. The main internal economic problems are budget deficits, which have often led to inflation; declining investment, which has led to shortages of certain goods; and, more serious, declining employment opportunities. The main external factors are slow growth of exports and relatively low prices of agricultural and mineral commodities in international markets. The total value of exports is no longer sufficient to meet Zimbabwe's import requirements, such as machinery and industrial raw materials, and to service external debt. In fact the present situation is such that capital outflow is now slightly larger than capital inflow.

To these problems we should add another exogenously determined force, the drought, which has wreaked havoc with Zimbabwe's agriculture for four of Zimbabwe's seven years of independence. This has implications for employment and exports as will be shown later.

Another destabilizing force is the political situation in the region. While this factor is an important one, it falls outside the scope of this chapter.

In order to put the problem of adjustment and economic management in its proper perspective, it is necessary to discuss the social and economic changes that have taken place in Zimbabwe since independence. Independence removed all social, economic, and political barriers which had been erected by past regimes to protect the white minority and the foreign capital on which they and their foreign partners thrived.

From the economic and social point of view, removal of these barriers necessitated rapid expansion of key social services. For example, education services were expanded to provide school places for all children, especially at the primary level, and the public service grew in size to cater to the increased tasks to be carried out by the government (resettlement programs, development of water resources, health services, and community development).

These and other revolutionary changes in the development of the society placed a heavy strain on the exchequer. It is important to note that before independence, the first charges to the national budget were the requirements of the white segment, which constituted about 5 percent of the population. The African population was treated as a residual group and the development of the areas in which they resided was dependent on whatever was left over after the needs of the white community had been met. This is why the issue of budget deficit did not emerge as an important problem in Rhodesia's financial publications.

Since independence, the strain placed on the budget has led to a progressive growth of the budget deficit which, in 1987–88, stood at about 10 percent of the gross domestic product (about Z$1 billion dollars).

In an attempt to reduce the budget deficit, the government implemented a number of measures, the most important of which are outlined below.

Removal of Subsidies on Food Items

Most subsidies on food items such as beef, milk, and mealie-meal have been removed in a phased manner. The remaining subsidies are those earmarked for parastatals to cover operating losses. The government is currently studying the situation in order to design a strategy for reducing the remaining subsidies where feasible. A committee on parastatals was established in 1986 to carry out an investigation into their operations. The committee has already made recommendations to the cabinet on a number of parastatals and the government has taken some decisions on the basis of these reports. The objective of this exercise is to reduce the growing dependence of statutory bodies on the exchequer. It is important to note that the very existence of the committee has kept many a manager on his toes. There is already some visible increase in the operational efficiency of some parastatals.

Restraint on Public Expenditure

As was indicated earlier, during the first two or three years of independence, the civil service grew by leaps and bounds in order to fulfil its expanded role. However, in order to contain public expenditure, the government imposed a freeze on recruitment, except in cases where the Public Service Commission felt a post must be filled for the efficient operation of a ministry or department. A wage freeze has also been used as a tool for restraining growth in public expenditure. For the fiscal year 1987–88, wages for both public and private sectors have been frozen at their 1986–87 level. This, again, has saved the government some Z$20 million. A freeze has been imposed on the prices of intermediate and finished goods. For this reason inflation has remained at its 1986 level.

THE PROBLEM OF EXTERNAL INDEBTEDNESS

One of the biggest problems and constraints to the development of Zimbabwe and, indeed, to the rest of the developing countries is the structure of their dependence on advanced economies for the growth and development of their economies. Like most developing countries, Zimbabwe's production system is largely dependent on imported machinery and industrial raw materials, and on a wide range of imported technologies employed in production and in other areas of social and economic activity. A greater proportion of the foreign currency earned through exports and external loans is spent on the import of machinery, equipment, and industrial raw materials. Thus, while it is true that Zimbabwe has one of the most sophisticated manufacturing sectors among developing countries, it should also be acknowledged that the manufacturing sector in Zimbabwe has no solid foundation, since its very existence is dependent upon events determined outside the country.

In this connection, one is justified to say that, for the greater part, *"the growth of the Zimbabwe economy is imported,"* because without imported machinery, industrial raw materials, and spare parts, the Zimbabwean economy could grind to a halt, especially now that the manufacturing sector is the dominant mode of production in the economy (contribution to GDP is 26 percent). The problem of dependence on advanced economies at the point of production is aggravated by the fact that the mining sector, which contributes about 8 percent to the GDP, is equally dependent on imported inputs and is externally owned and controlled.

The dependence referred to above is largely responsible for the debt crisis currently facing Zimbabwe and the other African countries

Zimbabwe's external debt problem is depicted in Table 12–1. As the table shows, Zimbabwe's external debt has grown from Z$100 million in 1979 to Z$2.5 billion in 1987. This is a 25-fold increase over an eight-year period. By its nature, external debt retards economic and social progress in two ways. First, external debt serves as a mechanism for exporting a significant proportion of the wealth of the indebted nation. Second, the wealth so exported is in the form of convertible currency, a valuable asset in the nation's production system.

The most important causes of the growth of Zimbabwe's external debt are:

1. Excessive borrowing during the early years of independence. The debt was contracted through the Zimbabwe Conference for Reconstruction and Development (ZIMCORD) which was held in April 1981. While the bulk of the borrowing consisted of soft loans and grants, the fact remains that the loans and interest will have to be repaid in the future and in hard currency. Many of these loans have already entered the repayment stream.

TABLE 12–1
External Debt and Debt Service Ratio
(Z$m, Cumulative, at 30 June)

Year	External Debt	Percent Change	External Debt Service Ratio
1979	100	–	–
1980	365	266	–
1981	488	34	9.5
1982	697	39	16.3
1983	901	34	24.6
1984	1,048	15	29.0
1985	1,735	66	28.6
1986	2,215	28	34.3
1987	2,513	13	35.0

Source: Reserve Bank of Zimbabwe, *Quarterly Economic and Statistical Review*, Sept. 1987.

2. The devaluation of the Zimbabwean dollar in December 1982, and the rapid depreciation of the Zimbabwean dollar, relative to currencies in which external loans are denominated, led to a huge increase in the value of Zimbabwe's external indebtedness. Suffice it to say that the depreciation of the Zimbabwean dollar implies that the nation is now paying for services which it never received. The same is true of all debt-ridden developing countries that have devalued.

For Zimbabwe the story of exchange rate realignment begins with the devaluation of 9 December 1982. Trends in the depreciation of the Zimbabwean dollar are shown in Table 12–2.

For Zimbabwe, the 1982 devaluation was not an event but the beginning of a process, a process intended to align in a meaningful way the Zim-

TABLE 12–2
Exchange Rates, 1979–86
(foreign currency units per Z$)

Year	U.S. $	Sterling	Rand
1979	1.48	0.66	1.24
1980	1.58	0.66	1.18
1981	1.39	0.73	1.33
1982	1.08	0.67	1.16
1983	0.90	0.62	1.10
1984	0.66	0.57	1.31
1985	0.60	0.42	1.57
1986	0.59	0.40	1.31

Source: Reserve Bank of Zimbabwe, *Quarterly Economic and Statistical Review*, March 1987.

babwean dollar with the currencies of its major trading partners. The government believes that this is an important instrument for attaining external economic stability. As Table 12–2 indicates, the Zimbabwean dollar, relative to the U.S. dollar in 1980, was Z$1 = U.S. $1.58, an obviously overvalued Zimbabwean dollar. With the devaluation of 9 December 1982 the exchange rate was set at Z$1 = U.S. $1.08 (see Table 12–2). It is interesting to note that early in 1983, when Zimbabwe was discussing the possibility of establishing a program with the IMF, the Fund included in its negotiation package a lower rate of devaluation. The devaluation of the Zimbabwean dollar was, therefore, not dictated by an agency outside the system. It was a policy deliberately instituted by the managers of the national economy.

After devaluation, the Zimbabwean government established a mechanism for making the Zimbabwean dollar responsive to movements in currencies of its major trading partners. Since 1983, the value of the Zimbabwean dollar is being determined by movements in the currencies of our major trading partners. The level of the Zimbabwean dollar is determined on the basis of a "basket of 14 currencies" consisting of currencies of the country's major trading partners. In the basket, weights have been assigned to currencies of the trading partners on the basis of the magnitude of the transactions between Zimbabwe and a given country. In this way, the country is able to adjust automatically the value of the Zimbabwean dollar in response to any significant movement in the trade in a given currency included in the "basket," thereby avoiding potentially major disruptions in external trade. This is a major achievement in the attempt at attaining external economic stability. These measures taken on the external front are probably the main reason why Zimbabwe could boast, albeit in a humble manner, that she could still honor external debt obligations. And in order to minimize the effect of devaluation on Zimbabwe's external debt, the government now attempts, in its loan negotiations, to denominate each loan in a currency which appreciates least, that is, relative to the Zimbabwean dollar.

Repatriation of Dividends and Profits

The Zimbabwean manufacturing and mining sectors are largely controlled by transnational corporations. In this connection, dividends and profits, whenever possible, must be paid to the owners of capital who reside outside the borders of Zimbabwe. This is a statutory obligation that Zimbabwe has always honored. In 1987, the amount to be repatriated was estimated at over Z$140 million. This is no small amount for a country like Zimbabwe. In fact, repatriation of such an amount, on a continuous basis, could bleed Zimbabwe to death. In this connection, the Zimbabwean government decided that every company located in Zimbabwe must bear part of the social and economic burden during difficult times. Hence on 28 May

1987, the government allowed payment of only 25 percent of declared dividends.

Earlier, around 1984, when an acute shortage of foreign currency threatened to lead the economy into stagnation and decline, the government froze the repatriation of dividends and profits until further notice. There was an outcry from the international community, which felt that this was the beginning of expropriation. The government was unmoved by these reactions. Essentially all dividends declared were put into "blocked funds" in Zimbabwean bank accounts where they would earn interest, albeit at a level lower than the average rate of inflation. The "block" on dividends was partially lifted in 1985 to allow repatriation of 50 percent of dividends. When the external economy began to show signs of instability in 1987, the government again imposed restrictions on the export of capital. The new program is as follows: (i) of all dividends declared only 25 percent can be repatriated; (ii) all blocked funds and surplus funds are now eligible for investment in expansion of existing capacity or in new ventures; (iii) the 25 percent dividends that qualify for repatriation can be used to import machinery or industrial raw materials, and in this case, import duty is waived. Several companies have responded to this arrangement, and it is hoped that many more would take up the challenge.

The Drought and Its Aftermath

On the whole, the people of Zimbabwe did not starve during periods of drought because the government maintains an adequate stock of grain and other foods. The effects of drought are felt directly by the agricultural sector and indirectly by the manufacturing sector.

Measured by its contribution to the GDP, agriculture is the second largest sector in the economy after manufacturing. Table 12–3 shows trends in agricultural output over a seven-year period.

As Table 12–3 shows, Zimbabwe has experienced only two good agricultural seasons since independence. The reasons the country has con-

TABLE 12–3
Agricultural Output, 1980–86

Year	Z$ (Millions)
1980	451
1981	515
1982	478
1983	403
1984	496
1985	614
1986	540

Source: Reserve Bank of Zimbabwe, *Quarterly Economic and Statistical Review*, March 1987.

tinued to reap a reasonable harvest during semidrought years are extensive crop diversification and the use of advanced farming technology and methods.

The major crops grown in Zimbabwe are tobacco, maize, cotton, sugar, wheat, coffee, tea, soya beans, and sorghum. All these crops do very well with a good rainfall. During a mild drought, cotton, tobacco, soya beans, and, of course, coffee still yield a reasonably good harvest, thus cushioning the effects of the drought.

The advanced technology referred to earlier is not restricted to equipment such as tractors and combine harvesters used by commercial farmers. It also includes the use of scientific methods of farming throughout a farming cycle, from ploughing and planting through harvesting and storage. It also includes use of pesticides and insecticides and proper crop rotation. These technologies and scientific methods of farming are used extensively by Zimbabwe's farmers, especially those in the commercial farming subsector.

The most serious effects of drought on Zimbabwe are unemployment, a decline in exports, and a decline in manufacturing activities. When the drought strikes, the farming community experiences a significant decline in employment and loss of income. The effects of a drought are also felt by many subsectors of the manufacturing sector that are dependent largely on agriculture for their inputs. Subsectors that process foods are affected almost immediately, while those that manufacture tobacco products, textiles, cotton lint, and clothing feel the effects within a time lag of a few months. On the average, manufacturing industries that depend on agriculture for their raw material inputs account for about 50 percent of the total value of manufactured goods. This implies, therefore, that during drought years, the manufacturing sector experiences a significant decline in employment and output, perhaps not nearly as much as the agricultural sector.

Another important result of a decline in agricultural output is the decline in agriculture's contribution to exports. During a good season, the sector accounts for approximately 40 percent of the total value of exports. The result is that foreign currency allocations are reduced in times of drought. In effect, therefore, drought in Zimbabwe leads to both internal and external economic instability, and, above all, to an increase in the degree of human suffering.

As indicated earlier, droughts have never led to starvation in Zimbabwe. Inevitably, however, the problem of malnutrition that is common to most African countries is aggravated during periods of drought because the supply of certain food items (such as milk and vegetables) is adversely affected by drought.

It must be stressed again that the droughts have not led to serious food shortages to warrant massive importation of food. During the three-year drought (1982–84), which was the worst in memory, only 20,000 tonnes of maize were imported to supplement domestic maize output (annual consumption = 900,000 tonnes). Some wheat was also imported. With respect to maize, the reason consumption requirements are always met is because of huge strategic stocks which are obtained from surplus years. The government uses part of the stocks to exchange with other countries for food items such as wheat and beans, which are often in short supply during drought periods. This as well as other recent measures adopted by the government have gone a long way in cushioning the overall effect of the economic crisis. The obvious lesson, therefore, is that creativity at the policy-making level is an indispensable element in overcoming specific economic problems (foreign exchange shortage, deficits in resource flow, and decline in agriculture production) as well as the general problem of maintaining the economy on a course of self-sustained growth.

BIBLIOGRAPHY

Central Statistical Office, Zimbabwe. *Quarterly Digest of Statistics* (September 1987).

Republic of Zimbabwe. *The First Five-Year National Development Plan, vol. 1, 1986*.

Reserve Bank of Zimbabwe. *Quarterly Economic and Statistical Review.* vol. 8, no. 1 (March 1987).

Socio-Economic Review 1980–1985.

CHAPTER THIRTEEN

ECOWAS Contribution to West African Efforts at Economic Recovery and Development

Momodu Munu

INTRODUCTION

The current economic situation has thrown out of gear such long-term development programs for the African continent as AFPLAN (for food), the Industrial Development Decade (IDDA), and the Transport and Communication Decade (UNCTADA). The continent's own Lagos Plan of Action has not been faithfully implemented. Only in recent years has the attention of African governments and the international community begun to focus on measures to halt the economic decline and achieve recovery. As the AAPAM conference theme makes clear, and as any serious consideration of what remedial action to take would reveal, Africa's economic recovery program should be conceived and executed within the context of a viable long-term development scheme if the cycle of the short-term crisis is to be broken. The development process needs to be accelerated through a massive and sustained effort to break away from the many restraining obstacles that have been the cause of the continued underdevelopment of Africa. This has been precisely the objective of such initiatives as Africa's Priority Programme for Economic Recovery, 1986–1990 (APPER), the United Nations Programme of Action for African Economic Recovery and Development (UNPAAERD), and the ECOWAS Economic Recovery Programme for the West African Sub-region.

APPER, UNPAAERD, AND ECOWAS INITIATIVES

In a forum such as this, where an assessment of the strategy adopted and the efforts made toward Africa's economic recovery is to be conducted, APPER and UNPAAERD provide the required point of reference. The review to be undertaken during this conference should, of necessity, cover both the content of these two programs and the measures taken to implement them.

The measures so far taken by ECOWAS to assist the economies of West African countries to recover were formulated in full awareness of the continental and global initiatives, and ECOWAS participated in the various preparatory measures that led to the formulation of APPER and "Africa's Submission to the Special Session of the United National General Assembly on Africa's Economic and Social Crisis." When the ECOWAS economic recovery program for West Africa was being finalized in October 1986, the relevant subregional components of APPER were carefully considered. It will be seen from the elements of the ECOWAS economic recovery program to be outlined presently, that, although the ECOWAS initiative to have an organized approach to West African economic recovery predates APPER, their strategies and orientations are similar.

West African Economic Situation

It should not come as a surprise to find West African countries and their economic community in the forefront of any attempt to stem the economic crisis that the African continent has been thrown into. West Africa has been one of the worst hit subregions. In West Africa, the economic crisis at the beginning of the 1980s followed nearly a decade of general economic stagnation and decline. The steady decline of agricultural production and the deterioration of infrastructural facilities in the 1970s and in particular, the inherent structural disequilibrium, rendered the West African economy quite incapable of coping with the world recession. In such a setting, the severe Sahelian droughts could only be devastating.

The effects of the economic crisis were widespread and severe in West Africa. The governments of the subregion, therefore, felt the urgent necessity to redress the situation. As far back as 1983, ECOWAS had proposed a comprehensive economic recovery program. The first meeting to plan the task of formulating such a program was held at the ECOWAS Executive Secretariat in January 1983, and had the African Development Bank (ADB), World Bank, and UNDP participating in the deliberations.

The ECOWAS initiative to have West Africa adopt a subregional recovery program was motivated by the following factors:

- Every ECOWAS member state clearly required a structural adjustment programme

- Countries would gain by coming together to assess and discuss the magnitude and seriousness of the economic crisis

- A minimum set of remedial measures needed to be adopted by each member state

- Synchronized and simultaneous action in some areas would be more effective than uncoordinated and isolated individual national initiatives

- Joint action at the subregional level in some sectors would supplement national recovery efforts
- A common subregional recovery program would be an additional measure that could attract additional external assistance to fill the considerable resource gap.

Lome Declaration on West African Economic Recovery

It was on the basis of considerations such as these that the issue of subregional economic recovery was raised at the Seventh Summit of the ECOWAS Authority of Heads of State and Government in November 1984 at Lome. In what came to be known as the "Lome Declaration on Economic Recovery in West Africa," the ECOWAS Authority recognized the need to adopt a subregional recovery program that addresses both short-term and long-term socioeconomic problems and identifies a series of actions to be undertaken at national and community levels.

In the "Lome Declaration," the West African heads of state and government pledged their individual and collective political and financial support to:

1. Adopt a common strategy for economic development based on a joint plan of action for the subregion, so as to make the best possible use of the resources

2. Promote the rehabilitation of the productive sectors of their national economies

3. Adopt and implement appropriate adjustment policies to combat the worsening balance of payments situation

4. Adopt, as soon as possible, measures to encourage the creation of an ECOWAS monetary zone, to promote stable monetary and financial conditions for a sustained growth of the regional economy

5. Take necessary measures to ensure the achievement of food self-sufficiency, the rationalization of manufacturing industries, and the improvement of their productive capacity. In the field of agriculture, every effort should be made to implement the decision relating to the establishment, on a zonal basis, of committees for agricultural development.

6. Continue to pursue the current community policies on infrastructure development in transport and communications, aimed at the promotion of social and economic intercourse among the peoples of the subregion

7. Initiate immediate joint action to combat desertification through the implementation of community afforestation programs

8. Adopt collective measures to minimize the effects of unemployment within the community

9. Take concerted action in the application of the findings of research institutions in the field of developmental problems in the subregion and provide the institutions with all the facilities necessary for the successful performance of their functions.

On the basis of the intentions expressed in the Lome Declaration, the ECOWAS institutions embarked upon an exhaustive study of both the immediate causes of the economic crisis and the basic structural problems facing the economies of the West African subregion. This analysis led to the formulation of a two-part economic recovery program. The first part of the program consists of measures to alleviate the effects of the global recession and achieve a revival of the national economies in the short run. The second part contains medium-term measures designed to lay the foundation for sustained growth and initiate the process of structural transformation required for the effective development of the West African economy.

The Short-Term Measures

Economic integration groupings in the Third World are mainly concerned with the long-term development problems of their member countries; their cooperation programs, therefore, tend to pay little attention to the short-term needs of national economies. ECOWAS felt that the time had come to depart from this practice and to be much more responsive to the immediate and pressing problems of the West African states. Apart from the reasons enunciated above, it was recognized that the economic crisis was threatening the very survival of many countries. Everything ought to be done to help the countries contain the crisis.

In line with these major concerns, the short-term recovery program adopted by the ECOWAS Council of Ministers in November 1986, focuses attention on priority sectors and measures which are crucial in the context of the current West African economic situation. The program concentrates on tackling the acute food situation and the declining agricultural production, control of drought and desertification, water resource development and management, the rehabilitation of infrastructural facilities and productive capacity. In addition, attention is paid to policy reforms to improve economic management, in general, and public sector performance, in particular. Other areas of concern that the program addresses are sound fiscal and monetary policies to curb inflation and eliminate domestic price distortion, correction of the overvaluation of weak national currencies, significant improvement of the balance of payments position, and controlling the rising external indebtedness. The implementation of the short-term measures will cost not less than U.S. $1 billion. This ($1 billion) investment program would have to be financed from internal and external sources.

The measures outlined above are the now-familiar policies contained in national economic recovery programs and one might rightly wonder whether the ECOWAS program was to be a substitute for national action. In any case, not all the sixteen member states had committed themselves to a serious economic rehabilitation exercise in 1984. The aim of the community was to create awareness for the need to take the challenge of the economic crisis seriously and to ensure that the minimum required policy measure was adopted by each member state. The short-term program is consequently divided into two parts: action to be taken at the national level by each member state and measures to be undertaken by the community at the subregional level.

IMPLEMENTING THE ECOWAS RECOVERY PROGRAM

Action at the National Level

The part of the ECOWAS recovery program to be executed at the national level was meant, in effect, to provide a checklist which would serve as a broad guide for the formulation of individual national recovery programs. These measures recommended by the community were to be modified to fit the specific requirements of each country. It was recognized that, although all the countries are going through an economic crisis, the severity of the economic difficulties would vary from country to country, and, therefore, different priorities would be established within the national recovery programs. The important point was that the community was able to get all the sixteen West African states to commit themselves to implement national economic recovery programs.

Subsequent developments have proved that, with or without the involvement of the International Monetary Fund (IMF) and the World Bank, all the countries of the subregion have made concerted efforts to rehabilitate their economies. The encouragement and guidance these countries received at the subregional (ECOWAS), continental (APPER), and international (UNPAAERD) levels contributed in no small way to the adoption of a series of bold economic reform policies within the past three years. The recent assessment of the economic situation carried out by the ECA concluded that the positive economic growth registered since 1985 could be attributed not only to the good rains, but also to national governments adopting recovery measures which, in many cases, entailed massive exchange rate adjustments, drastic cuts in public expenditure, privatization of state enterprises, and the dismantling of various economic controls.

Action at the Community Level

The purpose of the community-level measures is to supplement efforts being made at the national level and to assume responsibility for those measures that achieve greater effectiveness if coordinated and executed jointly. To a very large extent, the program elements reflect those subregional measures agreed upon in APPER. The sectors covered by the community are food and agriculture, ecological preservation, transport, industry, energy, trade, tourism, culture, economic management, money and finance, and external indebtedness.

Improving the Food and Agricultural Situation. In the field of food and agriculture, the following community actions are envisaged:

- creation or strengthening of community centers for production of selected cattle-breeding stock and improved seeds
- harmonization of livestock development programs of West African Inter-Governmental Organizations (IGOs)
- production of a subregional map on water and agro-pastoral resources
- participation in subregional programs on animal disease control
- promotion of cooperation in assessment of subregional fishery resources
- promotion of increased intracommunity trade in fish products
- coordination and assistance with establishment of national early warning systems
- establishment of subregional agricultural information system
- assistance with establishment of a system for organizing an emergency food aid and relief scheme on a bilateral and multilateral basis
- organization of systems for receiving, transporting, and delivering emergency food aid and other relief assistance
- coordination of food security systems
- harmonization of pricing policies on major staple foods

- organization of subregional seminars and workshops to debate major agricultural issues and encourage exchange of information between member states.

Drought and Desertification Control. In the area of natural environment and ecological preservation, the community is to formulate a comprehensive subregional plan to be used as guidelines by West African IGOs. The plan would also enable ECOWAS to coordinate their activities and identify issues and areas not adequately covered by these IGOs. ECOWAS is requested to develop close working relations with these IGOs to improve current programs on drought and desertification control, water resources and meteorological services, and soil erosion control. The community is to encourage the involvement and participation of nonmember countries in the programs of the IGOs to enhance their effectiveness. ECOWAS is also to lend its support to the IGOs in their search for international assistance, including multilateral resources such as are available under the Regional Fund of the EEC.

Rehabilitation of Transport. The short-term community-level measures adopted in the transport sector stress the need for an accelerated implementation of some of the ECOWAS cooperation activities in this sector. The program calls for the monitoring of the application of harmonized road legislation and the functioning of the Motor Vehicle Third Party Liability Insurance Scheme (Brown Card). The community is to devise means for improving transit facilities for moving goods within the subregion. The assistance being given in the construction of the Trans-West African Highway Network is to be stepped up, as well as continuing to encourage West African airlines to coordinate and harmonize their operations.

Industrial Development. The regular ECOWAS industrial cooperation program focuses attention on some selected priority subsectors and the short-term recovery measures adopted in this sector relate to the food and agro-allied industries. The community is to conduct an exhaustive evaluation of the agrochemical, agricultural tool, and food processing subsectors and to increase its assistance toward the establishment or expansion of enterprises in these subsectors.

Energy Priorities. The community short-term measures in the energy sector emphasizes conservation and efficiency in the utilization of energy. Some of the specific measures are:

- Continuation of the community energy conservation program including the electric-generating plant audit scheme

- Assistance with the rationalization and increased yield of existing oil refineries
- Increased search for better utilization of new and renewable sources of energy
- Cooperation between oil-producing and nonproducing countries.

Trade Promotion in Subregion. The objective of the short-term trade policies is to increase intracommunity trade. ECOWAS is requested to accelerate the utilization of harmonized customs documents, finalize the harmonization of the ECOWAS-CEAO-MRU liberalization schemes and ensure the effective application of a single community trade liberalization scheme. Every encouragement is to be given to the Federation of West African Chambers of Commerce in its efforts to strengthen cooperation among the business communities of the subregion. ECOWAS is further expected to speed up action on the harmonization and programming of national trade fairs organized in West Africa.

Economic Management. As a complement to national efforts to improve economic management and to cut down on government expenditure, ECOWAS is requested to assist in a study of West African intergovernmental organizations with a view to making proposals for the rationalization of the IGOs. Such rationalization is also to ensure the maximization of the contribution of subregional cooperation to the development of the West African economy.

Cooperation in Monetary/Financial Matters. In the field of monetary and financial cooperation, the community is to step up the preliminary studies for the establishment of a single monetary zone for West Africa. Meanwhile closer cooperation between the central banks of the subregion and their greater use of the West African Clearing House is to be encouraged. The community is to be used in the identification of additional sources of financial assistance for meeting the financial requirements of the national and community recovery programs.

Managing External Debt

Finally, the community is to bring its member states together through the organization of an international conference to discuss the issue of West Africa's external indebtedness. The conference is to determine the effects of the debt burden on the economies of the member states. Another aim of the conference should be to provide general guidelines on debt management and to determine tolerable limits for external debt service and debt ratios compatible with development requirements.

Short-Term Investment Program

Some of the short-term recovery measures agreed upon for implementation at national and community levels have to be translated into concrete projects. The ECOWAS recovery program therefore includes 136 projects. The total cost of the investment program is estimated at U.S. $926 million. Forty projects estimated at $548.5 million are of a regional nature, while the remaining are national projects. All the projects are drawn from national programs; that is, each project is sponsored by a member state or a number of member states.

The projects are drawn from the following priority sectors: rural development (consisting of drought, desertification and erosion control, plant protection, livestock and crop production), transport, communications, energy, and industry. All the selected projects are either ongoing or have reached the implementation stage and are capable of contributing to the recovery of the economy within the next three years. Other criteria used for the selection of the projects include the use of local raw materials, promotion of regional integration, satisfaction of basic needs, and supporting rural development.

At the community level, regular cooperation programs have been adjusted to reflect the priority and urgency accorded to particular projects. For example, there has been a heightened awareness for achieving greater monetary cooperation to complement national monetary reform measures. During the past twelve months, every effort was made to complete the studies on the creation of a single monetary zone and on the improvement of the West African Clearing House. Similarly, a joint ECA/ECOWAS report on the rationalization of West African IGOs has been completed which it is hoped will contribute to making subregional integration a more effective tool for West African development. Mention may also be made of collaborative efforts in respect of agricultural pricing policies, food processing industries, subregional programs on energy conservation (plant audits), and the implementation of the community transport program.

THE MEDIUM-TERM PROGRAM

Since the medium-term program is a prelude to a long-term development program, it is based on the development philosophy adopted by the countries of West Africa: subregional integration and collective self-reliance. The short-term program of agriculture, rural development, and related support measures is not just to redress the acute food and ecological problems of the subregion, it is a recognition that sustainable development must be based on the primary sector where the bulk of West African wealth is.

A mechanism involving community and national planning experts has already been adopted by ECOWAS for monitoring and assessing the implementation of the recovery program. One of the tenets of the medium-term program is the cultivation of the habit in national policymakers of seeing economic development in a subregional context. The medium-term program envisages the formulation of a master plan for West African development with the active participation of officials of all sixteen countries. Particular emphasis is given to staple food crop production, industrial crop production, livestock and fishing, rural infrastructure, water resource management, agro-industry, transport and communications, energy development, domestic and intracommunity trade, money and payments arrangements, external indebtedness, and balance of payments.

The medium-term program is largely an indicative one which will evolve and continue to guide future action. Indeed the community's effort in the entire economic recovery undertaking provides a general framework to guide individual member states. Some of these countries are quite advanced in their recovery programs and are already considering programs longer in duration and more development oriented. The pragmatic approach adopted by the community enables it to guide and be guided by developments within the member states.

The medium-term program has the following objectives:

- Consolidating the achievements of the short-term program, especially concerning major policy reforms

- Continuing with the reorganization of the economies of member states

- Initiating structural transformation and economic reorientation needed for accelerated and sustainable development.

CONCLUSION

The economic conditions prevailing in the first few years of the 1980s in West Africa obliged all the sixteen countries of the subregion to take the task of economic recovery much more seriously than on previous occasions. As the economic cooperation body most suited to render such a service, ECOWAS worked toward creating the necessary awareness among the countries for such an undertaking. Aided by the OAU and ECA initiatives to have all African countries adopt appropriate measures to stem the economic crisis, ECOWAS formulated its own economic recovery program which in a way translates APPER into West African terms.

So far a set of short-term policy measures and an accompanying $1 billion investment program have been fully formulated. These are based on the primary concern of rehabilitating agriculture and increasing the food production capacity of the subregion. Other policies and projects adopted are mainly in support of this critical sector. The short-term program has provided a useful guideline for individual national action in this field. In addition, the community has taken the necessary measures to supplement national efforts and make them more effective. By getting involved in this crucial exercise, ECOWAS has been able to draw attention to the need for sustained action going well beyond the short-term period. Indeed one of the main objectives of the ECOWAS medium-term program is to lay the foundation for the accelerated and self-sustained development that the countries of the West African subregion would have to embark upon at the end of the economic recovery exercise.

Part V

Manpower Development and Capacity-Building Implications

CHAPTER FOURTEEN

The Role of Management Training Institutions in Developing the Capacity for Economic Recovery and Long-term Growth in Africa

M. Jide Balogun

INTRODUCTION

This chapter begins by examining the dimensions of Africa's development crisis (with particular reference to the West African subregion) and looks at the measures so far adopted to achieve internal and external equilibrium. The second section of the chapter focuses on the administrative/managerial implications of the crisis. The third section discusses the current role of management development institutions within the context of the economic crisis and highlights some of the problems which these institutions might encounter in an attempt to formulate and implement a capacity-building strategy with an economic recovery and development bias. The fourth section looks at the future role of the institutions and proposes a mechanism for evaluating the role.

AFRICA'S DEVELOPMENT CRISIS: FOCUS ON WEST AFRICA

For some time now, studies have been produced alerting the countries of Africa to the danger of economic collapse and the accompanying social upheavals and political instability. Until recently, however, policy responses to the alarm signals have proved largely inadequate. In the meantime, Africa has been confronted with a whole range of problems: food, energy, terms of trade, balance of payments, external debt, liquidity, and economic management problems. As if the situation were not bad enough already, nature unleashed its own set of disasters in the form of desert encroachments, persistent droughts, crops failures, hunger, and famine.

Based on a paper presented at the subregional Workshop for Heads of Management Institutions sponsored by the Commonwealth Secretariat and organized at the Administrative Staff College of Nigeria, Topo-Badagry, 2–6 November 1987. The views expressed in the paper are the authors' and do not in any way reflect those of the UN and the ECA. I am indebted to the United Nations Institute for Namibia, Lusaka, for providing secretarial assistance and ensuring the timely production of the first draft of the paper.

The West African subregion was not insulated from the devastating effects of the socioeconomic crisis. As in other parts of sub-Saharan Africa, economic conditions in West Africa have deteriorated over the past two decades. Increasing external indebtedness is as much a topical issue in West Africa as in any other part of the continent.

Net Effects of Crisis

It was, in any case, a matter of time for the indices of economic trouble referred to earlier (food shortage, worsening terms of trade, galloping current account deficits, and increasing debt-servicing obligations) to manifest themselves as a major crisis of liquidity.

Both the public and private sectors immediately felt the impact of this sudden turn in economic fortune. Thus, faced with persistent current account deficits, the public sector was compelled to reduce recurrent expenses and scale down capital development projects. The "austerity" and "belt-tightening" measures almost invariably resulted in the retrenchment of staff.

The private sector was in even worse shape. It had to face the prospects of vastly diminished patronage from the public sector, in addition to being denied the foreign exchange which it required to procure raw materials, spare parts, and machinery. With decreased capacity utilization (illustrated by production interruptions, plant shutdowns, and outright liquidation), private enterprises themselves saw no alternative to large-scale retrenchment of staff.

Initial Response to Crisis

The countries of Africa have responded jointly and severally to the current socioeconomic crisis. However, the earliest attempts did not come to grips with the fundamental causes. Instead of taking a strategic view of Africa's development prospects and problems (as advocated in the 1979 Monrovia Accord and the 1980 Lagos Plan of Action and the Final Act of Lagos) the various countries saw the crisis as a series of nagging but discrete "problems," and for each of these, they had a short-term "solution." In general, the short-term measures were calculated to fulfil the stringent conditions laid down by the creditors for rescheduling Africa's debt, or for extending further trade credit. Examples are currency devaluation, import liberalization, reduction in public expenditure (as a means of "balancing" the budget), imposition of ceilings on public and private sector borrowing from the banking system, removal of subsidies, removal of price controls, as well as drastic reduction in the scope of the public sector. Not only do many of these policy options conflict with one another, they had the effects of slowing down (if not hampering) the recovery process, dampening public morale, and fanning civil unrest.

It must be added, however, that a few countries have, on their own, embarked on a comprehensive restructuring of their economies. An example is Nigeria, which has announced far-reaching policy changes in the past two years. Among them are the deregulation of the economy (illustrated by the abolition of the import-licensing system and the introduction of a Foreign Exchange Market), the implementation of a nationwide program of integrated rural development, and the formulation of a national employment policy the main components of which are agricultural development, small-scale business and entrepreneurial development, skills acquisition and apprenticeship, and public works programs.

Recent Concerted Efforts

Perhaps in realization of the fact that solo efforts were not adequate in combatting the recessionary forces, African countries have invoked the spirit of collective self-reliance in the Monrovia Accord (1979) and the Lagos Plan of Action (1980). Thus, in July 1985, the 21st Assembly of Heads of State and Government of the OAU accepted a major proposal titled *Africa's Priority Programme for Economic Recovery 1986–1990* (APPER). This was subsequently adopted by the 13th Special Session of the UN General Assembly in 1986 as the *United Nations Programme of Action for African Economic Recovery and Development* (UN-PAAERD).

To tackle the immediate problem of recovery, APPER outlines a budget of U.S. $128,104.5 to be allocated over a five-year period (1986–90). The emphasis is on the development of agriculture and other sectors in support of agriculture. The assumption is that, as a sector most likely to develop local linkages and induce growth in other sectors of the domestic economy, agriculture was crucial to the success of any policy designed to promote quick recovery and place sub-Saharan Africa on a course of long-term, self-sustained development.

While international support is essential to the success of APPER and UN-PAAERD (35.6 percent of the total budget is expected from external, non-African sources), the underlying philosophy is collective self-reliance. It is on the basis of this collective self-reliance that the African leaders themselves committed their countries to radical policy initiatives, among them:

1. Formulation of effective human resource development and utilization policy (with particular emphasis on the development of entrepreneurial capabilities in both the public and private sectors)

2. Improved management of the economy through efficient allocation of resources, improved public management systems, reshaping public services to make them development-oriented, im-

provement of the performance of public enterprises, and better management of external debt and foreign aid

3. Formulation of a balanced population policy, one that seeks to correct the disparities between population growth and resource endowments, and redress the urban-rural imbalance.

In addition, the African governments pledged to strengthen incentive schemes, streamline public investment policies, encourage domestic resource mobilization, and ensure grass-roots participation in the development process. In effect, *structural transformation* was to replace "structural adjustment" as an operational principle in the management of the African economy.

MANAGERIAL IMPLICATIONS OF THE RECOVERY AND DEVELOPMENT PROGRAM

There is no doubt that the socioeconomic situation is grim. Africa needs a new administrative/managerial order that is adequate to the challenge. The African governments themselves acknowledge the fact that "nothing short of radical measures can save the African economy from collapse."[1]

What are these "radical measures"? They should in no way be equated with pious declarations of faith in African brotherhood or with high-sounding but not-to-be-implemented resolutions on collective action. In the area of administration and management the "radical measures" go beyond the rhetoric on "administrative reform." To meet the challenge of economic recovery and long-term growth, Africa needs to completely streamline the policy-making and implementing institutions and imbue every role-player with a sense of purpose and urgency. As it is, no economic recovery plan is complete unless accompanied by a dynamic managerial strategy. It was in recognition of this fact that the ECA outlined a proposal for managerial revitalization and reequipment in support of APPER and UN-PAAERD.[2] The main components of the revitalization program are:

1. The restructuring, restaffing and reorientation of policy-making units

2. Restructuring of the civil service bureaucracy

3. Balancing of managerial autonomy in public enterprises with performance-indicating control

4. Encouragement of grass-roots participation in the development process, particularly, through genuine and meaningful decentralization

5. Optimizing the productive and self-reliant capacity of the private sector

6. Development of entrepreneurial capacity in both the public and private sectors

7. Improvement of economic and financial management through budget rationalization, expenditure control, and improved revenue administration, aid coordination, and debt management

8. Human resource development, management, and utilization

9. Dissemination of information about the goals, strategies, and tactics of collective self-reliance.

A way of interpreting ECA's proposal is to say that previous attempts to reactivate the battered economies of Africa failed largely because the institutions for policy-making and management lacked the capacity to anticipate and respond to changes in the external environment. Yet, institutional flexibility is what the continent needs to overcome the obstacles to growth. Insofar as the policy-planning framework is not equipped for this structural transformation role, and as long as the implementation agencies succumb to bureaucratic temptations, to that extent would the journey toward recovery be tortuous and unduly prolonged.

Open and Dynamic Policy-making

The major factor responsible for institutional rigidity at the policy level is the persistence of "closed" (as against "open") policy-making systems. Where "solutions" to contemporary problems are not refined by constructive criticisms and backed by reliable information and rigorous analysis, the framework is said to be "closed." In an "open" system, ideas flow freely from all possible quarters, and all possible scenarios are discussed before a final decision is made. But it is not just the environment that must be congenial to "homeostatic" policy-making. There should be a sufficient number of persons *willing and able* to make use of the open environment. This means that to be effective the policy-planning units need to be staffed by persons with "brains in their heads and fire in their bellies."[3] The alternative is to operate a system that does no more than recycle ideas and information.

Need for Managerial Adaptability

The obstacle to institutional dynamism at the managerial level lies in the career officials' preference for bureaucratic methods of dealing with complex situations. While the policymaker is interested in the substance (bridges, dams, highways, and irrigation projects) the bureaucrat is apt to focus on protocol. The dilemma of development administration is how to ensure that the substance is not lost in the intricate web of procedures—that *purpose* is not beclouded by *method*, important as the latter might be to the survival of organizations. In pursuance of the economic recovery objectives, the implementation agencies (in both the public and private sectors) would need to streamline their methods and procedures with a view to minimizing the effects of bureaucratic rigidity. In specific terms, they need to consider:

1. The implications of too many hierarchical layers for the *quality* and *speed* of administrative decisions
2. How the sometimes chaotic filing and record-keeping systems could benefit from the latest advances in information technology (or, at least, from the self-correcting logic on which the technology is based)
3. The impact of the frequent jurisdictional disputes (an inevitable outcome of rigid attachment to the principle of specialization/departmentalization) on information flow and concerted action in organizations
4. The consequences of the mismatch of *formal* academic qualifications and *actual* job requirements
5. The "opportunity cost" of protocol, empire-building, arbitrary job creation, and endless form-filling.

Public Service Restructuring

Apart from the general issue of institutional and managerial flexibility, a credible response to Africa's development crisis would have to address certain problems specific to the public service. This once proud and vigorous social institution has been reduced to a demoralized fighting force—and this at a time when Africa is engaged in a battle for survival! Perhaps the public service is now paying for years of ineptitude and resistance to change. In any case, there is no doubt that the generally negative perception of its role has assured ready acceptance of any idea suggesting that its wings be clipped. The recent move toward "privatization," for instance, is based on the premise that the high visibility maintained by governments in Africa has done the people little good. Proceeding from the philosophical assumption that unlocking the secret of human happiness essentially consists of doing nothing (of letting the world be), conservative economists have advocated the rapid dismantling of the governmental apparatus.

Yet the problems of our time dictate action not inaction. As long as societies want something, governments cannot remain inactive. While it is agreed that government intervention in socioeconomic life could be carried to a ridiculous extent, nothing is to be achieved by advocating the immediate closure of every government office. Indeed, the level of human happiness might be increased, and the equilibrium of the earth maintained, if governments and private individuals do what they are best placed by nature to do. The visible hand of government should complement the invisible hand of private entrepreneurs. When either (the visible or the invisible) does more or less than it is expected to, the result is large-scale human misery. Perhaps, the recent stock market crashes in the major centers of the advanced economies are a signal of an imminent global depression, and a warning that nature abhors a vacuum, particularly, in the corridors of power.

As far as the ongoing socioeconomic crisis in Africa is concerned there is a lesson to be learned from the New Deal Era of U.S. President Roosevelt. Apart from providing strong political leadership, Roosevelt enlisted the government bureaucracy in the fight against depression and attached utmost importance to the redynamization of government agencies.

Coming back to contemporary Africa, there is a need to reshape the civil service and equip it for the task of policy planning, implementation, and review.

As for the public enterprises, they have to ensure that in return for managerial autonomy, they accomplish the socioeconomic objectives of government. For this reason, it might be advisable to draw up management contracts that tie the career prospects of the key management staff of public enterprises to the attainment of the socioeconomic (including financial) objectives.

Decentralization is an essential aspect of public service reform. The generality of the people need to share the burden of development. That means efforts should be geared toward the establishment of representative local government authorities, and the "field" units of central government departments should be subject to local control.

New Service Ethos

In support of the public service restructuring measures discussed earlier, emphasis should be placed on the institutionalization of ethics of public service: accountability, loyalty (to the nation as against ethnic or primordial loyalties), integrity, and constant search for excellence. All these should be reflected in the way public funds are handled, development projects are designed and implemented, and government employees are recruited, deployed, promoted, and disciplined.

A Self-Reliant Private Sector

Finally, and taking into account the point made earlier about the need for public-private sector collaboration in the development process, Africa's private sector should itself imbibe the philosophy of self-reliance and structural transformation. It should spend less time asking what the government could do for it and more on what it could do for the people. It should become genuinely innovative and entrepreneurial and less of a burden to society. In specific terms, it should support the efforts of the government regarding local "sourcing" of raw materials, and the promotion of inter-African trade. It should work with regional and subregional organizations in making the dream of Africa's economic recovery a reality.

MANAGEMENT DEVELOPMENT INSTITUTIONS AND AFRICA'S DEVELOPMENT: A CRITICAL ASSESSMENT

This chapter started with an overview of Africa's development crisis. It then went on to discuss the managerial dimension. The conclusion is that institutional rigidity at the policy and management levels has been largely responsible for the persistent economic depression. If this is the case, what have the management development institutions done to promote structural transformation? Perhaps this is an unfair question. After all, they were seldom assigned this mandate at the time they were established.

It is true that the management development institutions were not set up with the aim of saving the African world from economic decay. However, they were more often than not part of the strategy of administrative reform formulated in the First and Second Development Decades. The reforming spirit of the two Decades, in fact, found its way into some of the enabling legislation. Let us take, for example, the Liberia Institute of Public Administration. It was established by an Act of the Liberian legislature in 1969 (which became operational in 1972). According to the Act, LIPA was to perform the following functions:

1. Operating training programs for public servants in *all* its forms (pre-entry service training, in-service training, initial post-entry training, and on-the-job training) including the provision of a basic academic background; such training shall cover the whole range of government positions

2. Creating and improving the capability needed for administering economic and social development programs

3. Enunciating a career development program by identifying specific career ladders, encouraging in-service training, manage-

ment internship, executive development programs and promotional programs based on merit

4. Providing leadership and guidance to the agencies of the government in developing more and better quality on-the-job training programs, serving as a research study group to analyze particular governmental organization and management problem areas

5. Studying and reviewing the indigenous situations and practices which affect social, economic, and administrative development in Liberia

6. Carrying out studies of systems and procedures and assisting in making improvements

7. Conducting research in administration to provide adequate, systematic, and precise information in critical areas of government for the purpose of improving planning and administrative capacities

8. Developing a library suitable for the needs of the research program and for the use of public officers

9. Performing such other functions as may be prescribed by the president, in accordance with the general policy of the government and the intent and purpose of the (enabling) act.

The laws setting up staff colleges and institutes of administration in other parts of Africa might not have said it in so many words or been as explicit as the Liberian Act on the "leading light" role of these institutions, but by and large, administrative reform is the "intent and purpose" of their founding fathers. And there is every reason to believe that this is not asking too much, considering the unique position occupied by the training institutions. To start with, they are a meeting place for theory and practice—for policy analysis and policy formulation. Second, the charter setting up each institution most frequently makes provision for its autonomy; this enables its instructional and research staff to carry out critical analyses of policy and management practices without fear of the consequences for their civil service careers.

However, if the intention was to establish the training institutions as agencies of administrative development, the general performance is well below standard. There is no doubt that they have turned out an increasing number of participants in the areas of general and functional management. They have carried out consultancy services to augment their dwindling subventions. A few of them must also have sponsored an occasional research project. In general, they have failed to influence development policy and public sector management practices. Above all, their contribution to the cross-fertilization of ideas between the public and private sector is minimal.[4]

Neglect of Development Policy

While some of the training institutes have hosted policy-oriented seminars and sponsored policy-oriented research projects, the majority are content to organize short-duration, technique-oriented training programs. Examples of institutes that have made important contributions to development policy are the Kenya Institute of Administration, which organized a seminar at which the idea of district focus was mooted, and the Administrative Staff College of Nigeria, which submitted a paper that might have directly or indirectly influenced the decision to begin the process of demilitarization in Nigeria with a restructured local government system.[5]

Neutral Attitude to Contemporary Issues in Management

In line with their "technical" orientation, the training institutes have not taken a clear stand on contemporary management problems, notably, those concerning the structure and organization of the civil service, the management of parastatals, and the status of local government and field administration. True, they respond to invitations to prepare consultancy proposals in these areas, but they seldom take the initiative to design, let us say, new management control and reporting systems for the civil service, profitability (or financial rescue) plans for ailing public enterprises, and service-delivery and productivity-monitoring models for local government. Their experts in operations management drive (or walk) past transportation and production bottlenecks every day without a sense of professional challenge.

Public Sector Bias

The institutes might have refined the structure and content of their training programs if they had combined public sector with business training. However, as creatures of the public sector, they tend to concentrate their attention on the training of public servants. In any case, both groups of clients (the public and the private sectors) have much to learn from each other.

Factors Accounting for Limited Role

The limited contribution made by the training institutes to administrative reform may be attributed to at least four factors: their perception of the policy framework as "closed," their confused orientation, the background of the staff, and financial resource constraints.

Staff colleges and institutes of administration tend to be located far away from the center of political and administrative action. Added to this physical distance is a psychological one which translates into the view that unless one "knows" someone high up, the chances of one's ideas seeing the light of day are slim. This is the prevailing view among the ranks of regular and associate staff of these institutes. It rarely occurs to them that the confidence of policymakers has to be earned—that the policymaker's mind could be made by a well-researched, logically reasoned, and lucidly presented policy document.

But the confused orientation of the training institutes makes it almost impossible for them to make up anybody else's mind. Many of them do not know where they belong, whether they are mere extensions of the civil service, departments/faculties in universities, or independent think tanks. There is also the fact that the factors inhibiting effective management in other arms of the public service (red tape, protocol, and hierarchy) might also be present in the training institutes. An institute unable to reform itself has no leg to stand on when it ventures to the world outside.

The background of the trainer might also have something to do with the limited effectiveness of the training institutes. Their experience tends to be confined either to the civil service or a university. The tasks before them require intimate knowledge of the workings of the civil service bureaucracy, as well as the analytical competence that is generally associated with an academic setting. Moreover, the ability to present a voluminous body of data lucidly and succinctly is imperative. Verbal and written communication is therefore a necessary asset. If one were to emphasize subject area specialization, a working knowledge of economics (with particular reference to Africa's development problems) would be compulsory for every staff member.

Perhaps the institutes would have accomplished more than they did if the required resources had been made available. In fact, they deserve to be commended for persevering in the face of all odds. For the majority of them, it has been one bad year after another in terms of budget allocation. Yet, they need huge financial provisions to be able to discharge their own obligations under the structural transformation program. Large sums of money have to be set aside for the expansion and renewal of physical facilities, procurement of suitable training material and instructional appliances, the training and retraining of staff, and the motivation and remuneration of staff.

TOWARD A NEW CAPACITY-BUILDING ROLE AND STRATEGY

For Africa's training institutes to perform effectively the task of developing the capacity for economic recovery and long-term growth, they need to carry out a critical assessment of their internal structure and revisit their mandate. In specific terms, they have to relate their organization as well as program structure to the demands of the external environment. That might mean creating new units, merging existing ones, retraining and reeducating staff, and reallocating resources in the light of new requirements. In addition, it is absolutely necessary for the chief executives of these institutes to deploy their forces in combat-ready positions. By this is meant ensuring that every member of the staff is made aware of the new mission, and that everybody's action is directed toward achieving the mission objectives.

Apart from reshaping and revitalizing the institutes' structures, it is essential that the programs be carefully reviewed. The training programs, for instance, should be made to reach all possible target groups, and should always emphasize the message of structural transformation or institutional reform. The research program should address the major issues in Africa's development experience. Each research report should focus on a major policy issue (e.g., local or regional "sourcing" of raw materials, pricing and tariff policy in public enterprises, countertrade and regional/subregional economic cooperation) or propose a new solution to an existing management problem. The consultancy program should be executed not only with an eye on the extra income that would accrue, but also with a view to tackling a major national or regional problem.

With the broad mandate now advocated, how could the institutes assess their effectiveness? For instance, it is proposed that they be more active in the areas of development policy and management improvement. How would the institutes know when they are making an impact in such amorphous areas?

There are techniques for evaluating the performance of training institutions. The most popular is quantitative: number of courses organized, number and grade of officers who participated, and their assessments of the programs (usually extracted from end-of-course questionnaires). As for research efforts, the "payoff" tends to be measured in terms of volumes of data produced and/or published as monographs or journal articles. The outcomes of consultancy programs are assessed in monetary terms and possibly in terms of the frequency with which consultancy teams get reinvited by "satisfied" clients.

For ordinary situations, the conventional evaluation methods described above are probably adequate. For a period of economic emergency such as Africa is witnessing now, a more comprehensive evaluation system is called for.

A New Evaluation System

It is perfectly in order to enumerate lower-level training programs and take a regular census of program participants. Periodic reports may be produced indicating how many officers "successfully completed" supervisory, middle-management and technical training programs. The reports could even be refined further to show what "skills" were acquired, and how general attitudes were "likely" to be influenced. If the (lower-level) training programs included some "educational" components, the "knowledge" gained might also be briefly stated.

However, if the "training programs" are in the form of seminars and conferences and are designed for policymakers and members of the higher civil service, it is not enough to enumerate them. The institutes which organized such programs would need to monitor the *policy changes* that come after the participation of senior functionaries in a seminar or conference. Even if the policy changes are "coincidental," the point should not be omitted in the institutes' role evaluation. The same applies to any *perceptible change* in management styles or philosophy which come in the wake of a senior policy seminar. This is important, bearing in mind the range of subjects (in the broad area of economic policy and management) that might be discussed in the institutions' seminar program.

A similar monitoring and evaluation technique should now be applied to the research and consultancy programs. It is no longer a question of how many research reports were produced over a period of time or how many manuscripts were "accepted" by, or published in, learned journals. We want to know—at least the suffering people of Africa want to know—which research projects produced what policy or institutional changes having a positive impact on living conditions. By the same token, the clients of national airlines and railways are not interested in how much an institution's consultancy team was paid for preparing a proposal, but in what impact this would have on the efficiency of operations. The economic situation is still precarious, but through determination and sustained efforts, Africa will vanquish the recessionary forces. However, instead of planning for minor skirmishes, we should brace ourselves for a long drawn out war. I see the management training institutions as forming the first line of attack on our common enemy—economic backwardness and declining productivity.

NOTES

1. OAU/ECA, *Africa's Submission to the Special Session of the United Nations General Assembly on Africa's Economic and Social Crisis* (OAU/ECM/2XV/Rev. 2, E-ECA/ECM. 1/1/Rev. 2, 1986).

2. UNECA, "Re-dynamizing Africa's Administrative/Managerial Systems and Institutions for Economic Recovery and Development," ECA/EDI Senior Policy Seminar on Development Management (Addis Ababa, 6–10 July 1987) (ECA/PAMM/PAM/87/1).

3. According to Adebayo Adedeji, the entire public service (and not simply the policy planning units) requires the services of men and women with "brains in their heads and fire in their bellies." See Adebayo Adedeji, "Administrative Adjustments and Responses to Changes in the Economic Environment," in *Ecology of Public Administration and Management in Africa*, ed. M. Jide Balogun (Addis Ababa: AAPAM, 1986).

4. M. Jide Balogun, "Building Management Capacity in Africa: The Role of Regional and National Training Institutes." (Paper presented at the IPS 25th Anniversary Conference, Hartford, Connecticut, 14 July 1986.)

5. See M. Jide Balogun, "Local Government as a Foundation of a Viable Political Order," Paper submitted to the Political Bureau. It may be a coincidence that the Bureau proposed, and the Government accepted, what the paper advocated, i.e., that military disengagement from politics should start from the local level and move gradually to the federal level. The paper also recommended a comprehensive program of political education for citizens.

Index

Abuja Statement, 122
Accountability, 137-138, 200
　in public service, 231
　weaknesses in, 143
Accounting, 137, 139
　deficiencies in, 142
Administration
　decentralized, 61
　flexibility in, 229-230
Administrative reform
　in CAR, 71-73
　content of, 75
　in Uganda, 71-73
　in Zambia, 73-75
Administrative Reform Agency, 75-76
African Association for Public
　Administration and Management
　(AAPAM), xvii-xviii, xxi-xxvii, 110
　programs of, 142
　role of, 30, 44
Africanization, 34
　of civil services, xxv-xxvii
Africa's Priority Programme for Economic
　Recovery (APPER), xxiii, 30, 55, 91, 123,
　227-228
　ECOWAS and, 211-212, 215-216, 220
　purpose of, 4, 135
　in Senegal, 178
　structural transformation and, 60-62
Agencies, central, 95-98
Agricultural Marketing Corporation
　(AMC), 166-169
Agricultural production
　organization of, 10
　per capita, 8
Agriculture, 53-54, 117
　crisis in, 6-8
　in Ethiopia, 150, 154-156, 160-162, 164-169
　growth rates of, 122
　incentives for, 11
　in post-independence period, 10
　private smallholder, 165-166
　problems in, 112-113
　protectionism in, 103
　in Tanzania, 187, 192-194, 198
　in West Africa, 216-221, 227

　in Zimbabwe, 203, 208
Agriculture Development Extension
　Programme (ADEP), 166
Algeria, 101
Allocations, 138-139
　budgetary, xiii
Analytical capacity, 95-98, 102
Angola, 40-41
Auditing, 137-139
　deficiencies in, 142
Austerity measures, 114, 171, 226
　in Senegal, 182-183
　in Zimbabwe, 37
　See also Belt-tightening
Awash Valley Authority, 158

Balance of payments, 112, 121, 214
　crisis in, 12, 14-17, 19-21
　in Nigeria, 59
　in Senegal, 183
　in Tanzania, 188, 190, 193-194, 198
　in West Africa, 215
Banking, reform of, 180
Bank intervention
　methods of, 80-82
　See also World Bank
Belt-tightening
　negative reaction to, 115, 117
　See also Austerity measures
Black (parallel) market, 192, 193
Botswana
　public sector management in, 97-98
Brandt Commission, 121
Budget deficit
　causes of, 140-144
　Gross Domestic Product and, 127-128
　in Zimbabwe, 204
Budgeting
　functions of, 138-139
　planning and, 99-100
　reforms in, 100
　responsibilities in, 139-140, 140
　scope and purpose, 136-140
Budget reductions, 116
Bureaucracy
　reductions in, 171, 182-183

239

240 INDEX

Capital flows, 13-14
Capitalism, 21, 45
  in Zimbabwe, 35-37
Central African Republic (CAR)
  economic recovery program in, 68-73
  PSM reform in, 81-83
  reforms in, 76-78, 87
Centralization, xxv
CESW (country economic and sector work), 80-81
Civil disturbance, 116
Civil service, 52
  in CAR, 77-78
  in Ethiopia, 170
  in the Gambia, 78
  management of, 68-72, 84
  reductions in, 82, 87
  restructuring of, 230-231
  in Tanzania, 188-189
  wage bill of, 71
  in Zimbabwe, 204
  See also Public service
Clean water, 163-164
Climate, 9
  changes in, 112-113
  See also Drought
Colonialism, 21, 33
Commodities
  prices of, 102-103, 121-122, 133
  shortages of, 112
Common Agricultural Policy, 103
Comprador, 33
Conditionalities, 55, 58
  SAL, 75
  See also International Monetary Fund
Consultants, 80-81, 237
Cooperation, regional, 63
Cooperatives, 196
Cooperativization, 168-169
  in Ethiopia, 154
Corruption, 127, 141
  in Tanzania, 201
Cost consciousness, 112, 114
Cost of living
  in Tanzania, 189, 190-192
Cote d'Ivoire, 14
Crop authorities, 194, 196
Currency
  shortage of, 62-63
  in West Africa, 218
  See also Monetary cooperation

Debt
  in Cote d'Ivoire, 14
  crisis in, 14-16, 19-20
  in Zimbabwe, 205-208
  external, 12, 14-15, 54, 113, 135, 178, 198, 201
  in Kenya, 56-58

  in Nigeria, 59
  in West Africa, 215, 218, 225
  in Zimbabwe, 205-207
  management of, 101
  policy in Senegal, 183
Debt servicing, 15, 54, 91, 102-103, 113
  effect on public service, 121, 133-135
  in Kenya, 56-58
  in Tanzania, 199, 201
  in West Africa, 218
  in Zimbabwe, 206
Decentralization, xxv, 95
  administrative, 80, 87
  of public service, 231
Defense spending, 132
Deficit budgeting, 194
Deficit financing, 190
Deforestation, 154
De-linking, xi, 45
Dependence, 29
  crisis of, 12-18
  structure of, 22
Depression, 52-53, 55
  See also Recession
Desertification, 122, 214, 217
Devaluation, 21, 56, 127, 226
  in Tanzania, 201
  of Zimbabwean dollar, 206-207
Development, 187
  administrative, 233
  approaches to, 10-11
  burden of for public sector, 109
  crisis in West Africa, 225-228
  dependent, 22
  in Ethiopia, 152-153
  ideology of, 94
  industrial, 217
  institutional, 79-80
  management of, 91, 96
  of policy, 93
  policy on, 234
  priorities of, 62
  rural, 61
  self-sustained, 227
  strategy for, 51
  in Zimbabwe, 36
Distribution, 138-139
Diversification, 53, 102
  of Senegalese economy, 179
Divestiture, xxiv
Dividends
  repatriation of, xiv, 207-208
Donor coordination, 77-78, 83-84, 87
Drought, xiii, 7-12, 20
  as cause of economic crisis, 122, 131
  in Ethiopia, 149-152, 156-161, 169, 172
  responses to, 23, 135, 141
  Sahelian, 212
  in Tanzania, 194

in West Africa, 214, 217, 225
in Zimbabwe, 203, 208-210
See also Climate

Economic Commission for Africa (ECA), 16-17, 63, 110, 215
description of African crisis, 5-7, 11-12
institutional reform and, 61, 118, 228-229
Lagos Plan of Action and, 4
on dependence, 23
planning and, 96
subregional integration and, 219-220
Economic crisis, 121-123
adjustment to, 29-47
administrative response to, 62-64
effects of, 135-136
in Ethiopia, 153-164
mediation of, 127-128
origins of, 3-27
recovery from, 51-65, 211-221
in Senegal, 177
in Tanzania, 187-202
Economic environment
international, 17-18
Economic integration
subregional, xv
Economic and Organized Crime Act, 201
Economic policy
limits of, 37-45
Economic Recovery Programme (ERP), 195, 197-200
Economic Recovery Programme for the West African Sub-region (ECOWAS), xv, 63, 123, 211-221
Economy
international, 29
management of, 227
Education, 9, 18, 132
shortages in, 115-116, 124
in Tanzania, 197
See also Training
Efficiency, 21
Employment, 128
in Nigeria, 227
public, 56
in Senegal, 179-181, 184
in Tanzania, 188
in Zimbabwe, 203
Energy
in Tanzania, 189
in West Africa, 217-218
Ethics
administrative, 64
of public service, 231
Ethiopia, xiii, 11
economy of, 149-153
financial management in, 142
response to economic crisis, 149-175
Exchange rates, 56, 206

in Tanzania, 194-195, 198
Expansion
institutional, 52
Export Retention Account, 197
Exports, 16-17
declining, 13
narrow range of, 53-54
Tanzanian, 188, 193
value of, 54
Zimbabwean, 203
Extension agents, 165-166, 179

Famine, 6-7, 18-20, 23, 121, 131
in Ethiopia, 149-150, 152, 156, 158
in West Africa, 225
See also Drought; Food; Hunger
Final Act of Lagos, 123, 226
Finance capital
international, 31-33, 37-38
First Development Decade, 52, 111, 115, 232
Fisheries, 180
Flexibility
institutional, 118, 229
in policy, 96
Food
crisis in, 6-7, 9, 11, 17, 20, 112, 135
growth rates of, 122
production of, 9, 110-111
per capita, 7-8
shortage of, 121, 124
in Zimbabwe, 209
situation in West Africa, 216-221
See also Famine; Hunger
Foreign aid, 38
Foreign capital, 31-33, 35, 37-38
Foreign currency
in Zimbabwe, 205, 208
Foreign exchange, 23, 56, 64
in Ethiopia, 171
reserves of, 14-15
scarcity of, 18-19, 226
in Tanzania, 194-195, 199
Formalism, 99
in budgeting, 100
Forward Budget, 101
Free market, 20-21
Fuel shortages, 124

Gambia, the
civil service reductions in, 78
PSM improvement in, 75
reduction of civil service in, 82
Ghana, 68
brain drain in, 127
institutional development in, 79-80
PSM reform in, 75-76, 83
Government
role of in reform, 181-183
role and scope of, 29-47

Gross Domestic Product (GDP), 9, 102
   budget deficit in, 125, 127-128
   decline of, 131-132
   growth of in Ethiopia, 152
   growth rate of, 111
   investment of, 8
   in Kenya, 57
   in Senegal, 179
   in sub-Saharan Africa, 5-6
   in Tanzania, 189
Growth
   declining rates of, 110-111
   self-sustained, 109
Guinea-Bissau, 68

Health, 9, 18, 124, 132
   measures taken in Ethiopia, 159-160
Hiving off, 80-81, 87
Housing, 18
Human resources
   development of, 117-118, 227
Hunger, 9, 18, 126
   See also Famine; Food

Imperialism, 33-35, 38-44
Imports
   agricultural, 54
   banishment of, 112
   dependence on, 13
   in Tanzania, 200
Import substitution, 16, 93
Incentives, 196, 228
   for farmers, 169
   in public service, 126-127
Income
   per capita, 131-132
Income tax, 197
Independence, 31-32, 34-35
   development plans for, 51
   early years of, 52
Industrialization, 93
Industry, 112
   in Ethiopia, 150
   in Tanzania, 194
Inflation, 121, 124, 141, 195
   in Tanzania, 190
   in West Africa, 214-215
   in Zimbabwe, 203, 208
Infrastructure, 132, 199
Institutional development (ID), 84, 88
Institutional reform
   effect of training programs on, 236-237
   trends in, 92
Institutional transformation, 109
Inter-African Public Administration Seminars, xxvi-xxvii
Interest rates, 54
Inter-Governmental Organizations (IGOs), 216-219

International environment, 53
International Monetary Fund (IMF), 37, 60, 94
   in CAR, 71
   conditionalities of, 20-22, 30, 58, 71, 78, 98, 122, 124-125
   debt service payments to, 133-134
   requirement for structural reforms, 113, 141
   in Tanzania, 192
   in West Africa, 215
International relations, 38-39
Intervention
   in socioeconomic life, 230
   state, 94, 103, 111
Investment, 8, 134-135
   in Ethiopia, 151-152, 172
   private, 181
   private foreign, 16
   public, 181
   in West Africa, 219

Kenya
   budgetary process in, 101
   debt of, 56-58
   planning cycles in, 99
Kenya Institute of Administration, 234
Keynesianism, 94, 99

Lagos Plan of Action, 20, 123
   development and, xxiii, 4, 60
   diversification and, 91
   implementation of, 211
   self-reliance and, 18, 226-227
   structural nature of crisis and, 30
Lancaster House Agreement, 33, 37-39, 42, 44
Liberia, 68, 142
Liberia Institute of Public Administration, 232
Liquidity, crisis of, 226
Living standard, 18-19
Lome Declaration on Economic Recovery in West Africa, 213-214

Malaria, 159-160
Malawi, 79
   debt service in, 133
   PSM improvement in, 75
Mali, 68, 78
Malnutrition, 7, 9, 124
   in Ethiopia, 159
   in Zimbabwe, 209
Management
   civil service, 84-87
   economic and financial, 68-72, 74, 84-87, 218
   financial, 100-101
   public sector, 67-89

Index   243

reform of, 98-102
review of, xx
role of, xix-xxii
techniques in Tanzania, 200-201
training for, 225-238
Manufacturing, 112
  growth rates of, 122
  in Tanzania, 187, 188
  in Zimbabwe, 205, 207-209
Marxist ideology, 40-41
Mauritius, 68
Medical supplies
  shortage of, 115, 124
Mining, 112
  growth rates of, 122
  in Tanzania, 187, 189
  in Zimbabwe, 207-208
Monetary cooperation
  in West Africa, 218-219
  See also Currency
Monetary reform, 63
Monrovia Accord, 226-227
Monrovia Strategy for the Economic Development of Africa, 123
Moonlighting, 124
Morale, 116
  of public servants, 126, 171
  in West Africa, 226
Morocco
  planning process in, 98
Motivation, xiii, xxii, xxv, 64, 116
  of civil servants, 171
Mozambique, 40-41

National Economic Survival Programme (NESP), 195
Nationalism, xxvi
  economic, 93
National Revolutionary Development Campaign Central Planning Supreme Council (NRDCCPSC), 153-154
National School of Public Administration (ENAP), 69-73, 77, 82, 87
National Villagization Coordinating Committee (NVCC), 162-163
Neoclassical theory, 20-23, 94
Neocolonialism, xi, 21-22, 29
New Agricultural Policy (NAP), xiv, 179, 184
New Industrial Policy, 179
Newly Industrializing Countries (NICs), 93-94, 103
Niger
  debt service in, 133
Nigeria
  Administrative Staff College of, 234
  debt of, 14
  economy deregulation in, 226-227
  external debts of, 101

structural adjustment in, 58-60
Nutrition, 18
  See also Famine; Health; Hunger

Official development assistance (ODA), 14
Oil import/export, 13
Oil prices, 121, 195
  impact of, 17
Organization
  reform of, 91-105
  review of, xx
Organization of African Unity (OAU), xviii, xx, 53, 63
  APPER and, xxiii, 122-123, 135
  Lagos Plan of Action and, 4, 123
  UN-PAAERD and, 117
Overseas Development Administration (ODA), 73, 78

Parastatals, 33, 52
  in Senegal, 181-182
  in Zimbabwe, 204
Paris Club, 97, 133, 201
Per capita income
  in sub-Saharan Africa, 5-6
  in Tanzania, 189-190
Performance monitoring, 100-101
Petite bourgeoisie
  African, 32-34, 38-39
Planning, 101-102, 139
  budgeting and, 99-100, 136-137
  limitations of, 99
Policy
  analysis of, 95-98
  development of, 93
  failure of, 20-23
  flexibility in, 63, 102
  formulation of, 142
  inappropriate, 30
  priorities in, 56
  reform of, 96, 98-99
  trends in, 92
Policy-making systems, 229
Political upheavals, 136, 149, 169
Population
  growth of, 8-9, 21, 110-112, 121, 131-132, 227
  in Ethiopia, 150
  in Senegal, 177
  in Tanzania, 188-190
Postcolonial state, 29-33
  central agencies in, 96
Post-independence period, 3
  agriculture in, 10
Poverty, 9, 18, 126
Preferential Trade Area (PTA), xviii, 63, 201
Price controls, 112
  abolition of, 114
Price policy

in Tanzania, 193
Prices
  declining, 13
  oil, 17, 121, 195
  producer, 196
Primary goods exports
  expansion of, 16
Private sector, 118, 231-232
Privatization, 182, 184, 230
  of public enterprises, 55-56
Production
  crisis of, 5-12
  industrial, 52
  rising costs of, 116
  in Senegal, 178
Productivity, 116
  enhancement of, 119
  morale and, 126
Professionalism, xxvii
Profits
  repatriation of, 207-208
Provisional Military Council (PMAC), 150, 153
Public administration
  orientation of, 30
  role of, xviii-xxii
Public debt, 138
Public employment
  in CAR, 71
Public facilities
  maintenance of, 143
Public sector, 118
Public sector management (PSM), 67-89
  bank operations and, 69-70
  diagnostic work, 81
  impact of improvement program, 75-79
  improvements in, 68-79
  in Uganda, 71-73
  in Zambia, 73-75
Public service, xi-xiv, xx-xxi, xxvi
  cost savings in, 125-127
  demoralization of, 110
  expansion of, 111, 118
  impact of SAPs on, 109-119
  personnel in, 121-129
  reduction of size of, 126-127
  restructuring of, 230-231
  retrenchment of staff in, 116, 124-127
  structural transformation and, 117-118
  in Tanzania, 188-189
  training for, 234
  in Zimbabwe, 203
  See also Civil service

Radical school, 20-23
Realism, 92-95, 102
Recession, 64, 116, 141
  1980-83, 12-14, 23, 42, 93, 111
  See also Depression

Recovery
  priorities of, 62
Reform
  administrative, 114-115
  of banking, 180
  in central agencies, 95-98
  content of agenda, 71, 79-80, 87
  development management, 102
  institutional, 114-115
  of management systems and practices, 98-102
  of organization and process, 91-105
  role of government in, 181-183
  structural, 92, 141
Refugees, 7, 19-20
Reintegration Fund, xiv, 179-180
Relief and Rehabilitation Commission (RRC), 156-158
Repatriation
  of dividends and profits, 207-208
Rescheduling, 133-134
Research, 236-237
Resettlement, 149, 157-161, 170
  in Ethiopia, 172
  in Zimbabwe, 203
Resources
  allocation of, 178
  conservation of, 166
  environmental, 11
Retrenchment
  effects of, 125-127
  programs of, 18-19
  of staff, 226
Revisionism
  neoclassical, 94
Revolution (Ethiopia), 149-150
Revolutionary Ethiopian Youth Association (REYA), 159
Rigidity
  bureaucratic, 229-230
  institutional, 232
  structural, 118
Rural development
  in Nigeria, 227
Rural land proclamation, 157

Savings
  domestic, 17, 134, 150-151
  in Ethiopia, 172
  public, 184
Secessionist movement
  Eritrean, 151-153, 169
Second Development Decade, 111, 115, 232
Second-tier Foreign Exchange Market, 58-59
Self-reliance, xii, 23-24
  collective, 62-63, 118, 219, 227
  economic, 29-30
  import prices and, 60
  Lagos Plan of Action and, 18

SAPs and, 115
Senegal, xiii-xiv
  civil service reductions in, 78-79
  institutional development in, 79-80
  PSM improvement in, 75
  response to economic change, 177-185
Sierra Leone, 68
  PSM improvement in, 75-76
Skilled staff
  shortages of, 143
Social change, 111-112
Socialism, 38, 45
  in Ethiopia, 150, 164-165, 168-170
  in Senegal, 181
  in Zimbabwe, 36
Social services, 5, 18-19
  in Zimbabwe, 203
Social upheaval, 136
Socioeconomic crisis, 51-55, 131-136
Soil erosion, 154, 217
Somalia
  invasion of Ethiopia by, 150-151, 158, 169
South Africa
  U.S. policy toward, 43
  Zimbabwean policy toward, 39-41
Southern Africa Development Coordination
  Conference (SADCC), xviii, xx, 41, 201
Special Economic Unit (Zambia), 97-98, 100-101
Stabilization, 138-139
Standard of living, 136
Starvation, 7, 126
State
  role of, 94-95
Structural adjustment, xix, 55, 109-110
  in Ethiopia, 165
  loans (SAL), 67, 69-75, 79-80, 84
  policies of, 110-113
  in Tanzania, 188, 195-198
Structural adjustment programs, xii-xiii, 21, 51, 56-60, 122
  adverse consequences of, 115-117
  budget deficits and, 127-128
  number of countries implementing, 114
  positive impact of, 113-115
  in Senegal, 180-185
  in Tanzania, 187, 195-196
Structural rigidity, 53
Structural transformation, 21-24, 232
  APPER and, 60-62
  depression and, 53, 55
  effect of training programs on, 236-237
  in Ethiopia, 155
  public service and, 117-118
  v. structural adjustment, 109-110, 228-229
  UN-PAAERD and, 60-62
  in West Africa, 214, 220
Subsidies
  in Algeria, 101

food, 56
petroleum, 58
removal of, 126
for services and commodities, 112
in Tanzania, 197
in Zimbabwe, 204
Sudan, the, 11, 14

Tanzania, xiv
  economy of, 188-189
  financial management in, 142
  response to economic change, 187-202
Taxes, 18-19
Technical assistance (TA), 80-82, 85-86, 142
  for PSM improvement, 83
Technical Assistance Loan (TAL), 68-70
Technology
  in agriculture, 11
Tourism, 180
Trade
  balance of, 183
  deficits in, 13, 54, 113
  external, 102
  foreign, 133
  inter-African, 232
  promotion of in West Africa, 218
  in Senegal, 180
  in Tanzania, 191, 198
  terms of, 53, 91, 134
Training
  institutions for, xv, 225-238
  public service, 77
Training programs, 142-143
  evaluation of, 236-237
  in Liberia, 232-237
  role of in reform, 234-235
Transitional National Development Plan, 37
Transport
  lack of, 115
  rehabilitation of in West Africa, 217
  services, 132
  in Tanzania, 189
Transportation, 18
  problems in, 116

Uganda, 68, 71-73
  PSM reform in, 78, 81-82, 87
  training in, 142
Underdevelopment, 10-12
  causes of, 45
  crisis of, 17, 22-24, 53
Underemployment
  in Senegal, 180
Unemployment, 19, 126, 214
  in Nigeria, 59
  in Senegal, 180
  in Zimbabwe, 209
United Nations, 122-123
United Nations Programme of Action for

African Economic Recovery and
Development (UN-PAAERD), 123, 211
  creation of, xxiv
  economic reform and, 215
  need for, 135
  self-reliance and, 227-228
  in Senegal, 178
  structural transformation and, 55, 62, 117
United States Agency for International
Development (USAID), 73, 78

Villagization, 149, 167, 170
  in Ethiopia, 161-164, 172

Water supply, 132
West Africa, 11, 211-221
Workers Party of Ethiopia (WPE), 155, 157, 161, 164
World Bank, xii, 20-22, 94
  ECOWAS and, 212
  in Ethiopia, 166-167, 170, 172
  mission of, 80-81
  PSM improvements and, 67-89
  requirements of, 30, 141
  study of Africa by, 128, 131-134
  in Tanzania, 192, 196-197
  in West Africa, 215
World trade, 133

Zaire, 14
Zambia, 58, 78-79
  debt service in, 133
  financial management in, 142
  PSM improvement in, 73-75, 81
  reforms in, 97, 98, 100-101
  structural adjustment loan to, 80
Zemetchas, 152-153
Zimbabwe, xiv, 29-47
  British policy toward, 44
  policy toward South Africa, 39-41
  post-white settler colonial state in, 33-37
  response to economic change, 203-210
  U.S. policy toward, 40-42
Zimbabwe Testimony, 42-43

The Kumarian Press
Library of Management for Development

Reforming Public Administration: Experiences from Eastern Africa, by Gelase Mutahaba

Managing Organizations in Developing Countries: A Strategic and Operational Approach, by Moses N. Kiggundu

Seeking Solutions: Framework and Cases for Small Enterprise Development Programs, by Charles K. Mann, Merilee S. Grindle, and Parker M. Shipton

Change in an African Village: Kefa Speaks, by Else Skjønsberg

Public Service Accountability: A Comparative Perspective, edited by Joseph G. Jabbra and O.P. Dwivedi

Community Management: Asian Experience and Perspectives, edited by David C. Korten

Local Institutional Development: An Analytical Sourcebook with Cases, by Norman T. Uphoff

People-Centered Development: Contributions Toward Theory and Planning Frameworks, edited by David C. Korten

Beyond Bureaucracy: Strategic Management of Social Development, edited by John C. Ickis, Edilberto de Jesus, and Rushikesh Maru

Bureaucracy and the Poor: Closing the Gap, edited by David C. Korten and Felipe B. Alfonso

Implementation for Sustainability: Lessons from Integrated Rural Development, by George Honadle and Jerry VanSant

Managing Rural Development: Ideas and Experience from East Africa, by Robert Chambers

Achieving Improved Performance in Public Organizations: A Guide for Managers, by Ian Mayo-Smith

Training for Development, by Rolf P. Lynton and Udai Pareek

Gender Roles in Development Projects, edited by Catherine Overholt, Mary B. Anderson, Kathleen Cloud, and James E. Austin

For a complete catalog of Kumarian Press titles, please write or call

Kumarian Press, Inc.
630 Oakwood Avenue, Suite 119
West Hartford, CT 06110-1505 U.S.A.
(203) 953-0214